Ringo Starr Solo Career

Got to Pay Your Dues

Aaron Badgley

NEW HAVEN PUBLISHING

Published 2025
First Edition
www.newhavenpublishingltd.com
newhavenpublishing@gmail.com

All Rights Reserved
The rights of Aaron Badgley as the author of this work, have been asserted in accordance with the Copyrights, Designs and Patents Act 1988.
No part of this book may be re-printed or reproduced or utilized in any form or by any electronic, mechanical or other means, now unknown or hereafter invented, including photocopying, and recording, or in any information storage or retrieval system, without the written permission of the
Author and Publisher.

Cover Design (C) Pete Cunliffe

Copyright © 2025 Aaron Badgley
All rights reserved
ISBN: 978-1-915975-25-6

For Harmony Marion Badgley

This book is dedicated to Andrea Badgley, Emily Badgley and Linda Badgley.

Content

Foreword by Ruth McCartney	5
Preface	6
Introduction	8
1 1970	11
2 1971	34
3 1972	48
4 1973	69
5 1974	89
6 1975	111
7 1976	128
8 1977	152
9 1978 - 1979	174
Conclusion	197
Ringo Starr – Discography	201
Acknowledgements	207
Bibliography	209

Foreword by Ruth McCartney

When I first read Aaron Badgley's manuscript, I was immediately struck by its sense of fairness and affection. Ringo Starr has often been the most underestimated Beatle, yet in truth he was the essential pulse of the band, the steady heartbeat that allowed the music to soar. Aaron's book reminds us that Ringo's story did not end when The Beatles walked away from the stage - it was, in fact, just beginning.

As Paul's step-sister, born and raised in Liverpool, I've seen firsthand how people around the world hold each Beatle in their hearts. Ringo, perhaps more than any of them, carried a universal accessibility. He was "the people's Beatle," the one who made fans feel they could know him, laugh with him, even chant his name in jest as "Ringo for President." That charm, however, was only the beginning. Behind it was a craftsman, a survivor, and an artist who refused to be defined solely by the greatest band in history.

The 1970s were Ringo's proving ground. While others might have questioned whether he could step into the spotlight, he charged forward - film roles, session work, hit after hit. 'It Don't Come Easy' may have been the perfect anthem for a man who had already overcome illness, hardship, and doubt. And yet, as Aaron so eloquently shows, Ringo made it look effortless.

This book is more than a chronicle of singles and chart positions. It's about resilience, reinvention, and joy. It captures the way Ringo embraced the freedom of the 1970s and established a career that was entirely his own - while never losing that mischievous grin or that deep Liverpudlian warmth.

Reading these pages, I was reminded of something my mum Angie often says: "You don't have to shout to be heard." Ringo Starr embodies that truth. His drumming, his arrangements, his voice, his personality - never the loudest, but always unforgettable.

Aaron Badgley has written a book that Ringo fans, Beatles devotees, and music historians alike will treasure. It shines a deserving light on a man who has given us more than just a backbeat - he's given us joy, laughter, and songs that endure.

So, with admiration for both author and subject, I invite you to turn the page and step into the world of Ringo Starr in the 1970s. It's a journey well worth taking.

Ruth McCartney

Preface

In 1973, when I was nine years old, I received, among other things, a copy of *Ringo* for Christmas. It was a cold and snowy Christmas. As Bing Crosby's 'White Christmas' played on the Fleetwood, and we opened gifts, my parents with their coffee, us kids with chocolate milk, I excitedly tore open the Christmas wrap to find a rather unique album cover. It was *Ringo*! Of course I knew who Ringo Starr was and I had the 'Photograph 'single, but this album seemed special. An illustrated book with lyrics, and Ringo on the record label. I could hardly wait for Bing to end so that I could slip *Ringo* on the hi-fi.

My mother bought it for me because she knew I loved The Beatles, but also because the salesman at the record store (Wilson and Lee in Oshawa, Ontario) told her that this was the biggest selling album of the Christmas season. So she bought me the album, which I loved and still love. She bought me *Goodnight Vienna* for Christmas in 1974, *Blast From Your Past* for Christmas in 1975, *Ringo's Rotogravure* for Christmas in 1976, and... well, you get the idea. This became a tradition to this day, only now my wife makes sure there is always a Ringo Starr album under the Christmas tree.

I tell this story for a reason. In 1973, Starr was a pop/rock star. He was not merely an ex-Beatle, but a fully fledged rock star. He had nine top 40 hit singles in America, with two hitting number one. Five of his albums made the top 40 in the US, with two of them going into the top ten. The salesman was not selling my mother an album that a nine-year-old Beatle fan would like, but rather what a nine-year-old music fan would like. He didn't push Lennon's latest album at the time, or even McCartney's. He pushed Elton John and Ringo Starr.

As for millions around the world, Ringo Starr has come to mean a great deal to me and has had a rather large role in my and my family's life. And this love has become multi-generational. My youngest daughter, Linda, still includes his 2008 album, *Liverpool 8,* as one of her favourite albums of all time.

Ringo Starr's success in 1973 was somewhat unexpected. His first two albums, while warmly received, did not top the charts and have the appeal that *Ringo* did. Nor did people have many expectations for Starr. While he achieved unimaginable fame as a Beatle, his solo career was not something many assumed would be as big as it was. It took Starr by surprise as well.

Richard Starkey, better known as Ringo Starr, must have been concerned about his future when he lost his full time job as one quarter of The Beatles. Since 1962, this had been all he knew. He was a musician, actor, and a member of the most influential and popular band of all time, and suddenly it was all over. Starr was married, a father of two (his third child, Lee, would be born in November of 1970) and in his eyes, he was unemployed. "The break-up was horrendous," Starr told Michael Parkinson in 1982. "I just sat around for a year. 'What will I do now?' I had to get out of the garden first and do something and then I started rolling again."

Introduction

Ringo Starr played his first show as an official member of The Beatles on August 18, 1962. As Paul McCartney has said on more than one occasion, he was the missing piece for The Beatles, and when he played with them, something clicked. The Beatles changed the landscape musically, socially, culturally and in other ways. Ringo Starr was a quarter of that band and was an essential member of the band. This book endeavours to show that Ringo Starr's career following the split of The Beatles was the beginning of a solo career that has been more than a handful of hit singles. The 1970s was the time when he established himself as Ringo Starr, not 'former Beatle Ringo Starr', but as a brilliant, relevant and vibrant artist.

When The Beatles officially called it a day on April 10, 1970, Ringo Starr had already released his first solo album (*Sentimental Journey*, which was a commercial success) and by the end of 1970, his second album (*Beaucoups Of Blues*) would be out and he would be on his way in establishing a solo career. In fact, along with George Harrison, Ringo was an early favourite. He had a number of hits, beginning with 'It Don't Come Easy', which surprised many when it made its way comfortably into the top ten worldwide. It was not a fluke, as he continued to release hit singles. The list of hits is impressive, including 'Back Off Boogaloo', 'Photograph', 'You're Sixteen', 'Oh My My', 'Only You' and 'No No Song'; all of these singles went into the top ten and a couple made it to number one. Not bad for the drummer of a band and not bad for an artist who takes his craft very seriously.

And that sums up Richard Starkey, Richie to his friends, Ringo Starr to the world. A person born into dire poverty and family problems, starting with his parents splitting when he was three. He was not a healthy child, and suffered medical and physical ailments. His health interfered with his schooling and he never had a complete formal education. Yet not only did he survive all adversity, he appeared to thrive from it. He had an innate positivity and seemed to gain strength from it. And he didn't express fear.

When The Beatles called it a day, Starr was honest about his concerns for a career. Whether it was making an album, acting in a film or designing furniture, Starr was not one to rest on his laurels. He had a number of interests and he was ready to show the world that he could do more than keep a brilliant backbeat.

It is important to remember that as he embarked on his solo career, he was already quite well known and loved. As a Beatle, in the US, he was the favourite. During the 1964 election in the United States, "Ringo For President" was often chanted. There was even a minor hit single by the Young World Singers called 'Ringo For President' on Decca Records.

There were other songs about Starr as well. Ella Fitzgerald released a song in 1965 called 'Ringo Beat', while a very young Cher (under the name Bonnie Jo Mason) recorded and released the song 'Ringo, I Love You', produced by Phil Spector and written by Spector and future Starr collaborator Vini Poncia. Future music critic Penny Valentine even got in on the act, releasing the novelty hit about Starr getting married in 1965, 'I Want To Kiss Ringo Goodbye'. And who can forget the hit 'Ringo Deer' by Gary Ferrier, about Ringo Starr joining Santa's reindeer team?

A lot of the songs Starr sang were fan favourites, again, especially in North America, where songs like 'Boys' and 'Act Naturally' were not only released as singles, but became well known hits. Starr even had a number one with The Beatles, singing lead on 'Yellow Submarine'. This was a huge accomplishment in 1966. That song and 'With A Little Help From My Friends' still receive standing ovations when Starr performs them with his All Starr Band. Ringo also co-wrote one song with John Lennon and Paul McCartney ('What Goes On') and had two of his solo compositions on Beatle albums ('Don't Pass Me By' and 'Octopus's Garden').

When it came to their films, Starr was the focus for both *A Hard Day's Night* and *Help!* He did so well with *A Hard Day's Night* - receiving the best reviews - that the story for their second film (the one in colour) was entirely built around him and his famous rings. Even *Magical Mystery Tour*, written by The Beatles, revolved around Starr and his aunt Jesse. Starr, it seemed, was a natural in front of the camera, so it was no surprise when he was offered a role in the famous (infamous?) star-packed film *Candy* in 1968. Starr holds his own with the likes of Richard Burton, Marlon Brando, Charles Aznavour, John Houston, Ewa Aulin and James Coburn (who would later appear on a Paul McCartney and Wings album cover) among many others. This led to a much larger role in the cult classic *The Magic Christian*, starring Starr and Peter Sellers.

His feature films also allowed him to appear on many television shows, such as *Laugh-in*, Cilla Black's television show, and other cameos. Starr was much loved and adored. Although he may have been nervous about the idea of a solo career, he seemed destined to have a very successful career as Ringo.

Starr made it very clear, in the book and television series *The Beatles Anthology*, that he didn't want The Beatles to end. Starr, who did not have siblings, suddenly had three brothers. "They became the closest friends I ever had," he said in *The Beatles Anthology* book. "I was an only child and suddenly I felt like I had three brothers." He continues to refer to The Beatles as such well into 2025. So the sadness, for him, was not wondering what he was going to do but rather not looking forward to doing it alone. "There was the possibility that we could have carried on," Starr said.

But the story of Starr in the 1970s goes beyond his worries and successes. He was also a well respected and in demand session player. He worked with a varied and diverse selection of artists playing everything from the blues to rock to folk to classical Indian music. He was fearless when it came to trying different styles and holding his own with superstars of that decade.

Starr's career goes well beyond the 1970s. He is in his sixth decade as a solo artist and bigger than ever. In 2025 he hit number one in the UK Country album charts, and his concert tours continue to sell out. But this story looks at an artist reestablishing himself. In the 1970s, in many ways, Starr had to rediscover his confidence and dig deep to find that survival instinct that he had and continues to have.

Without delving into his personal life, it is important to note that the 1970s were a critical time for Starr. He had to establish himself as a multidimensional solo artist, with forays into art, film and music. Unlike other bands and singers, he didn't make his way up in the 1970s by paying his dues in the small clubs, but he paid his dues in other ways. And he earned every success he achieved.

This is Ringo Starr in the 1970s.

1

1970

Ringo Starr was always my favourite, from the first time hearing 'Octopus's Garden' on *Abbey Road*, when I was five, to seeing him trying to get that ring off his finger in *Help!* (which I saw at the drive-in). I remember my mother having the *Sentimental Journey* album, because she loved all the songs. Family gatherings with aunts, uncles, grandparents and cousins were not complete without that album finding its way onto the turntable.

Ringo Starr started work on his debut album in 1969, which was a very busy year for Mr Starkey. Aside from his work with The Beatles, he was also working on the film *The Magic Christian*, as well as assisting George Harrison with a few Apple artists, and he took a great interest in Apple, signing artists to the label. Starr was also helping out friends in the studio. Although his debut, *Sentimental Journey*, would not be released until the spring of 1970, he set time aside in 1969 to begin working on it.

When Starr went into the studio to start recording the album, he was prepared. He had chosen the songs that he wanted to sing and had a very clear idea of how he wanted it to sound. His choice of material, to some, seemed very odd. An album of big band pop standards, even in 1970, seemed very out of date, and these songs seemed old. However, given the avant garde nature of the first three solo albums by John Lennon (with Yoko Ono), and George Harrison's first two albums, perhaps this could be viewed as another bold choice by an ex-Beatle.

George Martin, who produced *Sentimental Journey*, unknowingly set the formula for most of Starr's future solo albums. Rather than working with session players and one producer/arranger, Martin solicited help from a group of very famous people to provide an arrangement for each track on the album. Some were friends (Klaus Voormann, Paul McCartney, Maurice Gibb), and a couple would become great friends (Quincy Jones, Richard Perry), and others were well known and well respected arrangers. Martin himself arranged one track. But one can see how this became the template for most of Starr's future solo albums. Starr would do very well, with a little help from his friends.

To Starr, however, the whole project made total sense, from the song selections to the multiple arrangers. As far as Starr was concerned, writing an album's worth of material would take him a long time. He explained in 1970 to BBC's David Wigg, on the programme *Scene and Heard*: "I thought I would do an album, but because I don't write very fast, I write about one a year, it would take 20 years to finish it." Given that he thought that he was not, at that time, able to write an entire album, covers seemed to be the logical choice. Rather than having teams of writers writing for him, or covering early rock and roll, classic pop songs seemed more fitting for him.

For Starr this album really was a sentimental journey to his childhood and youth. As he told David Wigg during the interview: "I came into music with all these songs. They were my start in music. They are all the songs your mum, your dad and your aunties came back from the pub singing. These were all the songs they were singing and have great memories for me. And the fact that they are all great songs. Still nice songs, they stand up to today, they are powerful songs." Starr had a point: these songs had aged well and were now classics.

In an interview in 1977, Starr stated: "So I thought 'I'll go in and do all these standards,' you know, because I always liked them anyway - and it's me, right? So it's part of me. I'm not one of those people who won't admit to their past and their musical influences. So I thought, 'That's what I'll do'."

"I really dug all that old music, because it was the first I ever heard," Starr explained in the 1970 interview on *Scene and Heard*. "I thought my mum would be pleased if I sang all those songs." It is pretty certain that she was not only pleased but also very proud of her 'little drummer boy' (as she referred to him when he was a child learning the drums).

In 2001, Starr explained yet another reason for his decision to record *Sentimental Journey*. In speaking with Paul Du Noyer in *Mojo* magazine he said: "I was lost for a while. That's well-documented... And I just thought of all those songs that I was brought up with, all the parties we'd had in Liverpool at our house and all the neighbours' houses... So I called George Martin and said, 'Why don't we take a sentimental journey?'"

He also made things comfortable and familiar for himself by having George Martin produce the album - a producer whom he had not only worked with before, but a person from the inner circle of The Beatles. Starr felt comfortable with Martin, and more importantly trusted him. Martin would make sure that the album would sound fantastic and Starr would have a strong debut. Starr liked Martin's idea to hire a different arranger for each of the songs for the album.

"I thought it would make it interesting," Starr explained at the time of the release to Wigg. "If it was just one guy, it would be his scene, because I am just singing, not arranging. So I thought we would make it a bit exciting to get a lot of different arrangers doing each track, and I am the link."

Work on Starr's debut album actually began in the US in 1969. Richard Perry, who would work with Starr in the future as his producer, arranged the title track, 'Sentimental Journey'. The backing track was recorded in Los Angeles and sent to London for Starr's vocals. Quincy Jones arranged 'Love Is a Many Splendored Thing' at A&M Studios in Los Angeles as well. On 14 January 1970 Starr and Martin could be found in Olympic Studios recording vocals for both of the songs.

Starr was busy during the latter part of 1969, and due to his schedule, Martin had limited time with Starr in October and November to record songs for the album. Martin has never been one to waste time and he managed to record several backing tracks with the respective arrangers during this time, even if Starr would not record his vocals until the new decade. However, Starr was quite involved from the beginning. On 27 October 1969, Martin conducted his George Martin Orchestra at EMI Studios to record Chico O'Farrill's arrangement of 'Night And Day'. O'Farrill was a renowned jazz musician, composer and arranger who had worked with Stan Kenton, Charlie Parker, Benny Goodman and many others. He certainly introduced a big band sound to the album with this track. Starr recorded the vocals that day, and it was mixed and completed.

Wessex Sound Studios (where King Crimson recorded) was the place to be on 7 November 1969 when Paul McCartney helped out his Beatles colleague and friend by arranging 'Stardust'. Interestingly, the album was, at one time, named *Ringo Starrdust*, which was McCartney's suggestion. But wisely it was changed to *Sentimental Journey*. It was felt that *Sentimental Journey*, as a title, did a better job of capturing the overall feel of the album. The day prior to McCartney's recording with Starr saw the recording of the only known outtake from the album, 'Stormy Weather'. It seems it was a George Martin arrangement, and no reason was given for it not being included on the album, unless it was earmarked for a B-side for a single. Martin's arrangement for 'Dream' was recorded on 14 November at Trident Studios, and completed in February, while Oliver Nelson's arrangement of 'Blue, Turning Grey Over You' was recorded on 28 November. Again, that song was finished in February at EMI studios.

Oliver Nelson was well known for his landmark and classic 1961 album *The Blues and The Absolute Truth*. As well as performing and recording, Nelson also arranged songs/recordings for artists such as Thelonious Monk, Cannonball Adderley, Sonny Rollins, Eddie 'Lockjaw' Davis, Johnny Hodges, Wes Montgomery and Buddy Rich to name just a few. He also arranged the music for the film *Alfie*. Martin had had a hit with the title track from that film when he produced Cilla Black's version in 1966.

Work on the album intensified in early 1970. Martin busily prepared the remaining backing tracks for Starr to provide his vocals. Martin decamped into studio two at EMI studios and on 3 February 1970, he spent the day re-recording 'Love Is a Many Splendored Thing'. Quincy Jones and Martin were not satisfied with the first recording, so Jones flew to London to assist with the re-recording. Starr added his vocals that day, but re-recorded his performance on 5 February to get it right. In fact, more time was spent on this song than any other song on the album, as on 17 February strings and backing vocals were recorded and dubbed onto the track.

On 9 February 1970, Starr added his vocals to the Elmer Bernstein (an American composer and conductor best known for his numerous film scores) arrangement of 'Have I Told You Lately That I Love You?' Two days later, old Beatle friend and Manfred Mann member Klaus Voormann provided an arrangement for 'I'm A Fool To Care'. Voormann also conducted a fifteen piece jazz orchestra for the recording.

Les Reed was on hand on 12 February 1970 to put together the closing track on the album, 'Let The Rest of The World Go By'. Les Reed is best known as a composer and has composed some hits such as 'It's Not Unusual', 'Delilah' and 'There's A Kind of Hush'. Starr recorded his vocals two days later. Martin was not entirely satisfied with Starr's performance and encouraged him to try again on 17 February. On the same day, classical arranger Frances Shaw conducted a 17 piece string section for the song. It was a smart move, as the end result was a great vocal from Starr and one of the highlights from the album.

As February came to a close, Starr and Martin were busy in the studio completing *Sentimental Journey*. Final mixes and added vocals were completed as the album was taking shape. However, there were a couple of songs yet to be recorded. Moving to Morgan Studios on 5 March 1970, Martin and Starr completed the album. On this day, two tracks were recorded: Ron Goodwin's 'Whispering Grass (Don't Tell The Trees)' and Maurice Gibb's arrangement of 'Bye Bye Blackbird'.

Ron Goodwin was a British composer/arranger/producer who had worked with Martin in the early 1960s at Parlophone. He also produced and arranged hits for Petula Clark and Jimmy Young. He also worked with Pink Floyd's Roger Waters on the soundtrack for the film *The Body*. Martin was very familiar with his work and it seemed like a perfect collaboration.

Gibb was not only a friend but also a neighbour, residing across the street from Starr and his family. He was also one third of the very popular band The Bee Gees. Starr and Gibb would sporadically work with each other during the early 1970s, eventually recording an electronic/synthesiser album that has yet to see the light of day. But their professional paths crossed early in the 1970s.

Now that the album was recorded, mixed and mastered, it was time to design the sleeve. As mentioned, in December 1969 the album was announced with the title *Ringo Starrdust*. Wisely this was changed and in keeping with the theme of a sentimental journey, Ringo travelled to his birthplace of the Dingle area of Liverpool. Starr would revisit this area in music in the 2000s, especially with the album *Liverpool 8*, the postal district. The Empress Hotel was chosen for the sleeve, as it was a place where, no doubt, these songs had been played over the years. Photos of his family (including his mother and stepfather) could be seen in the windows while a black and white Ringo Starr stood in front of the tavern in a tuxedo. Although no credit was given for the design, Richard Polak (famed rock photographer) took the photos for the sleeve.

"There was a pub on the album cover. My family used to go to that pub and all Mum's friends and family would come back to our place, and at the parties everybody sang those songs," said Starr in *The Beatles Anthology*. That pub had to be on the front sleeve, as it represented the album and the songs perfectly.

The album was finished and ready for release on 27 March 1970 in the UK and on 24 April 1970 in North America. Starr was, rightfully, proud of the album. In many ways, his decision to tackle pop and big band standards was as avant garde and creative as anything Harrison and Lennon had released to date. The difference was that *Sentimental Journey* was an album which could attract a wider audience. Starr, a member of the biggest rock and roll band on the planet and a band that had changed music forever, was looking to the long past with his first solo endeavour. This was revolutionary in many ways and years ahead of its time. Bryan Ferry would turn to these songs in 1974, while other artists, such as Bob Dylan, Harry Nilsson, Linda Ronstadt, Carly Simon and Rod Stewart all took their turns with the great American songbook. Even Paul McCartney would record his own album of these classics in 2012 with *Kisses On The Bottom*.

The main difficulty for the album was that not only would Starr being competing with The Beatles (the *Get Back* project would finally see the light of day with the new title *Let It Be*, which was released 8 May 1970), but also with his former band mate, Paul McCartney, whose debut album, *McCartney*, was also scheduled to be released on 17 April 1970. No doubt these two albums impacted sales for Starr (and conversely, Starr may have had an impact on the other releases' sales as well). Competition was very steep, and fans may have had to make choices.

When looking back at the album, it should have not been that much of a shock. The Beatles themselves dipped into the old pop standards, even though they wrote the songs: 'Honey Pie', 'When I'm Sixty-Four', 'Your Mother Should Know', even their Hamburg, Germany recording of 'Ain't She Sweet' and their attempts at recording 'Besame Mucho' (which they revisited during the *Get Back* sessions). The Beatles even looked to Bing Crosby for inspiration for their song 'Please Please Me', which John Lennon said was influenced by Crosby's song 'Please', with the clever use of "Please lend your little ear to my pleas." However, here is the world's most famous rock drummer, not even drumming, and singing standards. Ringo knew there would be criticism and the album may not have been overly well received, but, much like Lennon and Harrison's avant garde works, he went ahead and recorded the album. In the future, however, such albums would not be out of place in a musician's catalogue.

Although The Supremes recorded and released *The Supremes Sing Rogers And Hart* in 1967, those songs were Broadway classics. Ringo Starr did 'The Great American Songbook' first. He was also the first solo Beatle to have a top ten solo album in the UK, and he was the first to release an album of 'pop' songs. He was the first solo Beatle to release an entire album of cover versions. Both John Lennon and Paul McCartney would look to the past, in 1975 with Lennon's album *Rock 'n' Roll* and for McCartney for three albums. But again, Lennon and McCartney focused on rock and roll, while Starr bravely took on jazz, big band and pop standards. As noted, McCartney didn't tackle the American Songbook until 2012.

The title track, 'Sentimental Journey', gets the album started and sets the stage. There is no mistake here: Starr is not trying to turn these songs into rock and roll, but rather record straight interpretations of these classic songs. No doubt Starr grew up with Doris Day's version of this song, which was a hit in 1945. Other artists have tackled it, but Day's version was the one that the young Richie Starkey heard on the radio. Starr's treatment of the song (with help from arranger Richard Perry) is very nostalgic and very warm. "Going to take a sentimental journey," Starr sings, "to renew old memories." Starr is welcoming all to his trip down memory lane, and given what was going on with The Beatles at the time, it made total sense for him to look backwards. The song is aided by Perry incorporating a 'singing guitar' solo in the song, a technique that was quite popular in the early 1940s but had somewhat disappeared by 1970.

Richard Perry was an interesting choice for the song and the album. By 1970, Perry was still a very young and not well known producer. Up until 1970, he had worked with and produced Captain Beefheart, Fats Domino (on his 'comeback' album *Fats Is Back*) and scored a top ten hit with Tiny Tim ('Tiptoe Through The Tulips'). He was a staff producer for Warner Brothers, but, like Martin, had formed his own freelance production company and went on to great success with Barbra Streisand, Harry Nilsson and Carly Simon, to name just three.

Given that a promo film was shot and aired for the song, there is no question that it was, at one time, considered as a single. For reasons unknown, or forgotten, that single never materialised. One has to wonder whether, if it had been issued as a single, it would have helped album sales. It is interesting to note that McCartney's debut solo album released at the same time also did not have any singles lifted from it.

The album continues with a very bold and swinging 'Night And Day', the Cole Porter classic. Chico O'Farrill (a Cuban composer, arranger, and conductor, best known for his work in the Latin idiom, specifically Afro-Cuban jazz or 'Cubop') brings in the big band sound and it works. It is certainly a side of Ringo Starr that fans have never heard before. The song made its debut in 1932, sung by Fred Astaire in the film *The Gay Divorcee*. Astaire also had a hit with it. However, the song managed to take on a life of its own, covered by many artists, and was featured in the 1942 film *Action In The North Atlantic* (starring Humphrey Bogart), performed by Julie Bishop.

This leads into a much more restrained 'Whispering Grass (Don't Tell The Trees)', a hit for the Ink Spots in 1940. Starr noted in an interview at the time that this was his favourite song on the album. He had also hoped that it would be a single. Sandy Denny recorded a lovely version in 1974. Perhaps she was more familiar with Starr's version than the original.

Up next is the much more sparse Maurice Gibb compact version of 'Bye Bye Blackbird'. This is the second oldest song of the collection, dating back to 1926. It was a pub standard. It was written by Milton Ager and Jack Yellen and, according to the Library of Congress, was first published in 1927 by Ager, Yellen & Bornstein, Inc. McCartney recorded the song on his *Kisses On The Bottom* album. This short burst of energy is one of the highlights of the album, with Gibb bringing the band in halfway through the song, creating a wonderful, engaging moment.

Side one continues with 'I'm A Fool To Care', a song made famous by Les Paul and Mary Ford and expertly executed by Klaus Voormann. The song also includes Billy Preston on organ. And with McCartney's

'Stardust', the side ends. McCartney sets the perfect backdrop for Starr and the song could have easily been a choice for a single.

Starr was quite correct in his assumption that a different arranger for each song would keep the proceedings interesting. Jazz musician Oliver Nelson's very jazzy version of 'Blue, Turning Grey Over You' comes from the Fats Waller songbook, circa 1929, made famous by Louis Armstrong. Nelson provides a solid, full on jazz/big band sound that may not suit Starr's voice, but Starr delivers a convincing vocal and in the end it is an interesting listening experience. Quincy Jones slows things down with 'Love Is a Many Splendored Thing' (again featuring Billy Preston on organ). This Academy Award winning song (1956, 'Best Song' category) is more in keeping with Mr Starr's voice and it is a perfect song for Starr on many levels.

George Martin continues the more mellow sounds with a dreamy version of 'Dream', a Johnny Mercer song with which The Pied Pipers had a hit. John Dankworth not only arranged 'You Always Hurt The One You Love' but also contributed his trademark saxophone to the song. Starr takes his turn with the Mills Brothers' hit and it is a great choice for Starr and the album.

Elmer Bernstein's somewhat comedic arrangement of 'Have I Told You Lately That I Love You' mixes with big band, swing and jazz. It is best left in the hands of Bing Crosby and The Andrew Sisters, who had a hit with the song in 1946. And the album ends with the wonderful 'Let The Rest Of The World Go By'. The song was written in 1919 and is the oldest song on the album. Interestingly, the original first verse is cut off, and Starr begins the song with the chorus. Composer Les Reed provides Starr with a choir and orchestra for the big finish for the album. It is the stand out track and Starr delivers it with tenderness and love. It bookends with 'Sentimental Journey' beautifully. Ringo would have most likely heard Dick Haymes' version of the song from the 1944 film *When Irish Eyes Are Smiling*.

The album was met with mixed reviews, although it did not get the coverage one would expect for a solo Beatles album. The major radio and retail magazine in America, *Cash Box,* didn't even bother to write up the album in their new and notable sections. Its counterpart, *Billboard,* did review, and noted the "dozen top arrangers", predicting that the album was a "sure-fire hit" and stating: "The Beatle takes us back to the good old band days in this collection of hits from the 40s and 50s as well as the 20s and 30s! Starr is featured as band vocalist on such favorites as 'Night and Day', 'Starlight', and the title tune."

Rolling Stone, not surprisingly, was somewhat negative. Greil Marcus noted that *"Sentimental Journey* may be horrendous, but at least it's classy. Or is it?" in his review for *Rolling Stone*. He also added, "There *is* a certain thrill to hearing Ringo swing immediately and finally flat on 'Stardust'." In the UK, Andy Gray in his review for the *NME* described the arrangements as "top class" and noted that Ringo's vocals may surprise many people, stating: "He sings better than you'd expect him to." In the same review he predicted the album would be a huge hit.

Ringo also did quite a bit of promotion for the album, especially in the UK. He appeared on radio and television (*Frost On Sunday*), and made his first promotional film for the title track. The film was directed by Apple's Neil Aspinall, with Ringo singing in front of The George Martin Orchestra. Apple artist Doris Troy is also there, with Madeline Bell and Marsha Hunt. Ringo performed his vocals live over a pre-recorded backing track. The film was shown in the UK (on *Frost On Sunday*) and on *The Ed Sullivan Show* on 17 May 1970 in North America.

According to Michael Seth Starr, in his book *Ringo With A Little Help*, the other Beatles weighed in as well, with Lennon saying he was embarrassed by the album, while Harrison reportedly thought it was "a great album...really nice". Although there is no official record of McCartney's thoughts, since he worked on the album, one would assume McCartney approved of the project.

The album was a success, peaking at number seven in the UK charts (Ringo's highest chart placing on the album charts in the UK), and number 22 on the *Billboard* charts, selling well over 500,000 copies. *Cash Box* and *Record World* had it peaking at number 20. In Canada, the album did not do as well, peaking at number 42. Ringo clearly had some stiff competition. Sitting at number one on *Billboard* when *Sentimental Journey* peaked at number 22 was *McCartney*, and number two was *Let It Be*. The soundtrack to Woodstock, Jimi Hendrix, and Crosby, Stills, Nash and Young rounded out the top five. But the album held its own, and it helped Ringo get back into the game. As he noted: "The great thing was that it got me moving, not very fast, but just moving. It was like the first shovel of coal in the furnace that made the train inch forward."

The one thing missing to promote the album was the release of a single from it. In talk with David Wigg, Starr does mention that two songs were being considered for a potential single: the title track and 'Whispering Grass (Don't Tell The Trees)'. He indicated that the staff at Apple seemed to like the two songs. "They seem to be the two biggest," he admitted. And he himself was leaning towards 'Whispering Grass (Don't Tell The Trees)'. But a single never materialised, and no reason has ever been given. The fact that he did shoot a promotional film for 'Sentimental Journey' clearly indicates that there was some serious consideration given to releasing that song as a single.

In North America, the album received virtually no airplay. Rock and roll FM stations would not touch it, and there was no single for AM stations. At this time, there were few AOR (Adult Oriented Rock) stations and while 'Beautiful Music' stations existed, playing the likes of Lawrence Welk, Acker Bilk and big band, they were not going to play a Beatle. Despite the lack of substantial radio play and very mixed reviews, the fact that it made it to number 22 on *Billboard*'s chart and sold the equivalent of a gold record in today's standard was quite an achievement. Keep in mind that the originators of some of the classics (Bing Crosby, Doris Day, Frank Sinatra) were struggling to chart and get radio play as well.

The release of *Sentimental Journey* brought some controversy too. Paul McCartney scheduled the release of his album for 10 April 1970, which was close to the original release date of The Beatles' *Let It Be*. Since Starr's album had been announced in December 1969, that date could not be changed. This scheduling conflict caused a great deal of strife for The Beatles and Apple. Suffice to say that when the three Beatles sent Ringo with a letter to argue with Paul about the release date, Starr was met with a great deal of anger from McCartney.

In the book *Anthology*, McCartney admits that he did lose his temper: "Ringo came to see me. He was sent, I believe – being mild mannered, the nice guy – by the others, because of the dispute. So Ringo arrived at the house, and I must say I gave him a bit of verbal. I said: 'You guys are just messing me around.' He said: 'No, well, on behalf of the board and on behalf of The Beatles and so and so, we think you should do this,' etc. And I was just fed up with that. It was the only time I ever told anyone to GET OUT! It was fairly hostile. But things had gotten like that by this time. It hadn't actually come to blows, but it was near enough."

While Starr was promoting the album he was also keeping himself busy with friends and artists that he admired. In fact he was keeping busy while recording *Sentimental Journey*. Leon Russell was in London recording some of his debut, self-titled solo album. While he was in London, some of his friends were there to help, including George Harrison and Ringo Starr. The Beatles had met Russell in the mid 1960s when he was a session player in Los Angeles. Through mutual respect and shared tastes in music they became friends. Once Russell relocated to England, it was only natural for him to make some calls. The album *Leon Russell* (Shelter Records) was released in March of 1970 and became a much loved album by future rock stars, such as Elton John, who regarded the album as an instant classic.

Harrison was busy helping other American artists who had settled in London. Doris Troy (born Doris Elaine Higginsen in 1937) was a rhythm and blues artist and songwriter who got her start singing back-up for artists recording for Atlantic Records but sold her first song ('How About That') at the age of 16 in 1960. It was an R&B top ten hit for Dee Clark, and a top 40 *Billboard* hit. Troy sold the song for $100.00. In 1962 she co-wrote 'Just One Look' with Gregory Carroll, a producer, writer and performer. In 1963 Atlantic Records released the single and it was a top ten hit in America (both *Billboard* and *Cash Box* singles charts) and a number one single in Canada. In the UK it was not as successful for Troy, but The Hollies took their cover version to number two in the official record chart.

After 'Just One Look', Troy struggled to have a successful follow-up and by 1969 she decided to move to England, as she had a minor hit with 'What'cha Going To Do About It' and seemed to have more work in England. She was also a friend of Billy Preston, and was working on his Apple debut album, *That's The Way God Planned It* (1969), which Harrison produced and provided guitar for. Troy ended up not only singing back-up but also co-writing 'Everything's All Right', 'Let Us All Get Together Right Now' and 'This Is It' with Preston for the album. 'Everything's All Right' was issued as a single.

It was during these sessions that Harrison met Troy. He was already a fan of her music, but in an interview in 1970 he said, "I first met Doris on this Billy Preston session. Doris had come over to England with a few demo tapes, because she'd decided that she wanted to live in England and try and do it from here like, I suppose, the thing that Jimi Hendrix did. She came to a session, and she's been there ever since!"

In fact, Harrison quickly signed her to Apple, giving her her own office on the third floor at 3 Savile Row, and began to assist her in recording her Apple debut album. Troy recalled: "George said to me after the second session, 'What are you doing, Doris? Are you free?' I said, 'Yeah, man, I'm free.' He said 'Do you want to sign with Apple?' I said 'Sure! Are you serious?' He said, 'Yeah.' I said, 'Well, I want to be a writer, producer and artist, OK?' He said 'OK.'"

Harrison called on some old friends, including Klaus Voormann, Leon Russell, Bonnie Bramlett, Delaney Bramlett, Peter Frampton, Eric Clapton, Steven Stills, Billy Preston and Ringo Starr. Troy later recalled: "We had Ringo Starr. He was one of my favourite people. He would be the first one there. He was so dedicated. I wish I could see him today and tell him how much I appreciate his enthusiasm and the way he worked, because he could play."

Recording of the album began in September 1969 and was completed in the spring of 1970. Not only did Starr drum on the album, he also co-wrote two songs, 'Gonna Get My Baby Back' and 'You Give Me Joy

Joy'. Starr met a number of artists during this recording that he would not only befriend but work with in the very near future.

With John Mayall's Bluebreakers, Eric Clapton, and Fleetwood Mac all topping the UK charts and selling out crowds everywhere, the blues were alive and well in England, and a lot of older blues musicians in the US took notice. A number of artists not only toured in the UK and Europe, but recorded there as well. Howlin' Wolf was one such musician, who was invited to come to the UK by Eric Clapton. It is worth noting that this was the first time Wolf had recorded outside of the US. He was somewhat nervous about the recording. He needn't have worried. Between 2 May 1970 and 7 May 1970, Wolf recorded an album featuring a virtual superband, including Clapton, Charlie Watts, Bill Wymen, Ian Stewart, Stevie Winwood, Stephen Stills, and one drummer named 'Richie'. Richie was, of course, Ringo Starr, who had to use a pseudonym due to record company issues (Wolf recorded for Chess). The resulting album, *The London Howlin' Sessions,* featured Starr on one track, 'I Ain't Superstitious'.

According to producer Norman Dayron, Starr was present on the first day of recording, along with Klaus Voormann and Alan White (Yes, Plastic Ono Band). According to Dayron, quoted in the CD notes of the reissue of the album, they "tried different combinations of things on the first day...I think we were trying to feel our way into it." He also noted that Starr didn't feel comfortable during the session, perhaps because he felt out of his element. Unlike The Rolling Stones and Eric Clapton, Starr's music included blues, and rhythm and blues, but there was a lot of other music in his musical education. It is noted that his drumming is captured on the track 'I Ain't Superstitious'. Dayron also noted in the booklet that Starr requested that he be credited as 'Richie', not at the request of EMI or Apple. According to Dayron, "I said 'how do you want to be listed on the album?' He said, 'just call me Richie'."

However, in the 31 July 1971 issue of *Melody Maker,* Starr has a different view as to why he contributed to only one track on the released album. Starr seemed to have an issue with Dayron as a producer and could not conform to Dayron's style. According to the article, Ringo said that Dayron was not precise enough in aiming for a musical direction, and that Howlin' Wolf seemed too dependent on the producer. Starr further stated: "after all, we'd gone there to play with Howlin' Wolf. It was him we dig, not the producer." Ringo was clear that he did not enjoy the sessions. "The sessions I played on I think were scrappy. I only played one night. Howlin' Wolf was great though. He'd come around to you, singing to you all the blues. You have to get through that thing first, 'well, look at me with Howlin' Wolf. One of the great blues singers of our time, and there's little old me playing with 'im'. That scene you go through. Some things blow your mind, you know."

The album was released in August of 1971 on Chess Records in the US and Rolling Stones Records in the UK. When the album was released in a deluxe form in 2003, Starr could be heard on two additional tracks, 'Goin' Down Slow' and 'I Want To Have A Word With You'.

Stephen Stills was another US musician based in London for a time. He knew The Beatles through their friendship with The Byrds. He was also featured on Doris Troy and Howlin' Wolf's albums and was also recording his debut solo album. Once again, Starr was available to help out, so during the early summer of 1970, Starr drummed on a couple of tracks for Stills: 'To A Flame' and 'We Are Not Helpless'. The album, *Stephen Stills* (Atlantic) became a worldwide top ten album, helped with the huge single 'Love The One You're With'.

Starr was also busy with Apple Records. While he did not sign as many artists as Harrison and Paul McCartney had since the label was launched in 1968, he did bring some interesting artists to the label, such as new classical composer, John Tavener. Tavener has since been hailed as one of the finest modern classical composers of the last 70 years. *The Whale,* his debut album for Apple, was his first major work, and he debuted it in 1968. Both Starr and John Lennon were big fans. Tavener met Starr through his brother, Roger Tavener. Roger Tavener was a very high end contractor, and Starr was meeting with him at his (Roger's) house. John Tavener recalled: "My brother had prepared caviar, but Ringo just wanted a jam sandwich. We finally agreed to record *The Whale* at that meeting."

Starr arranged for Michael Bremner to record *The Whale* at the Church of St. John The Evangelist, Islington, London, on July 22, 23 and 24, 1970. The actual recording was made by the BBC Transcription Service. Ringo can be heard shouting at the eight minutes mark as part of a crowd. *The Whale* was released on 25 September 1970 to critical acclaim. It also sold quite well in classical circles. Interestingly, Ringo obviously loved *The Whale*, as he would re-release the album in 1977 on his own Ring O' Records.

Finally Starr helped out his old Beatles Brothers, Harrison and Lennon, as well as Yoko Ono. His work with Harrison would lead to his second solo album, also released in 1970. From May through to October 1970 Harrison went to work on his triple album, the epic, classic *All Things Must Pass*. George had a huge supporting cast, and Ringo's contribution was not large. Meanwhile, Ringo was the sole drummer for Lennon and Ono for their *Plastic Ono Band* albums. Recording took place in June, September and October of 1970. For *John Lennon/Plastic*

Ono Band, Starr formed the perfect rhythm section with bassist Klaus Voorman. He did the same for *Yoko Ono/Plastic Ono Band*, although there was one track on that album featuring Ornette Coleman's band.

Luke Morgan Britton reported that Starr had told *Uncut* magazine in 2015 that working on *John Lennon/Plastic Ono Band* was one of his career's highlights. Calling the sessions "incredible," he went on to describe the recording with Lennon and Voormann as "the finest trios I had ever heard." Further, although Lennon came to the sessions with complete songs, Starr remembered that the recording was more like a "jam session." Lennon would kick the song off and Voormann and Starr would "kick it in and feel where [the song] should go. We knew Klaus anyway. John and I really knew each other, so we were psyched about where the atmosphere would go."

Starr even stated that he enjoyed playing drums on Yoko Ono's album, which was recorded while Lennon was putting his album together. "Her record was a lot of fun because it was like a jam," Starr recalled in the book *John & Yoko/Plastic Ono Band: In Their Own Words & with Contributions from the People Who Were There*. "And then she would do her crazy singing on top of it. I never felt with Yoko that there was the verse and the chorus, so we would just jam."

This was the only time that Starr appeared on a John Lennon album. Although Lennon would help Starr out with three albums, Starr never appeared on another Lennon album. He would work with Lennon on Nilsson's *Pussy Cats*, which Lennon produced, and he appeared in one television commercial for Lennon.

As for Yoko Ono, Starr would appear on her album *Fly*, released in 1971. In 1969, Starr drummed for Lennon and Ono's single 'Cold Turkey' and its flipside 'Don't Worry Kyoko (Mummy's Only Looking For A Hand In The Snow)'. Neither songs were initially on any album. 'Cold Turkey' would finally appear on the Lennon compilation album *Shaved Fish* (1976), and 'Don't Worry Kyoko (Mummy's Only Looking For A Hand In The Snow)' was included on the double album *Fly*, released in 1971 on Apple. Ringo's picture appears in the inner sleeve.

Lennon's *Plastic Ono Band* album received very lukewarm reviews when it was first released. It was a very personal and painful album, and some critics and fans found it difficult at the time. It was years ahead of its time, both in its bare production and primitive playing and in its deeply personal lyrics. The album reached number six in the US *Billboard* Top 200 Albums Chart, while it peaked at number eight in the UK. In Canada, on the national *RPM* chart, it got to number two, kept from number one by George Harrison's *All Things Must Pass* (which also featured Starr). One single was released from the album, 'Mother' b/w Ono's 'Why' from her *Plastic Ono Band* album. The single received positive notices in both *Cashbox* and *Billboard,* but the level of success was very different on their charts. *Cash Box* charted the single to number 19 on their top 100, while *Billboard* had it peak at 43. In Canada, on the *RPM* Top 100 singles, it made it to number 12. The single was not released in the UK, but was released throughout Europe and Japan.

Ono's album, at the time, did receive positive reviews and peaked in the US at number 182. Starr's drumming was singled out in the review in *Rolling Stone*, with Lester Bangs noting "John, Ringo and bassist Klaus Voormann working out accompaniments that are by turns as frenzied as Yoko herself and quite restrained. It always sounds thought-out, carefully arranged, *appropriate*; and with Yoko's music that's saying something."

Both *Plastic Ono Band* albums would age very well, and became very influential. Over the years both albums have been re-evaluated very positively. Both albums are now regarded as classics and deservedly so. A 50th Anniversary reissue of *John Lennon/Plastic Ono Band* was released on 23 April 2021, which featured unreleased material, all featuring Starr. These two albums were and are concrete examples of Starr's adaptability as a drummer, and this will be seen throughout the 1970s.

Starr was keeping himself very busy in early 1970 with his debut solo album and assisting other artists. However, it was his work with George Harrison that had the biggest impact on Starr's life. While recording *Sentimental Journey*, Ringo finished a song he had started writing in 1968. Harrison helped him quite a bit with the song that would become Starr's stand alone solo single in 1971, 'It Don't Come Easy'. In 1970, the song was known as 'You Gotta Pay Your Dues'. Although he did not receive an official writing credit, Harrison did finish the song off for Ringo. During the telecast of *VH1 Storytellers*, Ringo stated that Harrison co-wrote the song. In talking about his early writing abilities, Starr admitted that he was "great at writing two verses and a chorus" but really could not finish the song.

The first recording of the song was at EMI Studios (Abbey Road) on 18 February 1970. This was also the day that Starr completed his vocals for 'Let The Rest of The World Go By', the last track on the album *Sentimental Journey*. The session for 'You Gotta Pay Your Dues' could not have been more different from the *Sentimental Journey* sessions. At this session Starr was joined by Harrison, Klaus Voormann on bass and Stephen Stills on piano. However, for reasons unknown, although take

30 was marked as best, Starr discarded this version and returned to the song at a later date.

While working with Lennon, and on other Apple projects, Starr was more than willing to help his old friend George Harrison. As noted earlier, Harrison was putting together his third solo album, *All Things Must Pass*. Not only was it a great chance to work with Harrison, but this recording helped set up an opportunity for Starr to work with another individual who appeared on the album. On his website, Pete Drake wrote that he had received a phone call from George Harrison. Drake was a well known producer and lap steel player and Harrison thought it would be great to have him play on some songs on *All Things Must Pass*. Drake's name was passed on to him, no doubt, by Bob Dylan, with whom Harrison had worked during 1970 in Columbia Studios in New York City.

Dylan had worked with Drake on his Nashville albums (*John Wesley Harding, Nashville Skyline, Self Portrait*), and Harrison was a fan of those (and really all of Dylan's) albums. In fact, it was during the session in New York City that Dylan gave Harrison 'If Not For You' and co-wrote 'I'd Have You Anytime', both of which were included on the *All Things Must Pass* album.

Drake recalled getting the phone call from Harrison, and not knowing Harrison. "His name, you know, just didn't ring any bells - well, I'm just a hillbilly, you know... Anyway, I ended up going to London for a week where we did the album *All Things Must Pass*."

While Harrison was busy with *All Things Must Pass*, Harrison asked Starr if he would go to the airport to pick up Pete Drake.

"George was making an album and I sent my car for this steel guitarist and producer Pete Drake, from Nashville. So Pete came and he noticed in my car I had all these country tapes. I don't know why he was shocked at this but he goes, 'Wow, you've got all these country tapes!' 'Yeah. I love country music.' He said, 'Well, why don't you come to Nashville and we'll make a record?' Furthest thing from my mind. And I said, 'Oh no, I'm not going to Nashville for months to make a record.' With The Beatles I was so used to months and months making a record. He said, 'What are you talking about? We did [Bob Dylan's] *Nashville Skyline* in a day,' or whatever. Couple of hours! 'Oh, OK.' So I flew to Nashville because of him and we did *Beaucoups Of Blues*. And we actually did it in two days. Far out. We picked and learned five songs in the morning and we recorded five songs at night, and had a lot of fun in between. But these were all starters, I felt, for getting me back on my feet."

However, one of the musicians who appeared on the album, and contributed four songs, remembers it a bit differently. Sorrells Pickard, in conversation with Donald Sauter, recalled that Chuck Howard (who also wrote four songs on *Beaucoups Of Blues*), was in England with Pete Drake, and that Chuck became good friends with Ringo. According to Pickard, it was Howard who was the main influence in getting Ringo to travel to Nashville to record the album. Pickard said, "Ringo had some apprehensions at first, feeling like he didn't want to leave home for all the *months* it would take to record the album. It took some convincing that country musicians don't work that way!"

Whoever convinced Starr to go to Nashville did him a huge favour, as *Beaucoups Of Blues* would be a much more critically accepted album than *Sentimental Journey*. Drake, true to his word, brought together some of Nashville's hottest players and writers to provide Ringo with the basis of a great country album: Charlie Daniels, Jerry Reed, The Jordanaires (Elvis Presley's back-up singers), Sorrells Pickard, Jeannie Kendall (of The Kendalls), D.J. Fontana (Elvis Presley's drummer during his early years), Chuck Howard, Roy Husky, and Drake himself to name just a few. In fact, several of these musicians could be heard on Dylan's albums as well. Charlie Daniels would go on to great success with The Charlie Daniels Band ('The Devil Went Down To Georgia' was a worldwide top 20 hit in 1979) and Jerry Reed would go on to a very successful acting career as well as having several hits on the country and pop charts, such as 'Amos Moses' (1970) and 'When You're Hot, You're Hot' (1971), which Starr quotes in '$15 Draw'.

Session musician Charlie Daniels agreed about the country music musicians and their work patterns. "Those were pretty typical Nashville sessions. You know, three songs in three hours. It was to go in, sit down and work. Here's the songs, here's the chords, let's get it done. It was not a Beatles-type leisurely session. It was work." This goes a long way in explaining how the album was recorded in three days.

Having been through the *Get Back/Let It Be* sessions, Starr was not used to working quickly on an album. Not since the *Please Please Me* album had Starr experienced a recording at such a pace. "We went into the studio on Thursday and I had 10 tracks done by the Friday – the next night," Starr later remembered. "We did 10 tracks in the morning and 10 tracks at night."

Because this was a new way of working, "At first, I was nervous," Ringo admitted, "and Pete would say through the glass, 'Hoss, if you don't get loose, I'm gonna come in there and stomp on your toes.'" Pickard agrees with the pace at which they worked. According to Pickard, the daily routine was basically: "Each morning the writers of the songs Ringo was to record would go to his hotel room and teach him the new songs. Then they would record the songs that evening." One can see how this was a bit different for Ringo. But according to the players on the album, he rose to the occasion.

Drummer D.J. Fontana remembered Starr as being very committed to the project and very professional when they recorded. Starr was also a fan of Fontana because of his time with Elvis Presley. "Ringo was the nicest man in the world. We had some pretty well known players on that date, so we made him a little nervous, I'm sure. He made us nervous too."

Fontana added "We were thinking he was going to be a jerk. I mean, The Beatles, the No. 1 act in the world. This guy's got all these big monster records. But he came here and it was, 'Whatever you guys want to do, let's do it. You guys play the way you've been playing and I'll try to catch up'."

Pickard agreed: he remembered Ringo as a real nice guy and a hard worker. Pickard reported that sessions were "hard work". But as hard work as it was, Starr seemed to enjoy himself and the recording was a great experience.

Recording began on 25 June 1970 at 6.00 pm. By 9.00 pm, two songs were done: 'Woman Of The Night' and 'Without Her'. Later that night, after a late dinner, no doubt, they worked until 1.00 am and recorded 'Beaucoups Of Blues', 'Waiting' and 'Love Don't Last Long'. The tight schedule continued the next day, with '$15 Draw' and 'I'd Be Talking All The Time' being tackled and completed from 6.00 to 9.00 pm. Once again there was a break and work continued at 10.00 pm with 'Wine, Women, and Loud Happy Songs' and the unreleased 'The Wishing Book'. Once again, sessions came to a stop at 1.00 am.

Finally, recording was completed on 27 June. During the first session of the evening, from 6.00 pm to 9.00 pm, three songs were recorded: 'Silent Homecoming', 'Loser's Lounge' and 'Fastest Growing Heartache in the West'. Later that evening, 10.00 pm until 1.00 am, Drake got the musicians to record one song: 'I Wouldn't Have You Any Other Way'. With that, the album was done. However, two 'jams' were then attempted and recorded. First they recorded Ringo's 'Coochy-Coochy', the only song he wrote for the project and the only song on which he played drums. 'Coochy-Coochy' would not make it to the album but would be used as a B-side. The other song, a complete jam, was eventually trimmed down and given the title 'Nashville Jam' when it was released as a bonus track on the CD. It was originally titled 'Nashville Freakout', and because it was a jam, the song is credited to the musicians who attended the session: Starr, Jim Buchanan, Charlie Daniels, Pete Drake, D.J. Fontana, Buddy Harman, Howard, Junior

Huskey, Ben Keith, Jerry Kennedy, Dave Kirby, Grover Lavender, Charlie McCoy, Pickard, Jerry Reed, George Richey and Jerry Shook.

The album was released on Apple records on 25 September 1970 and was met with mixed reactions. However, a country album from Starr should not have come as a surprise to anyone. With The Beatles, Starr sang lead vocals on songs by Carl Perkins ('Honey Don't', 'Matchbox') and Buck Owens' 'Act Naturally' and contributed to the writing of a country based song with Lennon and McCartney ('What Goes On'). The Beatles also covered Perkins' 'Everybody's Trying To Be My Baby' and 'Sure To Fall' on their BBC sessions. So although a country album from Ringo Starr might not have been expected, it was not entirely out of the blue.

Starr himself would later say that "I think some of my finest vocals are on that album, because I was relaxed." Many critics agreed. Charles Burton wrote in *Rolling Stone*: "I am prepared to say that you won't be disappointed with Ringo's all-country and western album, *Beaucoups of Blues*. Shucks, you'll probably even *like* it." He further states: "Make no mistake about it, though, this record is a real winner. And finally all he had to do was act naturally. Natural Ringo Starr may not exactly be New Horizons in Pop Music, but, hell. He's really pretty good after all."

Robert Christgau in the *Village Voice* gave the album a 'B' and stated that "Pete Drake's production and song selection are superb, and Ringo, after all, is Ringo, which is still something. Recommended to country heads."

Even John Lennon was positive about the album, saying in his famous *Lennon Remembers* interview for *Rolling Stone*, "I think it's a good record. I wouldn't buy any of it. I think it's a good record and I was pleasantly surprised to hear 'Beaucoups Of Blues', that song. I felt good. I was glad and I didn't feel as embarrassed as I did about his first record."

In terms of sales, although *Beaucoups Of Blues* received positive reviews, the album did not do as well as *Sentimental Journey*. Starr did considerably less promotion for the record and as a result it did not chart in the UK and peaked at 65 on the US *Billboard* top 200 album charts, although it did get to number 35 on the *Billboard* country album charts, the first and to date only time any of The Beatles made that chart. In Canada, on 7 November 1970, the album entered the Canadian top 100 album chart at number 77, one behind James Taylor's Apple debut. It would peak at number 34 (Taylor did a little better, peaking at number 27).

In *Cash Box* (10 October 1970), the reviewer noted that *Beaucoups Of Blues* is "a happy easy going album of country music. Much of the 'good vibes' atmosphere credit must go to those backing Ringo...who lend their considerable talents to making the set sound authentic. Happily Ringo sounds right at home singing Chuck Howard's 'I Wouldn't Have It Any Other Way', Buzz Rabin's title track, and Sorrells Pickard's 'Without Her', among others."

Rolling Stone critic Charles Burton was very kind in his review, published on 29 October 1970. Not only does he hint that Ringo is breaking new ground with the album, he says "Make no mistake about it, though, this record is a real winner." He further added: "Coming from the lips of Ringo Starr, the songs sound terrific." Don Heckman, in *Stereo Review* (February, 1971), wrote: "With Pete Drake at the helm, the accompanying music could be expected to be excellent, and it is. Drake's superbly controlled steel guitar slips through every now and again, and the background singing - especially that provided by Jeannie Kendal - is always more than functional. According to Drake, the entire recording (including three unreleased tracks), was made in something less than a week. For that, alone, it should get a Grammy award. And for Ringo's singing, captured at last in an appropriate medium, the record should get - well, how about a lot of listeners?" Even Richard Williams, writing for *Melody Maker* in the UK, gave it a good review. "One can imagine ... that Ringo had a ball making this album. I had a ball listening to it."

Interestingly no singles were released in the UK, but the title track was issued as a single in North America and most of Europe. *Cash Box* noted that the single "is gentle and easy going and Ringo sounds right at home. The boys behind him are all top men in their field and add just the right touch to make it a winner." *Record World* reported that the "same guy sang 'Act Naturally' and 'Honey Don't'. C&W warblings will not go unnoticed in either the country or pop fields as he laments 'Beaucoups of Blues'." And made it one of their single picks of the week.

The single did not get a lot of airtime and this is reflected in the low placing on the US *Billboard* top 100, where it peaked at a disappointing 87. It peaked at number 43 in Germany, but in Canada it became Ringo's first post-Beatles single to make the top 40, peaking at number 35. Collectors will want to look for the US picture sleeve (with the incorrect catalogue number on the front of the sleeve) and the sleeve variations around the world. It was even released as a three song EP in Portugal.

The single is also notable for having the non-album B-side 'Coochy Coochy', a song Ringo wrote which features him on drums. 'Coochy Coochy' has the feel of a jam session with repetitive and silly lyrics. Yet the song works on a few levels. It is a fun country song, much more fun than most of the songs on the album. It is a cool bonus and for many years made the single very important to fans and collectors.

The album itself has aged extremely well, although it is very much an album of its time. Late 1960s country fans will enjoy the album, as it is very much of that era and genre. This is classic 1960s Nashville country. In many ways it is very similar to what Waylon Jennings, Willie Nelson, Conway Twitty, Dolly Parton and Johnny Cash were releasing at the time. The album opens with the title track, a very mellow, laid back song. 'Beaucoups Of Blues' guides the listener into the album. Drake and Starr picked the perfect songs for the album, but, as with many country albums at the time, the songs are somewhat depressing. Or, as country fans would say, this is an album full of "hurting songs".

Songs range from being about murder-suicide ('Love Don't Last Long') to being a loser ('Beaucoups Of Blues', 'Loser's Lounge', 'Wine, Women and Loud Happy Songs', '$15 Draw'), sex trade workers ('Woman Of The Night') and failed relationships ('Waiting', 'Without Her', 'Fastest Growing Heartache In The West').

The album ends with an anti-Vietnam War protest song ('Silent Homecoming'). The song tells of a mother waiting for her son's body to come home for burial. This type of protest song about the Vietnam War was quite popular in country music at the time. Kenny Rogers and The First Edition scored a big hit on both country and pop charts with 'Ruby, Don't Take Your Love To Town', while Waylon Jennings recorded the beautiful 'Six White Horses' on his very successful album *The Taker/Tulsa*. 'Silent Homecoming' is a powerful song and a brilliant way to end the album.

There was only one love song, 'I Wouldn't Have You Any Other Way', which was performed as a duet with the wonderful Jeannie Kendall. Kendall was a member of the family country band The Kendalls, who were highly regarded but had not yet had a hit record. She sounds great with Ringo, and it adds something different to the album.

Musically, however, it is a textbook country album, full of hooks, strong melodies and tunes that tend to get stuck in the listener's head. '$15 Draw' and 'Silent Homecoming' are two of the strongest songs on the album, with fantastic playing, great vocals from Ringo and strong melodies. Of course it did not hurt that Ringo had some of the finest Nashville writers giving him songs. Composers such as Chuck Howard, a noted country producer, who wrote for The Dillards and would go on to write for Reba McIntyre, and Sorrells Pickard, who wrote for Kitty Wells, Hank Thompson and The Statler Brothers, contributed multiple songs to the album. Larry Kingston, who had songs recorded by Don Williams, Kenny Price, and Reba McIntyre, also wrote or co-wrote songs for the album. With this amount of talent and Brill Building type of songwriting (but for country artists, not rock and rollers), the album was destined to sound great.

The sleeve and design of the album package was also quite stellar. John Kosh, who was the Apple label designer, did a fantastic job with the front sleeve. Using photographs taken by Marshall Fallwell Jr., Kosh put together a sleeve which showed most of the musicians who appeared on the album. Starr looks very relaxed in his photos and overall the sleeve reflects the high quality of music found within.

In many ways, this was Starr's *Nashville Skyline*. The main difference was that Dylan wrote his own songs, while Starr was able to pick from a crop of young, talented writers to come up with a cohesive and strong album. Drake knew how to produce Starr to get a strong vocal performance and Ringo was able to play the front man brilliantly. It is an album that was assembled quickly and served its purpose.

By the end of 1970, Starr had released two studio albums that could not be more different. And he had not even dipped his own toes into a rock career. Ringo Starr did not intentionally break new ground, but the fact that he recorded an album of standards and a country album demonstrated his ability to be diverse and open to experimenting with new and unusual genres of music. He was not afraid to try very new things, quite like Harrison's *Electronic Sound* and Lennon's first three albums with Yoko Ono. The main difference, one could argue, is that Starr's albums were much more accessible and pleasing to the ear.

Although Starr would return to country music throughout his career, it was not until 2025 that he recorded a follow-up country album. Starr had talked about recording another country album for decades, and in 2024, working with T Bone Burnett, he would finally realise his goal. The album, *Look Up*, released in 2025, proved to be one of the most successful albums in his career, giving him his first number one album when it reached number one in the UK Country Album chart. Although some fans and critics were surprised with Starr's return to country music, this is Starr returning to his roots. With *Sentimental Journey*, he provided nostalgia for his mother and, to a certain extent, himself. But with *Beaucoups of Blues*, and *Look Up*, Starr went back to his childhood, when he wanted to be a cowboy. Don't forget, his professional name, 'Ringo', partially came from Johnny Ringo. Johnny Ringo was an American historical figure from the old West that a young Richard Starkey loved to read about.

It is interesting to note that by the end of 1970, Ringo had appeared on three albums by ex-Beatles that were in the top 100 on *Billboard*. For a man who worried about his future once The Beatles split, he not only kept himself very busy during 1970 but had some substantial success with two solo albums and one solo single.

2

1971

To the casual fan, Ringo Starr seemed to take it easy from 1971 until 1973 and only released two singles. His third and most successful album, *Ringo*, was not released until November 1973. Although in those two years there were no Ringo Starr albums, he kept very busy with the two aforementioned landmark and classic singles, he appeared in three films (one of which he also directed), he filmed a fourth that was not released until 1974, he appeared in The Concert For Bangla Desh (the spelling at the time and title) and he started a design/designer furniture store. Not to mention the numerous albums on which he appeared. Starr may not have released any solo albums, but he was extremely busy during those two years.

There was also the small matter of court proceedings in which he was involved. The Beatles were beginning the dissolution of the band. McCartney filed court papers in London on December 31 1970, naming Apple and Lennon, Starr and Harrison. Eventually Alan Klein would become involved and the lawsuits really went into full swing. The Beatles would spend a great deal of time and money in the courts over the next six years, prompting Harrison to joke in 1976 that he felt he was a lawyer more than a musician. The court actions weighed on all four Beatles over the decade and at times seemed to get in the way of their friendship, at least initially. The problem was that much of the court drama played out in the press as well. *Variety* reported on the court actions almost on a daily basis.

During 1971, Starr made a point of concentrating on his acting. By then, he was already an old hand at being in front of the camera. Besides the films by The Beatles, he had made two other films (*Candy*, 1968, and *The Magic Christian*, 1969) as well as appearing on television programmes such as Cilla Black and *Laugh-In*. Starr was looking for suitable film roles, and he took one that came his way. Being asked to be in a film was not that surprising; what was surprising was the project itself.

Starr started 1971 by working with an artist that no one could imagine him collaborating with, Frank Zappa. Frank Zappa and The Mothers Of Invention made their debut in 1966 with the classic *Freak Out* album. Paul McCartney, at the time, and over the years, talked about how much he liked the album and hinted at it being somewhat of an influence on The Beatles. Zappa, however, was not always as complimentary about The Beatles. Although he has said he admired them, he also took his shots at them with the album *We're Only In It For The Money*, with the sleeve parodying *Sgt. Pepper's Lonely Hearts Club Band*.

However, Zappa was not above taking shots at himself. This can be seen in his film *200 Motels*. When he was ready to film *200 Motels*, it was really the other side of *A Hard Day's Night*. It is interesting that United Artists, the same film company that financed *A Hard Day's Night*, was behind the Zappa film. Whereas *A Hard Day's Night* showed the Beatles dealing with touring, fame and performing and having fun, *200 Motels* made it clear that life in a band is not always a good time. Zappa asked Starr to play 'Larry The Dwarf', a character who looked remarkably like Frank Zappa himself, and was not above stealing material for songs. Starr agreed and reported to the set on January 25 1971 at Pinewood Studios in Iver, Buckinghamshire, to begin rehearsals with Zappa and co-director Tony Palmer.

Zappa and his band, The Mothers of Invention, were joined by a very eclectic cast. Keith Moon joined his old friend for what promised to be an incredible experience and an incredible film. It is interesting to note that according to director Tony Palmer, *A Hard Day's Night*'s actor Wilfrid Brambell (Paul's grandfather) turned down a role in the film. Seeing Brambell interact with Moon and Starr would have been a sight to see. It would also have been great seeing Brambell team up with Starr again, given those classic scenes in *A Hard Day Night* between the two of them. Rehearsals were completed on January 29 1971, and filming began on 1 February 1971. Ringo would shoot his part in five days and he completed it on 5 February 1971. It is interesting that Starr's chauffeur at the time, Martin Lickert, has a cameo appearance in the film. He would quit Ringo's employment in April of 1971 to go to work with Frank Zappa and The Mothers Of Invention.

The movie used a new method of filming, using videotape instead of shooting onto film. This was much more cost effective. Videotape was relatively new at the time, and was typically reserved for short television shows. Feature films were shot on film. Videotape had (and has) a very different quality to film. The videotape would be transferred to film in order for it to be shown in cinemas. *200 Motels* debuted on 29 October 1971 in the Doheny Plaza Theater in Hollywood. It premiered in the UK on 16 December 1971 at the Classic Cinema in Piccadilly Circus, London. Starr can be seen on the front sleeve of the soundtrack album (released on United Artists Records on 4 October 1971), although he is not on the album itself. However, some of his dialogue did make it to CD when Rykodisc re-released the soundtrack on compact disc in 1997. Even more interesting to fans is the six CD box set released by The Zappa Estate in 2021 through Universal music, which not only features dialogue, but also outtakes and interviews featuring Starr.

In his review on 29 November 1971, Roger Ebert gave the film three stars and wrote "*200 Motels* is not the kind of movie you have to see more than once. It is the kind of movie you can barely see once: not because it's simple, but because it's so complicated that you finally realize you aren't meant to get everything and sort everything out." He further noted that "It is also not quite in the same family tree as the Beatles movie, but it's in a tree, all right. One with enough branches for everyone but wild tigers snapping at your toes." *Variety* made note of Starr's part as: "Starr's okay cameo has him dressed up like Zappa." And went on: "The film is a series of surrealistic sequences allegedly inspired by the experiences of a rock group on the road. The incidents are often outrageously irreverent. The comedy is fast and furious, both sophisticated and sophomoric."

Vincent Canby, in his review for *The New York Times*, points out that Starr "is easily recognizable but always slightly ill-at-ease." He further notes: "At its heart, *200 Motels* is a subjective *A Hard Day's Night* in desperate need of the early Beatles" . *TV Guide* was very kind, pointing out the technical advances of shooting the film on videotape and having it transferred to film. The critic for *TV Guide* also notes "*200 Motels* is a hodgepodge of color and sound linked by ex-Beatle Starr playing Zappa, complete with curly-locked wig and the signature goatee. The film is a marvelous whirl of color and visual effects, with some fine animation and Zappa's delicious wit present throughout the entire production."

The *Variety* critic said that Ringo's "cameo" was "okay" and summed up his review with "Overall the film is a literal trip which should excite, interest and amuse pop music fans. Those who don't dig the music might get a little more insight into the contemporary scene, but hardened squares will remain unconvinced."

With the film completed, Ringo was getting ready to release his debut rock single in April 1971: 'It Don't Come Easy' with 'Early 1970' on the B-side. The single was his debut single in the UK and his second single in North America. Although it was released on 9 April 1971 in the UK and 16 April 1971 in North America, on Apple, the song had been recorded in mid to late 1970, with a lot of work being done on it and several versions recorded. Starr wrote 'It Don't Come Easy' (with help from George Harrison) in 1970 as The Beatles were officially breaking apart.

"I'd written most of it, but I always had the problem that I found it hard to finish songs. But I used to take them to George. He would produce them and finish the last verse. He always wanted me to sing about God and Hare Krishna, and I said 'no no, that's your job, you do that,' and so we changed the words a little."

The song began life as 'You Gotta Pay Your Dues' or 'You Got To Pay Your Dues', and was first attempted during the *Sentimental Journey* sessions on 18 February 1970 at EMI Studios. That session was produced by George Martin and featured Starr on drums, George Harrison on guitar, Klaus Voormann on bass and Stephen Stills on piano. According to Barry Miles, in his book *The Beatles Diary Volume 1: The Beatles Years*, the recording went on until almost five in the morning of 19 February 1970, with 20 takes in the can.

On 19 February 1970, once Starr had finished 'Love Is A Many Splendored Thing', he returned to record ten more takes of what would become 'It Don't Come Easy', but Harrison was not present. According to Robert Rodriguez, Eric Clapton was present. Take 30 was marked as the best, and the sessions were completed. Sadly, this was all discarded, as Starr wanted to record a whole new version of the song.

In March, two days after the recording for *Sentimental Journey* was completed and the album had been mixed, Starr booked time at Trident Studios. Bill Harry has noted that on 8 March 1970, Harrison (who was producing the session) assembled Starr, Voormann, Stills, Mel Evans (tambourine) and Ron Cattermole (saxophone, trumpet). Additional overdubs were completed the next day at Trident, and then the song was left on the shelf. Starr and Harrison got very busy with Harrison's *All Things Must Pass*, and as noted in the previous chapter, Starr got involved with promotion for *Sentimental Journey* and the film *The Magic Christian*.

However, the song never left Starr's thoughts, and while he was working on *All Things Must Pass* and John Lennon's *Plastic Ono Band*, Starr and Harrison returned to finish 'It Don't Come Easy'. Starr sang the lead vocals, based on a guide vocal provided by George Harrison, and Badfinger's Tom Evans and Pete Ham provided backing vocals. Additionally, Gary Wright, with whom Harrison was working and had befriended, recorded a new piano part for the song, and Harrison employed a horn section. And with that, the song was done and was ready for final mixing.

The B-side, 'Early 1970', seems a bit more mysterious. Mysterious because no conclusive recording documentation exists for the song, which started life as 'When I Come To Town (Four Nights In Moscow)'. Documentation shows that recording started on 3 October 1970, at EMI

Studios, during the recording of Lennon's *Plastic Ono Band*. Although it is not clear if Lennon appears on the recording, Harrison once again acted as producer. Given that it was recorded during the *Plastic Ono Band* sessions, there is reason to believe Lennon is on the track. Peter Doggett wrote in his book, *You Never Give Me Your Money: The Beatles After the Breakup,* that Lennon plays on the track. Robert Rodriguez goes one step further in stating that Lennon not only played on the track but produced it. Because there is no documentation (at this time), it is difficult to say conclusively that Lennon was involved. Obviously Harrison is on the song, and in all likelihood Klaus Voormann was on bass. Starr sang, and played drums and assorted other instruments during the song (piano, guitar).

If Lennon did play on the track, with Harrison producing (and playing), this is the closest thing to a Beatles reunion until 1973's *Ringo* album, when the trio regrouped for Starr on Lennon's 'I'm The Greatest'.

Whereas 'It Don't Come Easy' was a song of worldwide peace and understanding, 'Early 1970' was a song to his three friends from The Beatles. He describes where they are at in 1970 and knows that Harrison will also play with him ("a forty acre house he never sees, because he's always in town playing for you with me"), and he knows Lennon will join him at times ("when he comes to town, I know he will play with me") but he is not so certain about Paul McCartney ("when he comes to town, I wonder if he'll play with me").

Quite simply, 'It Don't Come Easy' and 'Early 1970' were two songs written (or co-written) by a Ringo who was yearning for peace. One song was written with a more of a global slant ('It Don't Come Easy') and the other was more clearly a plea for peace between friends. At the core of both songs was a search for understanding and acceptance, a message Starr continues to expound.

The single was received as such by critics and the record buying public. Starr's new song received good reviews on both sides of the Atlantic. A new song from a former Beatle was still big news. Peter Jones in *Record Mirror* gave it a reasonably good review, even if he did take a few swipes at Starr's singing, but overall certified it a hit single and admitted that it has a "built in grow-on-you appeal". He also makes note of 'Early 1970' and states that because it has 'pertinent comments on how The Beatles as individuals are getting on…don't miss this side.' The *New Musical Express* (*NME*) was even kind in the review by Alan Smith, who notes that the song has a "very strong hook", and although he also takes a few jabs at Starr's vocals he does admit that it is "undoubtedly one of the best, thumpin'est things the Starr man has ever done."

Variety offered a very positive review of both songs, going so far as to state that 'Early 1970' could become the A-side. The writer also said: "George Harrison's production presence is evident in the guitar fills and brass riffs (reminiscent of 'Savoy Traffle')."

In America, in *Billboard* magazine, where it was one of two singles listed in their Top 20 Spotlight (the other was Wilson Pickett's 'Don't Knock My Love (Part One)'), the song received high praise, predicted to be a strong top 40 contender: "vocal workout has it to take him all the way". *Cash Box* was certain this was a Top 40 hit, with a "lavish new performance." In the 24 April 1971 issue, they went one step further, stating that the song harkens back to "the white-jacket double LP", and referring to the song as "stunning and delightful." Finally, *Record World* in the 17 April 1971 issue had it in the Pick Of The Week page, stating that Starr had "found his groove with this one."

On the charts, Ringo's debut single in the UK went all the way to number four in the national charts, while in America it got as high as number four on the *Billboard* top 100. *Cash Box* and *Record World* in the US both ranked it at number one, giving Starr his first number one in the USA. *Billboard* also charted the single in its Easy Listening Top 50, with it peaking at number 24. In Canada, the single topped the *RPM* national charts, giving Starr another hit in Canada. It became a worldwide top five hit. Starr himself seems to love this song, and has included it in all of his Ringo Starr and His All Starr tours. He would also perform the song at *The Concert For Bangla Desh* in August 1971.

Although Starr had his first worldwide hit, it is important to remember that he had some very stiff competition at the time. Paul McCartney's 'Another Day', John Lennon and The Plastic Ono Band's 'Power To The People' and Harrison's 'Bangla Desh' were all released at roughly the same time, and Starr won that race. Along with solo Beatle singles, there were other big hits at the time. One look at *Billboard's* top 100, and one sees that Starr was kept from the top three by The Rolling Stones ('Brown Sugar'), The Carpenters ('Rainy Days And Mondays') and the number one single at the time, 'Want Ads' by Honey Cone. In the UK, Ringo was kept out of the top spot by Dave and Ansell Collins ('Double Barrel'), The Rolling Stones ('Brown Sugar') and at number one, Dawn ('Knock Three Times').

Since the 1980s, it has been unheard of to release a single and not include it on an album. But Starr was not ready to record his first rock album, and was content to release the single as a stand alone single. A number of artists during the 1970s, especially in the UK, released singles that were not initially part of an album: David Bowie, Roxy Music and Elton John all had hits that were simply released as singles. In fact it was common practice for these artists; Paul McCartney and Wings did the same. Since neither side of this single appeared on any album at the time, fans had to wait until 1975 to purchase *Blast From Your Past*, a compilation assembled for Capitol/EMI, which did include both sides of the single.

Still, for an artist who one year ago worried about his future, he was proving to not only the music world but himself that he could be a viable force in the music arena. In many ways, 'It Don't Come Easy' felt like a debut. This does not discount his first two albums, but in terms of rock, 'It Don't Come Easy' felt like a hungry artist just starting out. It would become his signature song. It is also somewhat autobiographical. Not to put too fine a point on it, but Starr had paid his dues and he was attempting to demonstrate that he could be a solo musician at a time when the expectations for all four Beatles was rather high.

Because the song was a hit, Starr knew he would be expected to perform it on television around the world. He did not seem to have the inclination or desire to assemble a band and perform live, so, as with The Beatles, the answer was to shoot a promo film, the precursor to music videos. In April he travelled to Norway, where on 27 April 1971 he filmed the official promo. Basically, it is Ringo playing in the snow with clips of him sitting at a piano and playing a very small drum kit intercut. It is a charming film with a very homemade feel to it. The promo film was aired on *Top Of The Pops* twice and can now be found on the bonus DVD disc with *Photograph: The Very Best of Ringo* released in 2007.

One could never predict what Starr would do next, and again, fans could be forgiven for being a bit surprised when on 5 May 1971 an exclusive, modern, upscale design store opened in London. The store, Zarach, was not itself surprising, but in it was a kinetic sculpture which was described in Keith Madman's book, *The Beatles After The Break-Up 1970 - 2000,* as a "rich man's plaything". In 1971, in a short feature in *Playboy* magazine, it is described as "a work of art recently offered for sale…that its creator was none other than Ringo Starr. Zarach calls the piece a kinetic sculpture and, thanks to mass production, prices it only £60-$144. It consists of a clear Perspex rectangular box with mercury-filled discs inside that wind down a zigzag course, then spiral upward to repeat an interminable trip (with the help of a small motor in the opaque-lit base)." In 2025 money, £60 would be about £1500.

At the same time, Starr was working with a designer by the name of Robin Cruikshank, who came to his attention when his company, Design Associates, came to work for Apple Records. Design Associates was made up of Cruickshank and fellow Central School of Arts and Crafts students Robin Michael Wolchover and Roger Brockbank. When Starr moved to his new home in Hampstead in 1969, he called upon Cruickshank to help him and his then wife Maureen to decorate and design the home. Most importantly, he worked with Cruickshank and showed him some of his own design ideas. Not long after, the Chairman of Cunard approached the pair to design a 'disco' for one of their hotels. Although this did not pan out as planned and the plans were abandoned, it cemented a working relationship and partnership between Cruickshank and Starr.

In 1969, the pair became Ringo Or Robin Limited and had an office at Apple on 3 Saville Row. On 3 September 1971 they had a big launch at Liberty's department store in London. Available during their show at the store was a one sided single. The record 'Steel' featured Starr discussing their partnership and designs. The record was released on Apple (ROR 2001) and the official release date of that single is 13 September 1971. They would open their own showroom, near the Tate Gallery, in 1974, and the partnership lasted until 1986, when they both decided to cease operations. Cruickshank continues to design under the name ROR.

On 21 May 1971, The Radha Krsna Temple released their debut self-titled album on Apple. It was produced by George Harrison, and it included the UK top 20 hit, 'Hare Krishna Mantra', and the less successful but popular 'Govinda'. The track 'Govinda' was recorded in January 1970, and according to Radha Krsna Temple's member Shyamsundar Das, Starr played drums on it. Although there is no studio documentation to support this claim, it makes sense, given that Ringo was working with Harrison and Billy Preston, and Preston does appear on the album. Although the singles were both huge successes, the album failed to chart on either side of the Atlantic, but has been re-released several times since its original release.

When the single 'Govinda' was released, *Cash Box* gave it a good review (4 April 1970), noting that although there might be a barrier with the language, the exciting chant features "in a magnificent production that should climb from FM to top forty and possibly even MOR hit lists." It did receive a great deal of airtime on FM stations. *Billboard* gave the album a four star rating but did not review it.

Ringo was certainly keeping busy in the first half of 1971, and his name was appearing in the music and regular press. On 27 May 1971, Starr announced that he had signed on to play a Mexican bandit by the name of Candy in the film *Blindman*. The film was scheduled to start shooting in Italy and Spain on 1 June 1971. When asked about the film at the time, Starr was quite clear that this film was the next step in his acting career, which he was taking very seriously. "I want to be, like, in this film, a crazy cowboy or whatever part I get. We're talking about me being an actor now, not being used for the name like I have been. In this film, I really feel as if I'm acting."

However, before the cameras started rolling for the film, which was produced by Allen Klein's ABKCO and released through Apple, Ringo was asked to join an all star session for B.B. King, who was recording an album in London. The recording took place from 9 June 1971 through to 16 June 1971. The album, *B.B. King In London*, would be released on 19 November 1971 on Probe Records in the UK (it would be released a month earlier in North America on the ABC label) and featured Starr on three tracks ('Ghetto Woman', 'Wet Hayshark' and 'Part-Time Love'). 'Ghetto Woman' was also the lead off single, featuring Starr, and made the top 100 in the US and top 30 of the *Billboard* R&B charts. Others on the album included Gary Wright, Bobby Keys, Klaus Voormann and Alexis Korner.

In 1992, while being interviewed by Tom Petty, Starr said: "B.B. King called me the human grandfather clock." Overall, Starr seemed to enjoy playing with B.B. King more than he did with Howlin' Wolf. During an interview with Michael Watts of *Melody Maker*, Starr said: "B.B. you can get closer to because he's playing guitar." Starr went so far as to compare the two blues legends and his experience working with them. While he applauded King for his playing, Wolf was a different story. "Howlin' Wolf didn't play. He just sang. Eric played guitar, and another guitarist called Charles someone, I think his name was, who was with Howlin' Wolf." And Starr was equally clear that these sessions were not more important than working with his old friends. "But B.B. and Howlin' Wolf are no more important to me than sessions with John or George."

Starr was interviewed for *Melody Maker* at the time of the album's release. "The first night wasn't that good because no one knew each other and you couldn't get in with them. I played a bit crazy and they didn't know what was happening," Starr later related. But as far as Starr was concerned, it was the last night of recording that made it all worthwhile. "The last night with B.B. was the greatest session this year…it blows your mind. That's why music is important to me. Just for those days."

During the same interview, Ringo was very clear in saying: "That's why I think it's more important to me than acting." However, at the same time, he was trying to establish a career as an actor and wanted to be taken seriously. Following the recording, he made arrangements to fly to Italy to film *Blindman*.

Starr was also planning on writing the theme song for the film. He told Michael Watts in *Melody Maker* that "at the moment I'm working on the title song for this film which I've written, and when I get back I'll have to record and then take it back to Rome to fit with the film." During the same interview, Starr hinted at making a new album: "But then I think I'd like to get into an album. It'll be like 'Don't Come Easy', one of those. It'll be poppy." Before all this happened, however, Ringo was involved in the greatest event of 1971, *The Concert For Bangla Desh* (as the album was titled prior to the change to Bangladesh).

It is worth noting that during this time, on 15 May 1971, while holidaying on the yacht SS Marala in Majorca with George and Patti Harrison, Starr and Harrison begin writing a song which would evolve into 'Photograph'. Starr was getting ready for the B.B. King sessions and had accepted the role in *Blindman*, but a holiday was in order first. It turned out to be a working holiday, and the song that he and Harrison wrote would be finished, demoed and ready for recording in 1973.

Harrison and Ravi Shankar held a press conference on 27 July 1971 to announce the concert and debut Harrison's new single, 'Banga Desh', which was released the next day. Harrison invited all of The Beatles, but for various reasons only Starr accepted and turned up for both shows held on 1 August 1971. When Starr was asked to be part of the concert, he reportedly stated, "only if Keltner will do it with me", to which Jim Keltner replied later: "Of course, but I want to stay out of his way." Starr had performed in front of a television audience but hadn't appeared at a full scale concert since 1966. It is fair to say he was somewhat nervous about the event. The nerves seemed to get the better of him when he had the spotlight and sang 'It Don't Come Easy'. He forgot some of the words.

Besides Harrison and Shankar, many of Harrison's friends showed up to perform. Eric Clapton, Leon Russell, Billy Preston, Badfinger, Klaus Voormann, Jim Keltner, Jesse Ed Davis and Bob Dylan were also part of the iconic concerts. There was an afternoon and an evening show. Ringo performed during the entire show, providing a solid backbeat for all the artists and their songs. He got the spotlight once, to sing his then current hit 'It Don't Come Easy'. Although the version used on the album and film (the evening performance) has him forgetting some of the words, his performance is exciting, and fans certainly loved his solo song. He was met with thunderous applause and a great amount of goodwill.

Variety, in reviewing the triple album, stated: "The biggest pop musical event since the Woodstock festival...at Madison Square Garden a few months ago brought together another glittering constellation of hit-makers, including George Harrison and Ringo Starr." The reviewer also added, "The concert has been impressively packaged in a triple-platter album, whose profits will be committed to people of the newly established Bangla Desh. It shapes up as one of the blockbusters of the disk biz."

Both of the shows were filmed and recorded, and an elaborate triple album box set would be released on 20 December 1971 in North America and 10 January 1972 in the UK. Mixing and producing the album seemed to be the easy part for Harrison. Dealing with record companies, government taxes and Capitol Records was another matter. In hindsight it is a miracle the album and film ever saw the light of day. The film had several delays as well, and did not reach cinemas (20th Century Fox distributed the Apple film) until 23 March 1972 in the United States, while the UK had to wait until 27 July 1972 for its premiere. John Lennon and Yoko One attended the New York premiere in March, but reportedly left during Dylan's segment.

The film received rave reviews and did extremely well at the box office, especially for a concert film. It made $2.5 million in 1972, which is roughly $22 million in 2025 money. It was a chance for millions to view the concert who could not be in New York for the actual show. It was well filmed, but like the album, songs were left off the film. For the most part, the album set and film utilised the recording from the evening show. However, some songs were composites of the two shows, such as 'Wah-Wah' and Leon Russell's 'Medley: Jumpin' Jack Flash/Youngblood'. Interestingly, Dylan's 'Mr. Tambourine Man' (featuring Ringo on tambourine) made it to the album, but was not used in the film. Dylan performed 'Love Minus Zero/No Limit' during the afternoon show, which was later included as a bonus track for the 2005 DVD. Harrison's 'Hear Me Lord' was also performed at both shows but has not surfaced on any of the releases of the concert. The DVD did have a couple of interesting soundcheck moments included, such as Dylan and Harrison performing 'If Not For You' and Russell's 'Come On In My Kitchen'.

At the time of release, the film did receive a great many accolades. *Variety* was quite vocal with its praise, talking about the multi camera angles and stating that "the film benefits from a simple, uncomplicated style" (27 March 1972). In the *New Musical Express* (*NME*), John Pidgeon refers to it as "The Greatest Rock Spectacle of the Decade!" Roger Greenspun in the *New York Times* gave the film some positive points: "*The Concert for Bangladesh* exhibits less technical nervousness in the face of musical performance than any other remotely similar film I can think of. And because it is so little bothered with what it must do next, say, to turn song into cinema, it probably succeeds in moving with its people more closely, and surely differently, than the audience at

Madison Square Garden could have done." But he was also critical of the sound.

In March 1972, *Variety* noted that Allen Klein's company, ABKCO Industries, made a bid to buy out the Beatles' interest in Apple Corps Ltd. Not only was Apple the Beatles' label, it was also the collector of their royalties. According to *Variety*, Klein had already been talking with three of the Beatles, George Harrison, John Lennon and Ringo Starr, about the possibility of acquiring their respective interests in Apple. Each of these three owned 25% of the company. Such discussions and legal pursuits would lead to Starr forming his own record label, but that was a few years in the future.

It is worth noting that the film *The Concert For Bangla Desh* was directed by Saul Swimmer. He not only co-produced The Beatles' *Let It Be* but was also directing Ringo in the film *Blindman*. Both Starr and Swimmer had to depart to Italy and Almería shortly after the concerts to complete the filming of *Blindman*. Almería was also the location in which John Lennon filmed *How I Won The War* five years earlier. This location was a favourite of European and American filmmakers to shoot Westerns. And all of these films were ABKCO backed.

In an interview with *Variety* magazine (10 November 1971), Allen Klein discussed ABKCO. "Heavily involved in film operation will be the three Beatles with whom Klein is still on speaking terms, John Lennon, Ringo Starr and George Harrison, and two London-based staffers, producer Neil Aspinall and editor Tony Lenny. Upcoming ABKCO projects include *Along the Winding Road* and *The Sacred Mountain*, which *El Topo* director Alejandro Jodomsky will start shortly in Mexico."

Swimmer was an interesting filmmaker. An American-born fan of films, he was excellent at recognising opportunity when it arose. He directed the 1965 film *Mrs. Brown You Have a Lovely Daughter,* starring Herman's Hermits, and in 1982 produced and directed the Queen live film *We Will Rock You, Queen Live In Concert*. He also worked, for a time, with the writer-actor-director Tony Anthony (born Tony Roger Petitto in West Virginia). The two of them co-wrote and co-directed *Come Together*, which was released through Apple (the soundtrack on Apple Records is a very unique listening experience). It was through Allen Klein and Swimmer that Starr found himself in the cult classic *Blindman*.

The film *Blindman* was based on a Japanese film, *Zatoichi*, "about a blind samurai warrior". Anthony, as the blind gunman, is looking for fifty mail order brides who have been stolen from him by a gang which includes Ringo Starr's character, Candy. Coincidently, *Candy* was the first film Starr acted in, in 1968. *Blindman* had nothing to do with *Candy*, but it did give Starr a second opportunity to play a Mexican. If Starr was looking for a departure in his roles, he could not have picked a better one. He is the ultimate bad guy. Starr travelled to Italy and started filming on 17 June 1971, ten days after work began on the film, and then to the province of Almería in Spain. Famed Italian director Ferdinando Baldi (*David And Goliath*, 1960, and *Texas, Adios*, 1966, to name just two) directed the film. He would work with Anthony on *Get Mean* in 1975, filmed in the same location. Almería is where Ringo had visited Lennon when he worked on the film *How I Won The War* five years earlier. Filming was completed in August after *The Concert For Bangla Desh*.

The film had a very modest budget of 1.5 million US dollars, and would go on to earn 15 million US dollars. The film premiered in Rome (where some of it was shot) on 15 November 1971. *Blindman*, as it was shown in Italy, was entirely dubbed in Italian. In North America, it was a different story. It saw a limited release in North America after it premiered in Chicago on 12 January 1972. It would be over a year before the film was released in the UK due to concerns from the censor about the extreme violence.

The reviews for the film were not kind. *TV Guide* wrote: "Unbelievably stupid 'comic' spaghetti western that screams, gouges, yells, and shoots its jokes out." They did not seem to like the lead actor Tony Anthony and were less than enthusiastic with Starr's performance. "A complete waste of time, except for those who want to see Starr participate in one of the dumbest career moves in history. Let's hope that his role in this film wasn't a contributing factor in the breakup of the Beatles." Roger Ebert gave the film one and a half stars and said: "The movie itself is a greasy bill of goods." However, the film has gone on to achieve cult status, perhaps due to the complete oddity of it. Watch carefully for Beatle minder Mal Evans and Allen Klein's cameo at the beginning of the film.

Ringo was satisfied that his film career was becoming established, allowing him to avoid being typecast in comedy films. With his appearances in *200 Motels* and *Blindman*, he demonstrated his ability to play vastly different roles. He could honestly tell himself that he was not trapped in comedy roles, and in a sense, he altered his overall image, so that he was taken more seriously. As September began, Starr officially launched Ringo or Robin Ltd with Robin Cruickshank. The launch was on 3 September 1971. Also in September, Ringo would gather with Harrison, Gary Wright and Klaus Voormann in Apple Studios to record a song which would debut in March of 1972.

Starr was also laying the groundwork for a film that he would not only appear in, but direct. In 1971, Ringo Starr was introduced to Marc Bolan, who was riding his way to the top of the charts with his band T Rex. Starr approached him about making a documentary about the band and Bolan himself. Through this meeting, the two became fast friends, and their paths would cross professionally and privately until Bolan's untimely death in 1977. Bolan was not keen on a documentary, but when Starr became aware of a couple of shows Bolan was planning in London, he struck a deal with the artist. He would direct the film and Apple films would enter into an agreement with Bolan's Wizard Arts Company to produce it. The cost and ownership would be split 50/50. Bolan agreed.

As 1971 was drawing to a close, Ringo, along with his wife Maureen, attended the 9 October 1971 opening for Yoko's art exhibition *This Is Not Here* at The Everson Museum in Syracuse, New York. The opening was covered by television and news outlets. In fact, a television show, *John And Yoko In Syracuse, New York*, was filmed and shown on American television on 11 May 1972.

After the opening, Ringo attended John and Yoko's party in their suite and over the course of the evening a musical jam took place. Along with Ringo and Maureen, Lennon's friends in his suite included Eric Clapton, Klaus Voormann, Jim Keltner, Mal Evans, Neil Aspinall and Allan Ginsberg. Ringo even performed 'Yellow Submarine'. During the party, Ringo presented Lennon with a gift. Yoko had asked John's friends to record a message for John's birthday, and Ringo did a song, 'Happy Birthday, John', with help from Voormann, Billy Preston, Stephen Stills and maybe George Harrison. It was likely recorded during the 'It Don't Come Easy' sessions and presented to Lennon on 9 October 1974. It has been aired during the syndicated radio show *The Lost Lennon Tapes*.

Ringo had every right to be proud of his work in 1971. He scored an international top five single, appeared in three films and on television shows, and performed on several critically acclaimed and successful albums. He even started a design company and designed some of the pieces it sold. For an artist who two short years ago was worried about his career now that The Beatles were finished, Starr proved, beyond a shadow of doubt, that he had a viable and solid solo career. He excelled as a musician and he had started a healthy acting career. Ringo would find 1972 was much the same, but maybe a little better.

3

1972

For Ringo, 1972 would be another very busy and interesting year. Although there was no album in sight, he was putting the finishing touches on a single that he had recorded in September 1971 at Apple Studios. The B-side of the single was recorded a month earlier and a single with both songs would appear in March 1972. However, before that was to be released, Starr found himself involved in a rather interesting project.

During the 1960s, The Beatles became friends with many different artists in London. Starr befriended Keith Moon from The Who, so much so that Moon was the godfather of Starr's children. Keith Moon was an essential member of The Who, not only for his drumming, but for his off stage antics. He did not write many songs, but those that he did write were memorable, for example the two songs he wrote for the classic *Tommy*. The Who released this 'rock opera' in 1968. The album, about a child who is traumatised by seeing a murder committed by his father and becomes "death, dumb and blind", was not only critically acclaimed but also a worldwide hit.

Lou Reizner was at one time president of Mercury Records, but he was probably better known for producing records for Rod Stewart and Rick Wakeman. He also had a huge part in discovering Queen. He had decided to put together a symphonic version of The Who's *Tommy* album, with The Who's full cooperation. Not only did he use the London Symphony Orchestra and English Chamber Choir, he employed a number of rock stars to take parts in the original rock opera. This album set the stage for *Tommy* to be turned into not only a stage performance but also a feature film.

Members of The Who were involved, with Daltrey playing the lead role of Tommy. John Entwistle had the Cousin Kevin role, while Peter Townshend acted as narrator. Other artists who took part included Sandy Denny (The Nurse), Steve Winwood (The Father), Merry Clayton (The Acid Queen) and Richard Harris (The Doctor). Ringo Starr was asked to play the part of the sex offender Uncle Ernie, a character actually created by his good friend, Keith Moon, who would take over the role for the film and future stage performance.

According to Chip Madinger and Mark Easter, Starr recorded his part in January of 1972 in Olympic Studios. The album would not be released until October 1972, when it did extremely well, especially in the US, where it peaked at number five on the *Billboard* top 200 charts. The single from the album, 'I'm Free', did moderately well. It peaked at number 13 in the UK charts, while it scraped into the top 40 (number 37) in the *Billboard* top 100. No doubt the airtime the single received and the all-star cast help propel the album into the higher regions of the charts. The album also won a Grammy in 1974 for best packaging.

Lou Reizner put together a live show at The Rainbow in London (13 and 14 December 1972), in which Starr did not participate. As noted, Keith Moon took back the role, as he had performed the songs on the original album. Starr was busy with the premiere of his film *Born To Boogie*. Although the concert was staged to promote the album, the album failed to chart in the UK.

In January Starr was involved with an album that George Harrison was working on with a very respected musician. George Harrison wanted to help out a musician friend he first met when touring with the Delaney and Bonnie and Friends tour, Bobby Keys. Keys, who also worked on Harrison's solo album *All Things Must Pass*, was a respected and in demand session player. Perhaps to repay a favour, Harrison agreed to work on Keys' self-titled debut solo album. Starr got involved too, probably through Harrison, and the two found themselves at Command (or possibly Island or Olympic, according to Kristofer Engelhardt in his book *Beatles Undercover*) studio.

There is no clear information on the album or the CD reissue, so it is difficult to know what tracks the two Beatles appear on, but Engelhardt surmised they played on 'Bootleg'. Keys would later make an appearance in Starr's *Son Of Dracula* film, work on the *Ringo* and *Goodnight Vienna* albums and release a single on Starr's Ring O' Records label. The album *Bobby Keys*, when eventually released by Warner Brothers, was only released in the UK, Europe and Japan and failed to chart in any country. Although it is a good album, instrumental jazz-rock albums were not finding an audience in the UK in 1972.

Starr was also asked to help out with the recording of former Righteous Brother, Bobby Hatfield. Hatfield was trying to get his solo career off the ground and in doing so employed the very popular producer Richard Perry. At this point, Perry's career as a producer was really taking off, with credits such as Barbra Streisand's *Stony End* and Harry Nilsson's *Nilsson Schmilsson*, both top selling and critically acclaimed albums. Perry, who had worked with Ringo on his *Sentimental Journey* album, thought it would be a good idea to get Hatfield out of Los Angeles and record in London. Perry booked time at Apple Studios and asked Ringo to help.

Two singles were released at the time: 'Stay With Me' and 'Oo Wee Baby, I Love You'. Both singles featured 'Rock And Roll Woman' on the flipside. Ringo only played on 'Oo Wee Baby, I Love You'. Ringo would borrow the phrase 'Oo Wee' for his own song on 1974's *Goodnight Vienna*. 'Oo Wee Baby, I Love You' owes a great deal, musically, to 'Get Back'. The intro and Starr's drumming are lifted directly from the Beatles song, but then the song moves into the classic 'blue eyed soul' for which Hatfield was famous with The Righteous Brothers.

The single received a rave review in 18 March 1972 in *Cash Box* magazine, noting "Richard Perry's production blows the lid off" the song. But this did not help airplay or sales. The single sank without a trace. Given the success he had with The Righteous Brothers, the production and quality of the song, one would have thought it would have done better. Because neither single attracted much attention, the intended album was cancelled, even though it was pretty much completed. However, in 2020, an album was cobbled together titled *Stay With Me: The Richard Perry Sessions*, which features a couple of versions of 'Oo Wee Baby, I Love You' as well as other songs in which Starr was involved. It is interesting to note that Hatfield covered 'Sour Milk Sea', the song Harrison gave to Jackie Lomax as Lomax's debut single with Apple Records. Hatfield also takes a turn on another Harrison song, 'What Is Life'.

While Ringo was helping established rock stars kickstart their solo careers, and session players, he also befriended an up and coming musician who, with his band T Rex, was creating a stir that many compared to Beatlemania. Bolan, whose real name was Mark Field, was born in London in 1947. He was a musician from a young age and in the mid 1960s was involved with a couple of bands and ventures. But it was when he formed Tyrannosaurus Rex, which was wisely shortened to T Rex, that he found success. As Tyrannosaurus Rex, Bolan and his band found moderate success with the four albums they released, but it was with their second as T Rex, *Electric Warrior*, that they found international success.

According to Kristofer Engelhardt, Bolan actually came to The Beatles' attention when his paintings were used as decoration in the Apple Boutique, the clothing store The Beatles owned in 1968. At this stage, Bolan was a member of the band John's Children, before he formed Tyrannosaurus Rex. What is known for sure is that Ringo became friends with Bolan, and it was during a dinner at Ringo's house that Bolan was the inspiration for the lyrics of 'Back Off Boogaloo'.

According to Starr, Bolan had a unique way of talking. "He spoke like that: 'Oh, back off Ringo' or 'Boogaloo'," the drummer recalled. "So anyway, I became friends with him and he came to dinner one night. He was talking 'Back off, Boogaloo' so I went to bed and you know there's that zone just before you go off and I could hear 'Back Off Boogaloo... I said... Back Off Boogaloo'."

From that conversation, the germ of an idea hit Starr. He was able to turn it into a rock and roll classic. As Starr related during his VH1 Storyteller episode (1998): "I said 'Oh God, I'm getting a song here'," which proved very exciting for Starr. He was worried that he would not remember the tune in the morning, so he had to have some kind of record of his idea. "I've got out of bed and ran downstairs because I have no memory, I had none then and have not now. I was looking for the tape to put it on. The drag was that it was turned into 'Mack the Knife'. Anyway, I had to (steal) one of the batteries of the kids' toys to record the tape."

Starr would later say that Harrison helped him finish the song, as Harrison did with 'It Don't Come Easy'. Ringo recalled, "I'd got the melody down with my three chords and took it over to George's: 'Would you put in a few more chords?' It makes me sound like a genius."

Harrison not only finished the song but took Ringo into Apple Studios in September 1971 to record it. There has been speculation that this is a song was directed at Paul McCartney, with references to the McCartney death clues. "Wake up Meathead, folks pretend that you are dead," sings Starr. However, Starr has not confirmed this, and perhaps, as with the death clues themselves, fans were searching for ongoing strife in the music. Later in the song Starr sings "Get yourself together now, and give me something tasty", which many felt was another jab at McCartney. However, according to Keith Badman, in his book *The Beatles: After the Break-Up 1970-2000 : A Day-By-Day Diary,* this is actually in reference to British football presenter Jimmy Hill, who happened to be on television while Ringo was writing the song. Hill was famous for using the word 'tasty'.

One other controversy, or rather theory, about the song, is that Marc Bolan was the ghost writer of the song, especially the melody. Given that Starr was working with Bolan, they were friends, and the title is somewhat close to the title of the film *Born To Boogie,* one could make the connections and speculate that Bolan was involved with the song. However, the song sounds nothing like T Rex or Marc Bolan. It has a heavier sound than T Rex and it does not fall into the glam category of music.

Bolan would later play on Ringo's 1973 album *Ringo*, but there is no evidence that he was in the studio when 'Back Off Boogaloo' was being recorded. Harrison assembled the group of Klaus Voormann (bass and saxophone), Gary Wright (piano), Harrison (guitar, vocals) and, of course, Starr on drums, percussion and lead vocals. Madeline Bell, Lesley Duncan and Jean Gilbert provided backing vocals for the record. Once again, Harrison produced and the entire song was recorded at the newly refurbished Apple Studios which officially opened on 30 September 1971.

Apple Records' recording studio was set for a relaunch in 1972. After years of repairing and getting it set up for commercial use, the label was ready to open the doors of the state of the art recording studio. For the record, Harrison was the only Beatle who was there for the opening of the new Apple Studio. When the studio officially opened, Starr would go back to Apple to provide drums for the first recording sessions in the complex, Apple artists Lon and Derrek Van Eaton. Harrison used the Apple studio a great deal, as did McCartney in 1973. Many other artists used the studio while it was in operation, including Fanny, Nazareth, Roger Daltrey, Wishbone, Nicky Hopkins and Stealers Wheel.

With 'Back Off Boogaloo' recorded, Starr needed a B-side for the song. As it happened, he had written the song 'Blindman' for the film but the producer and director went with Stelvio Cipriani instead. Cipriani composed soundtracks for many films in Italy, and is perhaps best known for the 1979 film *The Concorde Affair*. Although the song did not make it to the film, this did not deter Starr from recording it. In August, Starr, along with Voormann, produced the song. It features Voormann, Starr and Badfinger's Pete Ham on guitar. The song is sparse and, in some ways, years ahead of its time. It has a drone-like chant and is not something one would expect from Starr. It is a song that has gained popularity over the years.

The single was released on 17 March 1972. In the UK, EMI set up a special phone line in London for fans to hear the song. EMI needn't have worried. The song received a great deal of airtime in the UK and became Starr's biggest solo hit to date, peaking at number two. It was kept from number one by 'Amazing Grace' by the Royal Scots Dragoon Guards Band. The single benefitted from a promotional film, directed by Tom Taylor, featuring Frankenstein's monster chasing Starr around Lennon's Tittenhurst estate (later to be purchased by Starr himself). Starr and the monster eventually make up and dance together at the end. According to Keith Badman, the film was not produced by Apple Records, but rather financed through Caraval Films. Caraval Films was often used by *Top Of The Pops* to film clips for the show. The film would appear on Starr's compilation CD/DVD *Photograph: The Very Best Of Ringo*. The picture sleeve of the single featured a similar Frankenstein's monster smoking a cigarette. This picture sleeve was used for print ads stating "Another monster from Apple". Very clever marketing.

As noted, 'Back Off Boogaloo' has been lumped in with glam rock, but it really isn't glam. It is a straight ahead rock song, leaning a little towards hard rock. It has Harrison's trademark slide guitar and some of Starr's most aggressive drumming, but it does not have the 'glam sound' of, say, T Rex, Bowie, Roxy Music or even Slade. Glam was much more about style and presentation. Glam rockers would wear out-of-this-world fashion, very flamboyant clothes and hair styles. Musically, it was a mix of pop, rock and an element of theatre or cabaret. 'Back Off Boogaloo' is a straight ahead rocker. The song is relentless and instantly recognisable. One could argue that it is a powerful piece of rock that really defies classification. It is simply a strong rocker. It is not hard rock, nor is it pop. Starr combined a great many elements into the song, which makes it stand out musically, then and now; these elements may seem to be a little uncharacteristic of Ringo, and yet, they are distinctly Ringo Starr.

Although it was not reviewed, 'Back Off Boogaloo' was listed in the 25 March 1972 '*Billboard* Picks section. In *Cash Box*, it was noted that 'Back Off Booglaoo' (spelled 'Bugaloo') was number ten on the chart that noted radio airplay for new releases. It is odd that *Cash Box* did not review the single as well. *Record World* did note the single and wrote "It's taken Ringo a long time to follow-up 'It Don't Come Easy', but he's come up with one here that should do at least as well, and that means top three." In the UK, it received mixed reviews, with Chris Welch, writing in the *NME*, stating "There's a touch of Marc Bolan in this highly playable rhythmic excursion... It's hypnotic and effective, ideal for jukeboxes and liable to send us all mad by the end of the week."

Roberta Flack's 'First Time Ever' kept Ringo from number one in Canada, where 'Back Off Booglao' peaked at number two, and on the US *Billboard* charts, the single peaked at number nine, when the number one song was Flack as well. What is interesting is that the single received a great deal of FM radio play in the US, which at the time was unusual for a 'single-only' release. FM was typically reserved for album cuts, but with 'Back Off Boogaloo' Ringo managed to attract a great deal of attention with a single that had no accompanying album. According to *Record World*, on 1 April 1972, it was the number one song added to radio station playlists.

The other interesting aspect of 'Back Off Boogaloo' is that the initial pressings in America, UK, Germany, France, Japan (which had a unique picture sleeve as well) and South Africa had a blue tinged or outright blue Apple. Bruce Spizer wrote in his book *The Beatles Solo On Apple Records* that perhaps this was done to satisfy Ringo's original choice for a blue Apple. There is no documented rationale for the label but it makes for an unusual collector's item, especially in the US.

Starr obviously loves the song, as he would record it twice more in his career. It appears on the 1981 album *Stop And Smell The Roses* (where he recorded it with help from Harry Nilsson, who repeated his medley format that brought The Beatles to his attention) and 2017's *Give More Love*, where it appeared as a bonus cut. He also performed it live with the Ringo Starr and The All Starrs band and it appears on several live albums, including *The Anthology... So Far* (2001), and *King Biscuit Flower Hour Presents Ringo & His New All-Starr Band* (2002).

However, as 'Back Off Boogaloo' was being released, Starr embarked on yet another project. During an interview with Hard Rock Cafe, Ringo talked about his working relationship with Marc Bolan. "I said to him one day, why don't we do a movie? He was very proud of his poetry. Every time he would come to say hi, he would say 'I'm the number one selling poet in Britain'. It was as important to him as his music. I said, let's make a movie. I'll bring the cameras and everything, you bring yourself, that's what we'll do and we did. We had a lot of fun, especially with the sketches."

One must keep in mind that Marc Bolan was one of the biggest rock stars in the UK at the time. Although T Rex are considered one hit wonders in North America, with 'Get It On' being their sole hit, in the UK and Europe it was quite a different story. Their album *Electric Warrior* was a number one album, and they had several number one singles, such as 'Hot Love', 'Jeepster' and 'Metal Guru'.

During the press conference prior to the premiere of the film, Starr elaborated: "I telephoned him one day and said, 'Come and see me. I've got this idea. See what you think, yes or no, and on that particular thing it was no. But through that meeting we got to know each other and became friendly. Then I heard he was going to be filmed at his Wembley show. Well, Apple has a film company so I said, 'Why don't you let me do it? I'm your pal' and he said, 'Okay. We'll do it together.' After the show we looked at the footage we had got and decided to add to it. You see, my theory about filming concerts is that you cannot create the atmosphere that was in the hall. So I needed to do more. We got him to write a few things and set up a couple more days shooting."

Not only would Starr be in the film, but he would also direct and produce it. *Born To Boogie* was intended to show off T Rex and Trectasy (instead of Beatlemania). On 18 March 1972, Starr turned up at the

Empire Pool, Wembley, with a full film crew. T Rex performed two shows that day to screaming and adoring fans, and Starr filmed both of them, although only footage from the second show would be used for the film. For reasons only known to Starr, he was dressed as a clown, perhaps so he would not be recognised. Starr would later admit that he enjoyed the screaming crowd and it was very nostalgic for him. "They were screaming and shouting and I love that. If they had been quiet when I played I would have died. I wouldn't have known what to do."

Starr also filmed the soundchecks, with some of the footage used for the closing credits of the film. On 21 March 1972, Bolan and Starr moved to Apple Studios to film segments for the *Born To Boogie* film. However, Badman states in his book that this was filmed and recorded in Lennon's studio in Lennon's Tittenhurst home. It was at Apple Studios where Starr said he took the photo for T Rex's 1972 album *The Slider*. Producer Tony Visconti challenged this and in his autobiography, *Tony Visconti: The Autobiography: Bowie, Bolan and the Brooklyn Boy,* he claims to have taken the front cover photo of Bolan and was not too happy when the album was released to see Starr credited for the photo.

Starr participated fully in front of the camera, and the two seem to have had a great time. Elton John joined the duo (and members of T Rex) later in the day for a jam session in Lennon's estate recording studio (where he had recorded much of *Imagine*).

Starr had the cameras rolling as the trio tore into Little Richard's classic 'Tutti Frutti' and two T Rex songs, 'Children Of The Revolution' and 'The Slider'. It is a spirited jam session, and the results are quite good. At times, Starr can be seen filming the jam himself, dressed as a clown, with full make-up. The next day, Starr, Bolan and crew returned to Tittenhurst to complete filming of *Born To Boogie*. They film the Mad Hatter's Tea Party, and T Rex's Micky Finn steals the scene with his eating habits.

'Tutti Frutti' and 'Children Of The Revolution' were released as a single on 13 May 2016 (with 'Born To Boogie (Original Version)'). It is interesting to note that neither the concert nor the soundtrack were released until 2005. When the concert and soundtrack were released, Tony Visconti was credited as the producer of the music.

The film premiered in London, at Oscar's Cinema in Brewer Street, Soho, on 14 December 1972. Elton John, Bolan and Starr were all in attendance, and the premiere received a great deal of press. However, the film did not do as well as hoped for Apple Films. It is interesting, given how huge T Rex were at the time and throughout 1973.

Bolan was very happy with the film. He said: "The film was made purely as a piece of rock and roll entertainment. I feel it documents the phenomenon that has been T Rex through the past year, and that was the purpose of the film, initially. But as Ringo and I became more involved in the making of *Born To Boogie* we decided to add several more scenes, bringing in 'accident' humour and also to shoot from recorded music, actually 'live' without dubbing. By doing so we were endeavouring to get a spontaneity which does not come naturally from some films. In some of the scenes outside of the concert we let our imaginations take their courses and, with the aid of props and a dwarf, let whichever happened, happen. We made the film strictly for a teenage audience who demand youthful excitement in the cinema - as well as on television and in the theatre. I think the film does that, no more, no less."

Reviews for the film were positive and negative. *TV Guide* noted "a suitably frantic document of Great Britain's collective bout with 'T Rex-stacy', and the definitive record of Bolan's strutting charisma." George Melly wrote a review in *The Observer* newspaper, commenting, "The film is directed and, in part, filmed by Ringo Starr. The incidental humour is drawn from the nursery surrealist world of *The Magical Mystery Tour,* but lacks that famous disaster's pretensions." *The Morning Star* newspaper reviewer wrote: "Made by Apple films and directed (?) by Ringo, this is the best teeny-bopper entertainment since The Beatles succumbed to insecticide." Fergus Cashin was perhaps the funniest, when he noted in *The Sun* newspaper that *"Born To Boogie* will open at boxer Billy Walker's cinema, Oscar…It's the nearest it will ever get to an Oscar."

The critic for *Variety* was not kind at all. "*Born to Boogie* is aimed at the teenagers and pubescents who rally to British rock group T Rex and their lead man, Marc Bolan. It probably will go down well with them as a programmer or in special bookings (the short running time could be a complication), but others are apt to find it a disappointment in both pop and cinematic terms, and scarcely an auspicious debut for Apple Films and former Beatle Ringo Starr (who also appears) as producer-director. Intercut with the concert footage is some labored location clown footage that shows even less invention." They thought that as a general rule, home movies should stay home (*Variety* 20 December 1972).

Starr summed up his relationship with Bolan and the times when he was interviewed by Paul Du Noyer in 1998: "Marc was a dear friend who used to come into the office when I was running Apple Movies, a big office in town, and the hang-out for myself, Harry Nilsson and Keith Moon. We'd go on to various venues, but we'd always start down in the office and Marc was so much fun, he'd tell us how many he was gonna sell, and what chart position he'd have. We were only 30, then, but we were looking at him like he was some crazy kid. We became friends, we had a holiday together. I took one of his album covers for him, that was just on the roof of Apple, actually. But Marc was such a cool guy, it's such a shame. We're all talking about him now he's horizontal, and I'd prefer to be talking about him vertical."

As noted earlier, Starr was at Apple Studios in September 1971 to help with a session that Harrison was producing. Lon and Derrek Van Eaton were a music duo (and brothers) who had been members of the band Jacobs Creek, who had released one album for Columbia records in 1969. When the band split, they decided to focus on writing and recording their own music and developed their own style and sound. The duo wrote and recorded a seven song demo tape, which their manager, Robin Garb, sent to various labels.

One tape was sent to Apple in New York City and landed on Allan Steckler's desk. Steckler, who worked at Apple for Allan Klein's ABKCO company, listened to the tape and loved what he heard. He played it for Harrison, who was impressed, and then Lennon, who agreed with Harrison. Harrison himself contacted the brothers expressing how much he liked their music. The duo were signed and sent over to London to record at Apple. Interestingly, their contact with Apple came through Tony King, in the London office, who was head of A & R for Apple. They received the letter on 11 June 1971.

On 21 September 1971, Lon and Derrek were not only at the Apple Studio launch party, but they were the first artists to use the new studio. Derrek Van Eaton recalled: "Yes, we were the first there to record. Beautiful studio in the basement of Apple London. Of course we had a few hiccups, there were glitches that you would expect being so fresh but nothing major that affected our work there."

Harrison had said that he wanted to produce the entire album but ended up producing just one song, 'Sweet Music'. Starr played drums. He also played drums for the song 'Another Thought', which Klaus Voormann produced. Voormann took over the production after Harrison had completed the one song as he had to move on to other things on which he was working. The album took three months to record. However, according to both brothers, it was not entirely recorded at Apple.

Derrek Van Eaton said, "On 'Sweet Music' we went to EMI to do the recording, and when we arrived all the musicians, a who's who were all there including Ringo and Jim Gordon as the second drummer...We assumed George set up the session with the same instrumentation as the *All Things Must Pass* session list. Great group to start our record in London. Before that, when we arrived in London, we were picked up at Heathrow by an Apple driver who first took us to Ascot John's White House, then over to Friar Park, when as we came to the Giant place

George and Klaus were sitting in front with guitars and were playing 'Sweet Music' when we arrived."

The single 'Sweet Music' was released on 6 March 1972 in North America, with the non album B-side 'Song Of Songs'. It was not issued as a single in the UK, even though Harrison had thought it would be a huge hit. In the UK, the song 'Warm Woman' was chosen instead, which featured a song from their album on the B-side, 'More Than Words'. 'Warm Woman' is an interesting song, because Lon Van Eaton said, during an interview, that the version released was the original demo, and that a re-recording of the song was attempted which featured Ringo on drums. This version has not yet been released. Both singles received very little attention, and Harrison was quite upset when 'Sweet Music' failed as a single, going so far as to send a letter to Klein and Steckler asking them why the single was not at the top of the charts. Given the popular music at the time, one can understand Harrison's frustration as both songs are custom made for AM radio, and should have been hits.

Neither of the singles charted or were reviewed, even though Apple ran full page ads for the single and the album in *Billboard*, *Cashbox* and other publications. The album, *Brother*, would not be released until 22 September 1972 in North America, while fans in the UK had to wait until 1973 (9 February 1973) for it to be ignored. It is a shame, as the album and respective singles are quite good. Stephen Holden, writing for *Rolling Stone* on 23 November 1972, said: "This staggeringly impressive first album…displays more energy, good feeling, and sheer musical talent than any debut record I've heard this year. Derrek's lead singing is amazing. His style ranges from a weird, tremulous falsetto to the hardest rock holler, and he is capable of shading in the difference as well." *Rolling Stone* included the album in an article from 2019, '20 Rock And Roll Albums *Rolling Stone* Loved that You Never Heard.'

Lon And Derrek Van Eaton would continue to play with Starr and have the distinction of having worked with three different producers while working with Starr, the producers being George Harrison, Klaus Voormann and Richard Perry. The three were very different in their approach and style. Lon Van Eaton would also work with two additional producers, Arif Mardin and Vini Poncia.

Lon Van Eaton reflected back on the working styles of the producers: "George was George as I would have thought. Straight ahead, no frills but such a wonderful, caring person. Great mind and nice, even got us all his special tea. Detail beyond detail. I remember once in New York where he was playing a lead on one of our songs that we can't find, he played in the control room, direct recording for at least two hours so he got it just as he wanted - wish we could find a copy of that song. Great tune I really loved! Klaus was also so nice. He tried for us to be ourselves more than any other of the three. He was very feel oriented. Liked funky feels and was more of a rudimental thinker. Now Richard was the Hitmaker. Reminded me of the successful wealthy man who knew what he wanted to go with the songs. Very nice guy but he tried to add himself to the songs as in ideas. Hard to argue since he did have so much success! All three were great in their unique styles."

Peter Frampton was a member and founder of the band Humble Pie (along with Steve Marriott), and got to know Ringo through George Harrison during the recording of *All Things Must Pass*. It was no surprise that Starr would be on hand to assist Frampton with his debut solo album, *Wind of Change*. The album was recorded at Olympic and Island studios in London from November 1971 through to February 1972. Ringo can be heard on two tracks, 'Alright' and 'The Lodger'. According to Kristofer Engelhardt, Starr also drummed on the track 'Lady Lieright', but Frampton opted for a more acoustic version of the song for the album. Frampton is quoted in Engelhardt's book as saying that Ringo wanted to hear the songs prior to the sessions, and according to Frampton, "he liked everything."

Wind Of Change was released in the UK on A&M records on 26 May 1972. North Americans waited patiently until 10 July 1972. The album didn't chart in the UK and didn't make it on to the *Billboard* Top 200 until 7 October 1972, and peaked at number 177 the following week. However, according to *Billboard* magazine, the album was playlisted on several FM radio stations across America. It is worth noting that *Billboard* did give the album a positive review and thought it would do very well: "...succeed he did, first as Humble Pie's guitarist and scoring with his first solo album. Peter has gathered as some of his 'session men' a most illustrious crew including R. Starr, B. Preston, J. Price and K. Voormann."

Peter Frampton would go on to great fame with his 1976 classic album, *Frampton Comes Alive*, which featured live versions of songs from *Wind Of Change*. It is an album that people rediscovered once Frampton was a household name. Frampton would repay the favour by appearing on Ringo's 1976 album *Rotogravure* and later being part of the All Starr Band from 1997 through to 1998.

During 1971, Ringo struck up another friendship, one that lasted for many years. The Beatles became aware of Harry Nilsson in 1968 when they discovered his music through Derrek Taylor. Taylor invited Nilsson over to London to record and do publicity. The Beatles were fans of Nilsson, especially his debut album for RCA Records, *Pandemonium Shadow Show*. Besides writing his own songs, he covered Ike and Tina

Turner's 'River Deep-Mountain High', which The Beatles loved. Ringo later said that "it was bordering on madness, and so we thought, 'We gotta meet this guy'." Nilsson also covered a couple of Beatles songs, including 'You Can't Do That', into which he wove a medley of other Beatles songs. All four Beatles thought this was brilliant.

Nilsson later recalled receiving a phone call between three and four in the morning in early April 1968. It was John Lennon, although Nilsson didn't quite believe it was him. According to Nilsson, Lennon said, "Hello, Harry. This is John. Man you're too fucking much, you're just great. We've got to get together and do something." He finished the call by saying "It's John Lennon. I'm just trying to say you're fantastic. Have a good night's sleep. Speak to you soon. Goodbye." The following Monday, he received another call early in the morning, this time from Paul McCartney. "Hello, Harry. Yeah, this is Paul. Just wanted to say you're great, man! John gave me the album. It's great; you're terrific. Look forward to seeing you."

On 14 May 1968, during a press conference to promote Apple Records, Lennon and McCartney name checked Nilsson when giving their opinion of American music. The stage was set, and later, when Nilsson received the invitation from Taylor, he jumped at the opportunity. Upon landing in London, Ringo's Daimler limousine was at the airport for Nilsson and later all the Beatles would meet up with him. Over the years Nilsson would lose touch with three members of The Beatles, but he remained very close friends with Starr until his death in 1994.

John Lennon was very enthusiastic about Nilsson. He loved Nilsson's version of 'You Can't Do That' because Nilsson incorporated other Beatle songs in the form of a medley. Lennon played it for the other Beatles, and they equally shared in Lennon's delight. But it was Starr with whom Nilsson felt the closest. In fact, when he bought his apartment in London (in Mayfair), in 1971, it was Starr and Robin Cruikshank's designer firm, Ringo Or Robin Limited, that decorated it for Nilsson.

By 1971, Nilsson had experienced limited success with hit singles 'Everybody's Talkin'' (from the film *Midnight Cowboy*) and 'Me And My Arrow' (from *The Point*). But even with The Beatles promoting Nilsson, he could not crack the album market, and he had not yet made an album with which he was entirely satisfied. According to the Nilsson website, he approached Richard Perry, who was developing a name for himself, having just made Barbra Streisand cool with young people with the classic *Stoney End* album. He even took Tiny Tim into the top ten with *God Bless Tiny Tim*, which made it to number seven on the

Billboard Top 200. If he could do that for Tiny Tim and Streisand, just think what he could do for Nilsson.

Richard Perry first met Harry Nilsson in 1968 at a party in Phil Spector's home in June of 1968 to celebrate the release of Tiny Tim's new album, which Perry had produced. The two hit it off immediately, both fans of each other's work and, as Perry put it, "both Geminis". In March of 1971, Nilsson went over to Perry's home on a mission. According to Perry, in his book *Cloud Nine - Memoirs Of A Record Producer,* Nilsson was "never one to mince words" and asked Perry: "How would you like to produce my next album?" Perry was thrilled to be asked but before he said yes, he had two conditions. First, Nilsson would let Perry call all the shots, and second, they had to record the album in London. Perry wanted to record in London to reproduce a sound close to The Beatles. Nilsson agreed to both, and the pair went to London and recorded *Nilsson Schmilsson*.

This pairing proved to be very fortuitous for Perry and for Nilsson. *Nilsson Schmilsson*, released in November 1971, was Nilsson's only US top ten album, and it featured his three biggest hit singles, 'Coconut', 'Jump In The Fire' and 'Without You'. 'Without You' was written by Pete Ham and Tom Evans of the Apple signed band Badfinger. Much to the chagrin of Nilsson, 'Without You' became his only number one hit. For a singer who was also known as a songwriter, this never sat right with Nilsson. Two of his hits (the other being 1969's 'Everybody's Talkin', which peaked at number six) were covers. The only top ten single that Nilsson wrote and recorded was the novelty hit 'Coconut' which got as high as number eight; although Three Dog Night did take his song 'One' to number five on Billboard's top 100.

Nevertheless, *Nilsson Schmilsson* got to number three, with help from a core band that included many Beatle friends, such as Klaus Voormann (bass), Gary Wright (piano), Jim Keltner (drums), Bobby Keys (saxophone), and Jim Gordon (drums). Perry himself, although having never met Ringo, worked on Ringo's *Sentimental Journey* album and provided an arrangement for the title track (and closest thing to a single from the album). As *Nilsson Schmilsson* ascended the charts and was garnering rave reviews, RCA Records (to whom Nilsson was signed) was eager for a follow-up. Richard Perry went back in the studios with Nilsson and some very famous friends to record the follow up, and Nilsson insisted on calling it *Son Of Schmilsson*.

The album was recorded in Trident Studios in London and the newly re-opened and updated Apple Studios. The sessions lasted from March to April 1972. However, the sessions did not go as smoothly or as well as *Nilsson Schmilsson*. In fact, according to Perry, his relationship with

Nilsson was somewhat strained during the recording and he wrote that Nilsson underperformed. Nilsson wanted the album to be raw ("warts and all") and on that level he succeeded. According to Perry in the liner notes of the *Son Of Schmilsson* CD reissue, "My approach would have been to just pick up where *Nilsson Schmilsson* left off...Typically brilliant Nilsson vocals, songs that maintained our artistic integrity but at the same time had great commercial value. If *Nilsson Schmilsson* was our *Revolver*, [let's] make *Son of Schmilsson* our *Sgt. Pepper*. *Son Of Schmilsson* was as far away from that goal as humanly possible."

The addition of a film crew was not helpful either. Nilsson insisted the recording sessions be filmed for a documentary of the recording and his time in London. Nilsson was not an artist who performed live often, so the film could serve as an excellent promotional tool and allow fans to get a glimpse of him performing. Unfortunately, the proposed documentary was never completed and released. Some of the footage would be used for the 2010 documentary *Who Is Harry Nilsson (And Why Is Everybody Talking About Him?)*.

For *Son Of Schmilsson*, two Beatles would be assisting Nilsson. George Harrison (appearing as George Harrysong) played slide guitar on the scathing 'You're Breaking My Heart' and Starr (as Richie Snare) provided drums for 'Take 54', 'Spaceman', 'At My Front Door', 'Ambush', and 'The Most Beautiful World In The World'. The front cover, showing Nilsson with a cape and looking very much like a vampire, was taken at Harrison's Henley-On-Thames estate. The photo was not only used for the album sleeve but was a nod to a film that he and Starr were working on, *Son Of Dracula*.

Son Of Schmilsson was released on 10 July 1972 in the US and three weeks later in the UK. Perry wrote in his autobiography that the timing of the release of the album was very odd. The album hit the stores as 'Coconut' from *Nilsson Schmilsson* was still going up the top 100. In Perry's mind, the fact that 'Coconut' was ascending the charts would bring attention to *Nilsson Schmilsson* and detract from *Son Of Schmilsson*. Clearly, a new album in the racks in stores was bound to have caused some confusion for the record buyers, since the single being promoted was not on it. *Nilsson Schmilsson* was still in the top 100, so it does seem RCA jumped the gun somewhat with the release of *Son Of Schmilsson* and Perry had every reason to question the timing of the release. This also meant that the first single released from the album, the brilliant 'Spaceman', had to wait until September to be released in both the UK and the US. This is a full two months following the album release, which in rock time in 1972 is very long. While FM stations immediately latched on to *Son Of Schmilsson*, the record buying public did not, perhaps due to lack of AM radio play.

Billboard reviewed the album in their 28 July 1972 issue: "*Son of Schmilsson* is a binding album. He is no longer content to be a singer of merely pretty songs, rather he has become a chronicler, a jurist of sorts. Every cut on this album is a unique vignette, a subtle tale." They highlight 'You're Breaking My Heart' as a top 40 hit except for the use of a "four letter word".

The album peaked at number 12 in the *Billboard* top 200, and a disappointing 41 in the UK.

The first single from the album, 'Spaceman', as noted, was released on 4 September 1972 in the US and ten days later in the UK. 'Spaceman', of course, featured Starr on drums. The single did extremely poorly in the UK, not making the top 100, while in the US it peaked at number 23. In Canada, the single was a huge success, just missing the top ten and peaking at number 12. In Australia, the first single was 'You're Breaking My Heart', which appeared on the B-side of 'Spaceman' in the rest of the world.

The second and last single from the album was 'Remember (Christmas)', a beautiful song that deserved a better chart placing than it received. Released in December 1972, with the charming 'Lottery Song' on the flip side, this single did even worse, peaking at 53 on *Billboard's* Top 100, but again, in Canada it was a fairly big hit, peaking at number 14. It failed to chart in the UK. Oddly, the song 'Joy' was released as a single but under the name Buck Earl, with an older Nilsson track on the B-side ('I Guess The Lord Must Be In New York City'). Perhaps because it was under a pseudonym, it failed to get airplay and as a result it did not chart.

Although the album *Son Of Schmilsson* was not the success RCA or Perry had hoped it would be, a couple of important connections arose from the recording. One was that Ringo met Richard Perry, who suggested to Ringo that they should make an album together. In much the same way Peter Drake got Starr to visit Nashville, Perry was inviting Starr to Los Angeles to work on some music. Although Starr did not immediately say yes, the idea was planted in his mind.

The second important connection became Nilsson himself. Nilsson would work on the next three Starr albums and Starr got Nilsson to agree to star in a film that he (Starr) was bringing together for Apple films. Starr, having finished *Born To Boogie*, for the most part, was eager to start a film that he had planned to make. Through the mists of time, there is no documentation as to how Ringo came upon the idea, but he, acting as the producer, was smart enough to hire famed cinematographer and film director Freddie Francis to direct the film. Francis made his name working on such classics as *Room At The Top, Saturday Night And Sunday Morning, Sons And Lovers* (as the cinematographer) and *Dracula Has Risen From The Grave, Tales From The Crypt* and *Hysteria* (as a director) to name just a few. Given his history with Hammer Film Studios, Francis was the perfect choice.

Francis was not the problem with the film. The original title for the film was to be *Count Downe*, which was very wisely changed to *Son Of Dracula*. Starr's *Son Of Dracula* had nothing to do with the original 1943 Universal film starring Lon Chaney Jr. and directed by Robert Siomak. After the film was released, Apple tried to recoup some of the loss by retitling the film *Young Dracula*, to cash in on the success of Mel Brooks' *Young Frankenstein*. It didn't work or help in attracting patrons. According to Richard Scheib, Francis brought his usual crew to help him make the film. This included actress Jennifer Jayne, who, under the name Jay Fairbank, wrote the script. Filming began in August of 1972 and wrapped up in September. The film, however, had a number of problems and would not be released until 1974.

According to D Cairns, a writer for the website *Shadowplay, Son Of Dracula* was one of the reasons Francis cited when he decided to "give up directing." It was shot at Surrey Commercial Docks, Rotherhithe, in London. It had a formidable cast featuring Ringo Starr as Merlin, Harry Nilsson as Count Downe, Freddie Jones as the Baron, and Suzanne Leigh as Amber. Led Zeppelin's John Bonham, Peter Frampton, Keith Moon, Klaus Voormann and Leon Russell make up Count Downe's band. Although the film has little plot, the concert scenes featuring those musicians are quite wonderful.

When the film shoot was over, Francis removed himself from the picture. "I said Ringo, look, I'm ill at the moment, you better cut the film yourself. He had made it with a lot of his friends and that, the less said the better." Not to be deterred, Starr did finish the film, but there were still issues with it. Starr brought in *Monty Python's Flying Circus* member Graham Chapman and his writing partner, Bernard McKenna, to write some new dialogue for the film. Starr, by the way, made a cameo appearance on a *Monty Python's Flying Circus* episode, which aired in the UK on 26 October 1972, having been filmed in January. Said Starr, "We went into a studio with Graham Chapman and re-voiced a lot of it, so it makes even less sense now." Chapman's contributions were not used.

According to writer and Harry Nilsson expert, Curtis Armstrong, Nilsson was not Starr's first choice for the role of Count Downe. Starr originally wanted David Bowie, but that did not work out. Bowie would play a vampire later in his career in the 1983 film *The Hunger*. Also, Nilsson, and many others, felt that Ringo was inspired by the *Son Of Schmilsson* album cover, in which Nilsson looks very much like a vampire. According to Keith Badman, the idea came to Ringo long before the sleeve was designed and in fact he was unaware of the album design until his wife, Maureen, bought him a copy. Finally, Ringo's and the film's shooting was a year prior to *The Rocky Horror Show*, which would debut in London in 1973. Again, Ringo was somewhat ahead of the curve with the idea and film.

The soundtrack for the film featured songs by Nilsson from his *Nilsson Schmilsson* and *Son Of Schmilsson* albums, with instrumental music from Paul Buckmaster. However, one new song was written and recorded for the film, 'Daybreak'. 'Daybreak' was written and produced by Nilsson and recorded at Trident Studios in London in September during filming. The song features Starr on drums, as well as Voormann, Frampton, Keys and Price. It also features George Harrison on cowbell. Due to the film's release date, the song was not released until 1974, although Nilsson arranged and performed with Micky Dolenz, who released the song as a single in May of 1973. Two versions of the song by Nilsson exist. The album/film version features the line "Here comes the daybreak, it's making me cough, it's causin' me sunburn, it's pissing me off". This line was replaced on the single version by repeating the line "It's making me cough". Dolenz sang the censored version.

Although it is a very strong song, and features some inspired drumming from Ringo and a great vocal performance from Nilsson, the single did not perform as hoped, peaking at number 39 on the *Billboard* top 100. It was to be the last time Harry Nilsson troubled the top 40. As usual, it did much better in Canada, where it made number 14. However, Nilsson would never chart in Canada's top 40, or any top 40, after this single. It did not chart in the UK. It certainly did not help the soundtrack album or the film. *Billboard* did include the single in the 'Recommended' section of their new pop releases. There was no accompanying review, but it was noted in their 30 March 1974 issue. *Cash Box*, however, were much more complimentary and even predicted the single to be a smash hit. In their 30 March 1974 issue the reviewer wrote:"From *Son Of Dracula* superstar flick comes Harry's version of this track, a delightful pop/reggae outing certain to make new friends for the artist." Without naming Starr the reviewer also notes the song is "...complete with steel drums, flute and assorted percussion. All that and Nilsson's super fine vocals."

The soundtrack was released prior to the film's release, which provided some confusion to fans. As a way to please both Apple and

RCA records, the album was on the Rapple label, a nice combination between Nilsson's RCA label and Starr's Apple label. Both artists are crested on the sleeve, and it has the appearance of a collaboration. The album featured songs from Nilsson's *Nilsson Schmilsson*, and *Son Of Schmilsson*, which made sense in 1972 when those albums were released. But in 1974, it seemed odd. *Billboard* reviewed the album in its 6 April 1974 issue and noted: "With the film collaboration of Nilsson and Ringo Starr yet to hit the screen, Nilsson's fans may find this freewheeling aural precis a bit confusing and rather disappointing for its lack of new material." But they are quick to point out that with the use of dialogue from the film, "Nilsson favorites included derive a new spunk from often funny new intros." The review recognises 'Daybreak' as a clear highlight. The writer also acknowledges the new label with the comment: "someone deserves a pat on the back for the one shot label art."

Cash Box was even more excited and complimentary about the album. In their 6 April 1974 issue, the reviewer wrote: "This album is one of the most exciting and interesting of the new year and provides one with yet another insight into the genius of Harry Nilsson, who is so ably assisted by Ringo, George Harrison, Jim Price, Bobby Keyes, Peter Frampton, and Klaus Voormann." Special note is made of a spoken word portion of the album, and 'It Is He Who Will Be King' is also highlighted, as is the single 'Daybreak'. The album peaked at a disappointing number 106 in *Billboard's* top 200. It failed to make the charts in the UK. Nilsson was not able to steer his career out the nosedive he found himself in, and after 1974, he never made the top 100 again.

Although *Son Of Dracula* was completed in 1972, much like Count Downe in the film, it would not see the light of day for quite awhile. When the film was released in 1974, it had a huge premiere at the Cherokee Theatre in Atlanta Georgia on 19 April 1974. The Cherokee Theatre is a famous movie house that was the location for the world premiere of *Gone With The Wind* in 1939. *Son Of Dracula* did not have the same impact as *Gone With The Wind*. Sharing a theatre is where the similarities ended. Oddly, they tried again on 27 November 1974 for a second premiere, this time in Los Angeles at the famed Beverly Canon Theatre. Again, while both premieres were well attended, the film was not well distributed and could not find an audience.

When asked about the film in 1998, Ringo was quite vague about it and non committal. "I produced it for Apple. We had this script, Drac takes the cure, marries the girl and goes off into the sunlight - and it was the only movie we wanted to make. I called Harry because he was a blonde bombshell and we had his teeth fixed, which his mother was always thankful for. We had a lot of fun, there's a lot of musicians in it -

John Bonham, Keith Moon, Peter Frampton. We had the premiere in Atlanta, the first movie since *Gone With the Wind* to open there, and we had 12,000 kids screaming, we had bands... but we left town the next day, and so did everyone else. In America, the movie only played in towns that had one cinema, because if it had two, no matter what was on down the road, they'd all go there! It's a bit of a shambles now."

As 1972 was coming to an end, Starr had to have been happy with his career. For a man who, in 1969, was worried about his future, things had turned out just fine. Since 1970, he had released two albums, become an in-demand session musician, firmly established an acting career, directed his first film, produced a film, and performed at the most important concert of the decade and one of the most important of all time. Not to mention the success of his first two singles (not counting the 1970 single 'Beaucoups Of Blues' because it was not released in the UK), two top tens, which was better than any solo Beatle at this time. Whether intentionally or not, Starr took his time in establishing himself as a solo artist and as a rock musician, and it worked.

Ringo was also setting the scene for 1973. He had an offer from an established producer and was ready to put together his first rock album, and he would continue to find roles in films. In 1973 he found one of his greatest film roles of all time. Starr, and the other Beatles, would also be surprised to experience Beatlemania again, three years after the split of the band. But before all that could happen, Starr had to make the decision whether to work with Richard Perry or not.

"I got to Richard Perry, who'd worked with Harry Nilsson. And it was, 'Why don't we do an album?' Richard said, 'Why don't you come to LA and we'll see what happens.' And we did. We started the Ringo album, we had The Band on it, and Dr John, all people who were in town. And just by chance, so were John Lennon and George Harrison, not that we'd planned anything, it was just one of those days. And that has sort of been the way I've kept my career going. On albums I've always had lots of friends come and play, and on the All-Starrs, the live gigs, I have lots of really interesting musicians to play with. That's the way I do it." (Paul Du Noyer)

During 1972, Starr brought an artist to Apple, Chris Hodge. Hodge sent a tape to Apple in 1972 and Tony King, Apple's A&R man, liked the tape and played it for Ringo. Starr liked the UFO theme and the song itself. He requested a meeting with Hodge to discuss the record. Starr signed Hodge to Apple and suggested some changes to the song, which Hodge rejected. Starr let Hodge record the song as he saw (or rather heard) it and Tony Cox (formerly of the band The Young Idea) was brought in to produce it. According to Stefan Granados in his book *Those*

Were The Days – An Unofficial History Of The Beatles Apple Organization 1967-2002, Phil Spector remixed the single in New York.

Other than signing him to Apple, Starr had nothing to do with the recording of the song. Apple took out full page ads in *Cash Box* and *Billboard*, and the single was released with a picture sleeve. Hodge's debut single, 'We're On Our Way' b/w 'Supersoul', was released on 3 May 1972 in North America and one month later on 9 June 1972 in the UK and Europe. The single did reasonably well in the US, where it peaked at number 44 on the *Billboard* charts, number 36 on *Cash Box*, and number 35 on *Record World*. It got to number 26 in the Netherlands, and 25 in Canada.

Harrison and Starr signed the last two artists to Apple, Lon and Derrek Van Eaton and Chris Hodge. Although Hodge had a minor hit, neither artist received the appropriate promotion and attention from Apple. As Lon Van Eaton said, "Apple was collapsing and we got lost in the shuffle." The same could be said for Hodge. Both artists went on to record for other record labels. Lon And Derrek Van Eaton ended up on A&M with an album that was to be produced by Bill Schnee (who engineered two albums by Starr), but ended up being a joint production with Richard Perry. Chris Hodge signed to RCA but, again, got lost in the shuffle.

Hodge released one more single on Apple: 'Goodbye Sweet Lorraine' b/w 'Contact Love'. The single was released only in North America and a few European countries. It was produced by the production team of Andy Black and Ray Hendricksen. Black had some production credits under his belt (The Slender Plenty and The Fidd), while Hendricksen had made a name for himself working at Pye Records and producing Fire, and engineering recordings by Robert Fripp and Brian and Peter Sinfield. Starr recorded a song by Sinfield in 1978 ('Hard Times'). Perhaps in an effort to be more 'hip' or 'current', when Hodge released his first single for RCA he went under the name Chris Hodge (The Sunshine Kid). 'Goodbye Sweet Lorraine' failed to chart anywhere and was basically ignored by the music press, with the exception of *Cash Box*, which reviewed the single on 21 January 1973 and wrote: "Following the success of 'We're On Our Way', Chris comes to bat with a sensitive ballad geared especially towards top 40 and MOR formats." They predicted it to be a hit.

4

1973

For Ringo, 1973 started off much the same way 1972 ended. He was, once again, helping his friend George Harrison with Harrison's next studio album. Little did Harrison or Starr know that 1973 would turn out to be the first Beatlemania revival, with The Beatles topping the album charts, not to mention Harrison, Starr and Paul McCartney and Wings all hitting number one on the US singles charts, and Harrison and McCartney both having number one albums in America, with Ringo just missing the top spot (although *Cash Box* did chart his album *Ringo* at number one). But that was later in the year. In late 1972 and early 1973, Ringo could be found at Apple Studios in London providing the steady beat for Harrison.

Living In The Material World was Harrison's first studio album following his massively successful *All Things Must Pass* and his first album since the award winning and chart topping *The Concert For Bangla Desh*. Whether Harrison acknowledged it or not, there was a great deal riding on this album. The album was recorded at Abbey Road studios and at Harrison's newly built F.P.S.H.O.T studios in his stately home, at Henley-on-Thames. The house was known as Friar Park, so the studio was known as Friar Park Henley On Thames (F.P.S.H.O.T.).

According to Klaus Voormann, who also played on *Living In The Material World*, much of the album was also recorded at Apple Studios. Unlike *All Things Must Pass*, which seemed to have a revolving door of musicians, Harrison kept to a smaller unit for most of the album, which included Voormann (on bass and saxophone), Jim Keltner (on drums), Jim Horn (saxophones), Nicky Hopkins (keyboards) and John Barham (orchestrations). Harrison handled the guitars and The Beatles' old engineer Phil MacDonald recorded the sessions. Ringo, who was busy with a couple of other projects, appeared on only two songs, 'Living In The Material World' and 'The Day The World Gets Round'.

When the album was released on 30 May 1973, it reached number one in the US *Billboard* charts but strangely missed the top spot in the UK, where the soundtrack to a film, *That'll Be The Day*, kept it from number one. The album received mostly positive reviews, but it could never live up to the hype following *All Things Must Pass*, although in some ways, to this author's ears, it is a much stronger album. The fact that a soundtrack album, featuring hits from the 1950s, stopped it from hitting number one would have been frustrating for EMI and Harrison, especially when one considers that Ringo Starr had a major role in the film and is on the sleeve of the album.

The film *That'll Be The Day* is now considered a classic. Initially, Starr was not considered for a role. It was only later, after a meeting with the producer and writer, that Starr was included in the film.

"I first met Ringo, probably on the *Magical Mystery Tour* and then I went to his house...we had a very good afternoon and I enjoyed it. It was nice. I got to know him pretty well," recalled Ray Connolly. Connolly is a writer who not only wrote for the *Daily Mail*, as well as *The Sunday Times*, *The Times*, *The Daily Telegraph* and *The Observer*, but was also a playwright of note. *That'll Be The Day* would become his first film script. According to Connolly, producer David Puttnam asked him to write a film. "I said, I don't know how to write a film, I don't even know how to lay one out." But Puttnam persevered and convinced Connolly to write what would become *That'll Be The Day*.

Connolly reported that "the idea came from a Harry Nilsson song, '1941'. David [Puttnam] was born in 1941 and I was born in 1940, so it was about our generation. In the song, Harry runs off to join the circus, and David said, 'why doesn't our boy run off to join a fair?' So we planned it out that day, and I went home and began writing it."

The film had a modest budget and it was agreed that David Essex would star, but who could play one of Essex's friends, Mike? Because it was about famed British holiday camps, Puttnam was worried that neither he nor Connolly had ever been to Butlin's (the most famous of the holiday camps). Connolly remembered that Ringo had not attended the camp but worked at it. "I arranged a meeting with Ringo, purely for information really. Ringo turned up with Neil Aspinall and Derrek Taylor. We had lunch at Apple. Ringo and Neil were so funny and made us laugh the whole time. On the way out, I said to David, 'maybe we could get Ringo to be in the film'." Initially Puttnam thought Ringo could play the leader of the band at the holiday camp, since Ringo performed there with Rory Storm and The Hurricanes, but Connolly thought Ringo would be better as the character Mike.

After discussing the idea "on the steps of Apple", they offered Ringo the role, and he jumped at it. The script, the cast and the crew were arranged and filming began on the Isle of Wight on 23 October 1972. The Isle of Wight would double for the holiday camp. Ringo also had the comfort of having some friends involved as well, with Neil Aspinall, Billy Fury, Keith Moon of the Who, and John Hawken of the Nashville Teens and The Strawbs all having roles in the film.

The filming was quick and the schedule on the Isle of Wight was very tight. According to Connolly, "Ringo on the first day of the shooting, he turned up wearing a tailored Teddy Boy outfit, not something you would wear at fifteen, it was much more glamorous than that. He had it made for the premiere of the *Magical Mystery Tour* film and had never worn it since. But we had him for ten days, that is all we had him for. We shot the film around his availability. On the tenth day we realised that we worked so well we had time. David Puttnam asked if we could write another scene. So I wrote the scene in the pool hall. We shot it on the Monday, and he said 'if we're not finished and I miss the boat, I am going anyway, so make sure we are finished', which put a bit of pressure on the director."

Connolly recalled that he, the director (Claude Whatham) and producer David Puttnam were very impressed with Starr's acting. "He was brilliant in the film, just brilliant. We didn't know he would be that good. We were astonished. He was happy to do it. He liked the part. He put a kind of life to those scenes because he lived it. But he could live the character and he was really good."

Starr was excellent at taking direction and seldom deviated from the script; however, he did on a couple of occasions, and those 'ad libs' were kept in the film. For example, in one instance Ringo was with his date and Essex's character. Said Connolly, "There was one line, when he was in the bar with David Essex, and he said 'one drink and she wants the world'. That was his line. He would say later that he wrote half of it, but come on Ringo. What he did was he said the lines with such distinction."

Connolly also said that Starr could have easily become a serious actor. "He could have been a proper actor. It really bothered me, he made a couple of terrible films after it. I just thought, you are better than that. You shouldn't be in that, they are just using your name. I guess we were to a certain extent, but he was playing a character he understood. He had lived the part. I think he liked the part, he liked living it for a couple of weeks. Because it did remind him of walking with the lads, as he would say. It was exciting for him to be playing that part again."

During the filming, perhaps due to the long standing relationship he had with Ray Connolly, "in between the shooting, he would talk about life with The Beatles." However, when the sequel, *Stardust*, was in production, Ringo declined to reprise his role of Mike. "When I wrote *Stardust*, I thought Ringo was going to play the part. Then I got a call from David Puttnam, who said 'we lost Ringo.' I said 'why?' He wouldn't give a real reason, but I think it was too close to home because he had already been through all that with The Beatles. And I think he got bored with *That'll Be The Day*. It was only a couple of weeks. He may look back now, and think, 'I should have been in *Stardust* too'."

One of the more disturbing scenes in *That'll Be The Day* features Starr's character, Mike, being beaten up by a gang. Against everyone's wishes, Starr did the scene and they did not use a stunt double. Connolly remembered that Starr had fun with the scene, but just in case, "We did that scene at the end, the last night of the fair. We said we will do that scene last." It was saved until the end of shooting, just in case anything went seriously wrong. Nothing went wrong and the scene was shot without incident.

Although there were hopes for the film, no one knew that *That'll Be The Day* would become as big and well received as it was. The film was released in the UK on 12 April 1973 and went on to be one of the top grossing films of the year. *The Guardian*, in their review on 12 April 1973, said the film was "an accurate and shrewd…summation of the late 1950s" and noted that it was "well written by Ray Connolly." The review also singled out Starr, saying: "Ringo, in fact, is a revelation. And the couple's girl chasing scenes are a joy in themselves."

The film earned two British Academy Film Awards for Most Promising Newcomer To Leading Film Roles (Essex) and Best Supporting Actress (Rosemary Leach).

When *That'll Be The Day* was released in North America on 29 October 1973 it did not do as well and became somewhat of a cult film. Distribution in the US was a bit more complicated. Early in 1973, a deal was signed with Continental Releasing, and sneak previews were held, although exact dates are unknown. Reportedly reception was poor, and the company decided not to put the film into general release. However, when the film was screened in Los Angeles a film programmer, Jerry Harvey, was so impressed with the film that he wanted to get it into cinemas. Along with his partners Richard Chase and Kenneth Greenstone, a small company, Mayfair Film Group, was formed to distribute the film. This meant, however, that the film had to be rolled out in North America, rather than hitting numerous cinemas at once.

The New York Times, in typical fashion, had little good to say about the film (23 December 1974). Nora Sayre found the film boring ("Movies about boredom aren't ever likely to make the blood leap, and 'That'll Be the Day' proves that there's no such thing as a rousing soporific") and pointed out that "Ringo Starr makes a "phlegmatic appearance—he looks a bit sheepish, as though apologizing for making no music at all." *The Los Angeles Times* was a bit kinder, calling it "a very special, strange and fascinating movie." A film about the beginning of rock and roll in the UK was certainly lost on the critics in North America.

Once Ringo had finished *That'll Be The Day*, it was time to think about working on a new album. Starr had not released an album in over two years and he was ready to record. No doubt the success of his two singles also gave him the encouragement he needed to record a full album.

Richard Perry helped with Ringo's debut album, *Sentimental Journey*. In fact, he arranged the title track, but as he wrote in his memoir, *Cloud Nine: Memoirs of A Record Producer*, "I never got to meet Ringo during the process. I cut the track in LA, and sent it to him in London where he did his vocals and finished the album." Perry did finally get to meet Ringo, first while working on Bobby Hatfield's solo single ('Oo Wee Baby, I Love You'), and then while working on *Son Of Schmilsson* with Harry Nilsson. Perry produced both releases.

According to Perry, he approached Starr during the Nilsson sessions but "he was resistant; he did not want to devote five months to making a record." This was the same response Pete Drake received when suggesting Starr record an album in Nashville. Starr did not want to spend a lot of time working on an album, nor did he want to stay away from home for long. That would change, but Starr was economical with his time when recording an album. He still is.

Perry, however, was very clear with his desired outcome for the album. "I envisioned it like a Beatles record, but with Ringo singing lead on every track." He very nearly got his wish.

Starr himself enjoyed making the album. In 2023, he told Ken Sharp, in *Goldmine* magazine: "I have really great memories of working on the album. We were originally going to record in New Orleans and it was my producer Richard Perry who decided upon recording the record in LA. In many ways, it's the first example of my All-Starr band as many close friends of mine played on the album. John, George and Paul played on the album and also contributed songs. There's still songs we perform from the album every time I go out on the road with the All-Starrs."

Starr had agreed to appear with Harry Nilsson at the 1973 Grammy Awards to present an award. He called Perry and said that since he was coming all the way to do the one show, he may as well see what they could do in the studio. Perry quickly agreed and suggested they record in Los Angeles. Starr had suggested Nashville. Perry won out, and Starr soon relocated to Los Angeles at the very least to meet with Perry. But Starr came prepared and brought a song that he had been working on for over a year. A song he co-wrote with Harrison.

Perry sat with Starr to hear some ideas for songs, and according to Perry the first song Starr played him was 'Photograph'. Starr had written the song with George Harrison in 1971 on a yacht off Cannes following

Mick Jagger's wedding. Harrison and Starr recorded a demo in 1972. It was the only song to be credited to Starr and Harrison.

On 12 March 1973, Starr entered Sunset Studios in Los Angeles with Perry, Harrison (playing 12 string acoustic), Nicky Hopkins (piano), Klaus Voormann (bass), Jim Keltner (drums), and Jimmy Calvert (rhythm guitar). Later Apple artists Lon and Derrek Van Eaton would overdub backing vocals and some percussion. Both Lon and Derrek Van Eaton received a gold disc as a thank you for their help on the song. Derrek Van Eaton later commented during our email exchange: "You go out, put on your headphones, listen to the track, get your levels good and sing. As always you find your own parts then after you get what you want the producer adds their ideas and you finish with what was best for the song."

Bobby Keys provided a fantastic saxophone solo. Famed arranger Jack Nitzsche, who made his name working with Phil Spector, arranged the stunning orchestral arrangements to accompany the song. Ringo had attempted to record the song twice, both times with Harrison producing, once at Apple Studios in 1972 and later in that year at Harrison's Friar Park Studios (F.P.S.H.O.T.) during the recording of Harrison's *Living In The Material World*. For various reasons, Starr was not happy with the results, so he was interested to see what would come of the sessions in Los Angeles.

According to engineer Bill Schnee, who worked on the entire album, "when they brought in the version from England that George had done of 'Photograph', Richard thought it was a little too mournful. You know, this guy just lost his girl, and all he has is this photograph. Richard came up with the idea of doing it kind of 'wall of sound'. Then we went down that road."

One song did survive from the Apple sessions. While recording at Apple Studios, Harrison produced a song that Starr had written with the title 'Down And Out'. The session included Gary Wright (keyboards), Harrison (guitar) and Klaus Voormann (bass). The song was entirely written by Starr and it is a song he has always seemed to like and one of which he should be proud. It is a basic rocker, with some great slide playing from Harrison. During the sessions for *Ringo*, Perry would add a horn section, which earned him a co-production credit. Although there is no confirmation it was ever considered for the album, it is interesting that when the song was added to the UK CD release it was sequenced between 'Photograph' and 'Sunshine Life For Me (Sail Away Raymond)', rather than tagged on at the end as it was in the North American version. This may be an indication of where the song would have originally been placed. But until the CD re-releases, the song remained as a non-album B-side.

While Starr was hard at work on *Ringo*, an article appeared in *Variety* on 4 April 1973 stating that: "The four-year business relationship between Allan Klein's ABKCO Inc. and the Beatles' Company, Apple Corps, came to an abrupt end April 1." While the reasons and issues are complex and well beyond the scope of this book, it was important news for Starr, George Harrison, and John Lennon. According to the article, the original contract expired on 31 March 1973 and would not be renewed, because Apple would act as their manager, instead of ABKCO. It was also noted that ABKCO continued to have "the unresolved legal actions brought by the fourth Beatle, Paul McCartney, against his onetime colleagues." However, ABKCO countered with Yoko Ono: "Apple has been picking up the tab for her various album enterprises which have not been particularly successful." For the world at large, this gave fans a chance to hope that it might pave the way for a Beatles reunion.

It is also worth noting that in April it was reported in *Variety* that "Harry Nilsson, Ringo Starr and George Harrison screened their *Son Of Dracula*...at the Charles Aidikoff screening room on Sunset with a small group...Micky Dolenz and Davy Jones (of Monkees fame)". Dolenz was not only a friend of Nilsson, he also helped on the next two Nilsson albums.

With 'Photograph' and its B-side recorded, the songs were released as a single on 29 September 1973 as a taste of what was to come. Ringo shot a promotional film for the song, with him wandering around his Tittenhurst Estate (which he had purchased from Lennon). The single was released in North America and the UK with the same picture sleeve. The picture of Ringo in a star, poking his head out, was also used for the label of the single (and the upcoming album, *Ringo*). 'Photograph' was immediately embraced by radio in North America with saturation level radio play.

It became Starr's first number one solo single in the US and his second in Canada. In the UK it peaked at number eight, even though *Record Mirror* (in their 'Discorama' page) certify it as a hit single, further stating: "It's an instantly commercial single which will be sung along with for the next ten years, at least." Further, the reviewer stated: "Just about everything in, then, but nothing so overdone as to take away from the song. Obviously a giant smash for this promising all round entertainer". This was high praise indeed.

In the US, *Cash Box* gave the single a positive review, predicting it to be a huge success. In the 6 October 1973 issue, in the singles review, the writer notes: "Already one of the hottest records in the country, this new Ringo outing is definitely headed for the Top Five. A moderate paced rocker with a strong blues feel and good vocal performance adds up to another solo Beatle success." In the same issue, the song is listed as the most added song to playlists in America. In the 6 October 1973 issue of *Record World* the reviewer predicted that the single would hit number one and said: "From his forthcoming LP comes this strong pop tune penned by Starr and George Harrison." 'Photograph' would go on to become one of Ringo's classic songs and one he performs on every Ringo and The All-Starr Tour, and on many television appearances. He also sang a very emotional version at *The Concert For George* held on the first anniversary of Harrison's death.

It is a classic pop-rock song. The beautiful orchestration by Jack Nitzsche adds so much to the song, along with the stunning backing vocals by Harrison and Starr's emotive, melancholy vocal. As far as pop songs go, it is near perfection. It was understandable why radio embraced the song then and continues to play it to this day. It may not be his best song in his vast catalogue, but it is a custom made radio song. A promo copy, featuring stereo and mono versions, was sent to radio and set the single on its way to success.

According to Perry they also started working on Starr's cover of 'You're Sixteen (You're Beautiful And You're Mine)' at the same time. In the first week, quite a bit was accomplished for the *Ringo* album. Harrison contributed a song he had written, 'Sunshine Life For Me (Sail Away Raymond)', for which Starr and Harrison got to play with their old friends, The Band. According to Schnee, "The song was George's, but I think that it was Richard's idea to bring the band in. Richard did most of the driving."

All but one member played on the track, with Richard Manuel being the hold out. Robbie Robertson, Levon Helm, Garth Hudson and Rick Danko (along with David Bromberg) put in an incredible performance and the song became a highlight on the album. Harrison reportedly wrote the song in Ireland in 1971 and was influenced more by Irish traditional music than country, although the song has a definite country flavour to it. George Harrison's original demo and an instrumental version were released in 2024 on the Deluxe version of George Harrison's *Living In The Material World*. One can hear Harrison asking Perry about the arrangement.

While Starr was beginning to record his album, something odd was happening in America. In 1972, an album was offered on late night television, an album being advertised that could only be bought through mail order. It was titled *Alpha Omega,* and it promised to be a greatest hits compilation of The Beatles. It was not on EMI, nor was it authorised by The Beatles or Apple. But one thing was sure: it was selling. Klein and Apple moved fast to not only halt the production and sale of the box set, but to come up with their own. Thus, *The Beatles 1962 - 1967* and *The Beatles 1967 - 1970* were both born, and released on Apple Records on 2 April 1973. This must have come as a bit of a shock to Paul McCartney (and Wings) and Harrison, both of whom had albums scheduled for April and May. This meant that once again McCartney was battling his former band (remember 1970's *McCartney* and *Let It Be* fought on the charts) and Harrison would be thrown into the mix as well.

Both albums were apparently assembled by Klein with all four Beatles giving their approval to the track selection. Neither compilation had any cover versions, and all of their hit singles were included as well as album cuts that had done very well on radio. George Martin was also asked to be involved. In 1980, John Lennon remembered, "I didn't want lousy versions going out, I wanted them to be as was. And I asked Capitol/EMI, or EMI/Capitol whichever, please ask George Martin would he take care of this, so at least he knows what to do. I didn't want some strange guy, you know, making dubbed versions of it and putting it out..."

Both of the sets were warmly received. In North America, there had never really been a 'best of' The Beatles, and the UK had not seen a compilation since 1966's *A Collection Of Beatles Oldies*. They may have introduced The Beatles to a whole new and younger audience. Both sets received rave reviews and were nicely packaged, with the *Please Please Me* cover and the photo taken for the proposed *Get Back* album. The set clearly showed how much The Beatles changed physically and musically over a very short eight years.

One look at the charts at the time, and one could see a mini Beatlemania happening worldwide. Both of the compilations did very well, *1967 - 1970* even reaching the number one spot in the US, while both Wings' *Red Rose Speedway* and Harrison's *Living In The Material World* made it to number one in the US, and both had number one singles, with McCartney's 'My Love', which has become a standard, and Harrison's 'Give Me Love (Give Me Peace On Earth)'. Starr and Perry had to have been keeping an eye on the charts while recording what would become *Ringo* in Los Angeles.

In the UK, *The Beatles 1962 - 1966* and *The Beatles 1967 - 1970* peaked at three and two respectively, held out of the top spot by David Bowie's *Aladdin Sane*. McCartney was kept to number five by The Beatles, Bowie and a compilation album.

And as The Beatles and solo Beatles were dominating the charts, once again, work continued on *Ringo*. According to Perry, he introduced Starr to Vini Poncia, a songwriter and producer of note. He was also a member of Trade Winds, who had a minor top 40 hit in the US in 1965 ('New York Is A Lonely Town'), and he had written songs for The Ronettes, Bobby Bloom and Darlene Love. Once they met, the two formed a songwriting partnership that lasted for a number of years and was extremely important in the 1970s. Poncia would even produce Starr's last album during the 1970s, *Bad Boy*. Poncia played acoustic guitar on 'Photograph', and the two seemed to hit off immediately. The first song they wrote was 'Oh My My', which Perry wanted to include on the album.

Schnee remembered, "Vini was an old friend of Richard's from New York. And he had come out a year earlier. Richard had been asked to produce Melissa Manchester, and because he was working with Ringo he couldn't do it, so he brought out his buddy Vini who produced it. I engineered that record too, it had 'Midnight Blue' on it. He was a friend of Richard's who was a songwriter, and he thought it would be good to get Ringo involved in the writing with someone. So that was Richard's idea."

Perry brought 'Oh My My' to life with Billy Preston on keyboards, session player Jimmy Calvert on guitar, Klaus Voormann on bass, Tom Scott on saxophone and Jim Keltner along with Ringo on drums. The end result is a thumping, pounding rocker that became yet another hit for Starr when it was released as the third single from the album. In some ways, 'Oh My My' is the unofficial follow-up to 'Back Off Boogaloo'. It contains the same energy and Starr (and Keltner), along with Voormann, created a powerful rhythm. The song is catchy and has a hook that stays with the listener long after the needle has been lifted.

According to Perry, Starr told Perry that there was a lot of buzz about the album, and John Lennon had heard about the recording sessions in New York. It seems that Lennon had some business in LA and wondered if he could contribute a song. Perry wrote in his memoir that when he played Lennon the tracks they had recorded, he was very enthusiastic about 'You're Sixteen' and predicted it would be a hit single. Then it was time for Lennon to play Starr and Perry the song he had written for Ringo, called 'I'm The Greatest'. Perry wrote that Lennon had not finished the song and that he and Lennon were working on it when they were interrupted about a telephone call.

It was Mal Evans on the phone and he said he was with George Harrison, and George was wondering if he could come and play in the session too. Perry said, "When I asked John, he replied, 'Fucking Hell!

Tell him to get down here and help us finish the song'." Harrison arrived about twenty minutes later as the band was laying down the track. This included Ringo on drums, Lennon on piano, Klaus Voormann on bass, Billy Preston on keyboards and now Harrison on guitar.

'I'm The Greatest' is the perfect song for Starr and the only song that could start the album. Lennon custom made the track for Ringo, and Lennon acknowledged that he (Lennon) could never have gotten away with singing 'I'm The Greatest'. With Starr, however, the song doesn't sound arrogant or bragging, just charming. Starr's public persona let him get away with the song, and many listeners, this author included, saw the humour in it. The bonus was that there were three Beatles playing on it, which was the closest thing to a reunion up to that point. Perry could also say he met his goal of creating a 'Beatle' album.

Ringo, in 1977, said, "We were like big girls again. We were all looking at each other smiling. We hadn't played together in four years. We were just smiling while we were playing. It was nice."

Thanks to Bill Schnee's quick thinking, the world has the original Lennon demo/guide vocal to enjoy today. "I recorded it because Ringo needed a guide to sing it, but what was in those days recording on a sixteen track, you ran out of tracks. Richard said, 'erase John's vocal' and I said, just give me five minutes. I put it down, the mix I had going. Thirty years later when they were doing a retrospective on John, they called me up for anything I had to say, and as we were talking, I said 'I have something you are really going to enjoy'. And sent it off to the record company."

Perry, in an interview with the *Los Angeles Times,* was clear: "The other Beatles know that this is Ringo's show." Perry was concerned that the celebrity element of the album might overshadow the actual music, and perhaps even impact the overall sound of the music. Said Perry in the same interview, "I just didn't want the party to dominate the work; and in the end we had fun, but we got a great album too."

Starr also recalled, during an interview with Robert W. Morgan in 1978, "I'm friendly with most people. I've always been friendly with everyone. It wasn't being a diplomat. They're my friends, so we came to LA, while I was here, John was here, and I didn't know George came into town. And I was talking to John and I said 'have you got any songs? I'm doing an album.' He said, 'I'll write you one.' George comes into town. He asked, 'what are you doing?' I said 'I am making an album, do you have any songs?' And he said, 'yeah, I have a song. I'll come down and play'. It just fell into place. It wasn't a major sensation for any of us. When the album came out, that's when it got big. I phoned Paul, and said 'you can't be off this, I got the other two, what have you got?' He said 'I got a song too.' But he wouldn't play bass."

At this point, the *Ringo* sessions were becoming big news. Perry noted that "Every night when we arrived at Sunset Sound, an avalanche of TV crews and photographers was waiting in the parking lot to greet us." He also noted that famous friends, like Peter Sellers, would often drop in to hear what was going on. For Perry, who had always dreamed of producing The Beatles, he was almost living the dream. The only Beatle missing was Paul McCartney, who wanted to contribute but could not get a visa due to his recent run-in with the law regarding marijuana being found on his farm.

Plans were then made for Starr and Perry. If McCartney could not come to LA, then they would go to him. Perry states in his memoir that they had gone to London to record more material for *Ringo*, and McCartney requested that Perry assist him with the live recordings of segments that would be part of a television special McCartney was filming featuring Wings. Perry accepted the position because McCartney wanted someone in the booth who "knew what his music should sound like." This gave him the opportunity to pitch the idea of McCartney now contributing to the *Ringo* album. Not surprisingly, McCartney agreed. Remember he was the only Beatle to help Ringo with Starr's first solo album, *Sentimental Journey*. McCartney, with help from his wife Linda, composed 'Six O'Clock'.

A recording session was set up. Starr (who had come from the premiere of *That'll Be The Day*) sat behind the drum kit, with McCartney (piano, synthesiser, backing vocals), Voormann (bass), Vini Poncia (guitar, percussion) and Linda McCartney (backing vocals) gathered together at Apple Studios on 12 April 1973 to record the basic track. McCartney has never recorded a version of the song, and his demo has never surfaced. However, the song could have fit easily on McCartney and Wings' *Red Rose Speedway*, while at the same time, it is the perfect vehicle for Starr.

On the same day, McCartney also recorded his famous 'mouth sax' solo for 'You're Sixteen (You're Beautiful And You're Mine)'. McCartney simply made the sound of a kazoo with his mouth and performed a solo for the song. It added a great deal and sounds fantastic. It was the missing ingredient for the song and contributed to it being the huge hit it became for Starr. Starr also recorded his famous tap dancing segment for the song 'Step Lightly' at Apple Studios.

Ringo's cover of 'You're Sixteen (You're Beautiful And You're Mine)' (simply titled as 'You're Sixteen' on the single and album) adds a great deal of energy to the original by Johnny Burnette. The bottom line was, the song was a great choice for Starr. 'You're Sixteen' was written by Disney favourites, The Sherman Brothers (Robert B, and Richard M). Burnette's version peaked at number eight in 1960 in the US *Billboard* charts, while it was a much bigger hit in the UK, going as high as number three. Starr's version was recorded in March 1973 and features studio musician Nicky Hopkins (piano), Klaus Voormann (bass), Jim Keltner (joining Ringo on drums), Harry Nilsson (backing vocals), Vini Poncia (guitar) and Jimmy Calvert (guitar). McCartney's mouth sax solo completed the recording in July 1973.

Although The Beatles did not talk a great deal about Johnny Burnette, they were obviously fans of his. The Beatles had previously covered Burnette's 'Lonesome Tears In My Eyes' for their BBC sessions in 1963 (and eventually released on the Beatles' 1994 album *Live At The BBC*). In 1969, the Beatles had performed a straight cover of Burnette's version of 'Honey Hush' during the *Let It Be* sessions. McCartney would take another turn at 'Honey Hush' on his 1999 album, *Run Devil Run*. Starr was also never shy about covering songs. With The Beatles he recorded several cover versions, and his debut album entirely consisted of covers. Quite frankly, it was the perfect choice for Starr. His cover charted higher than the original and became Starr's song. He would perform it on some of his tours and he also included a new version in his 1978 television special, *Ringo*.

'You're Sixteen' was chosen as the second single from the album. It was released on 8 December 1973 in North America, but the UK and Europe had to wait until 8 February 1974. It was released with a picture sleeve, and as with 'Photograph' a promo copy was sent to US radio stations with the stereo album mix on one side and a mono mix on the flipside. Starr did not shoot a promo film for this single, but it was released with a picture sleeve.

In the 15 December 1973 issue of *Record World*, it was noted: "'Photograph' went to number one, and Mr. Starkey followed it up with the Sherman brothers tune that was a hit for Johnny Burnette in 1960." They add that Harry Nilsson's backing vocals fit perfectly and add a great deal. Upon release, radio and the trade magazines were all very complimentary about the song and the choice of it as the second single. Radio immediately pounced on it and within a very short time 'You're Sixteen' was topping the US *Billboard* charts. In *Cash Box*, for the week of 8 December 1973, in their singles review, it was clear they loved this song as a choice for a single. "Ringo is digging the '50's and you know what? This track is simply fantastic and perfect for the '70's. Not only is the vocal perfect, and steady, for this delightful easy going rocker, but the music is the perfect complement." The same week, the single was at number two for most added song on the radio, and the single was merely a day old.

It peaked at number two in Canada, and was kept out of the number one spot by Canada's own Terry Jacks and his hit 'Seasons In The Sun'. 'You're Sixteen' charted higher than 'Photograph' in the UK, going all the way to number four. Peter Jones, writing in *Record Mirror* (16 February 1974) states: "A natural-born hit. This chap Starr has a style, and sense of big-time - he'll take chart stardom in his stride. There's a good-time feel to the whole thing, oohs and aahs, a bit of a dated atmosphere, and it's a giant hit in the States. Ringo Starr may not turn out to be a Stevie Wonder or a Johnny Mathis, but he's definitely a lad to watch. I believe he plays drums, too." Starr was beginning to be taken very seriously in the UK. For the record, Paper Lace's 'Billy Don't Be A Hero' was at number one, and Starr placed higher than Paul McCartney and Wings' 'Jet', which had peaked at number seven the week before (16 March 1974).

The B-side for 'You're Sixteen ' was the rocker 'Devil Woman', written by Starr and Vini Poncia. This hard driving song, taken from the *Ringo* album, has more in common with glam than it does with the 1950s rock and roll. Jimmy Calvert's electric guitar playing, in combination with Tom Scott's flawless horn arrangement, make for one exciting and rocking song. Starr and Jim Keltner provide one of Ringo's heaviest beats in his career and Starr's vocals have a sense of urgency not heard in his music up to this point. Richard Perry provides backing vocals that borrow from his arrangement of Harry Nilsson's 'Spaceman' (which Starr played on).

However, the song has not aged well when it comes to the lyrics. Some of the lines are somewhat questionable ("I want to beat you up and then I want to be kind, and one of these days I'm going to make you mine") and are on the aggressive side. However, keep in mind that this was not out of the ordinary in 1973. David Bowie's 'Queen Bitch', Jim Hendrix 'Hey Joe', The Rolling Stones 'Brown Sugar', or even songs by Alice Cooper ('Dead Babies') were released prior to *Ringo*. Today such songs are viewed in a more negative light. However, 'Devil Woman' is tame in comparison to the others, and although lyrically it may not have aged well, musically it is a great example of mid 1970s rock.

Days later, without Starr present, McCartney and Perry finished 'Six O'Clock' during an all night session at Abbey Road Studios (Perry later wrote, "coincidently, we wrapped the recording of 'Six O'Clock' at six o'clock in the morning"). McCartney added synthesisers, and arranged a string quartet for the song. Finally he and Linda provided the trademark backing vocals. Collectors note that the song originally ran for over five minutes (5:26 to be exact), featuring a coda at the end. This part of the song was cut off, but not before North American labels were printed, and the song, which now ran for 4:05, still had the original (and incorrect) time of 5:26. To further people's confusion, the long version of the song could be found on the original cassette and eight track releases in North American and on very early promotional albums. It was then added as a bonus track to the 1992 CD release of *Goodnight Vienna*.

It is frustrating/interesting to fans that the label of the album always bore the incorrect time. Also, another track on the album, 'Hold On', has the wrong time listed on the label. To further add to confusion, when the album came out, the original sleeves and booklets incorrectly listed 'Hold On', which was later changed on the second pressing to 'Have You Seen My Baby'. Many booklets also kept the title as 'Hold On' included with the second sleeves printed. And there was a third pressing, where the song is listed as 'Have You Seen My Baby (Hold On)'.

Like 'I'm The Greatest', 'Six O'Clock' was perfect for Starr. While Lennon's demo has survived and been released, McCartney has never shared his demo of 'Six O'Clock'. It is a great, loving song of regret and sadness that Ringo could sink his teeth into. His delivery is perfect and the song, like 'Photograph', is very touching. It is a brilliant track and both of these songs would not have been out of place on any Beatle album, but they found a home with Ringo and they are perfect where they are.

Upon returning to Los Angeles, Starr met up with Marc Bolan and got him to get to A&M Studios for him to overdub some fiery guitar on the Randy Newman track 'Have You Seen My Baby'. Bolan's guitar is quite strong and it lifts the song into a more exciting arena. The track features Jim Keltner along with Starr on drums, Voormann on bass, Tom Scott (horns and horns arrangement), and James Booker and Milt Holland on percussion. The song was originally released in 1970 on Randy Newman's *12 Songs* album. No doubt Starr heard the song through Harry Nilsson, who was a fan of Newman's and recorded an entire album of Newman covers.

'Step Lightly' was recorded on 9 March 1973, with overdubs being completed in July of 1973. It is the only song on the album that credits Starr as the sole composer. It is a lovely, harmless song with Starr really giving himself advice. It is very middle of the road, and features Starr on drums, Steve Cropper and Jimmy Calvert on guitar, Nicky Hopkins on electric piano, Tom Scott on clarinet and Klaus Voormann on bass guitar. Starr, as noted, provided a tap dance for the song.

Richard Perry in 1974 told Chuck Thegze of the *Los Angeles Times* that "'Step Lightly' was especially fun because that night Ringo showed up with some tap shoes; I don't know where he got them. And at 5am, a drunken Ringo Starr, holding on to a music stand to keep his balance, made his tap-dancing debut." (24 March 1974)

Bill Schnee also, in his memoir, remembered Starr recording his tap dance. "Ringo came in with a set of tap shoes and we overdubbed him dancing. I wish we had all the sessions on film, but that one in particular was a blast and would be the most entertaining to watch."

The last track, 'You And Me (Babe)', was the perfect song to complete the album. The song started with lyrics by Mal Evans. Evans had been with The Beatles since The Cavern days (he was the doorman/bouncer) but graduated from roadie to confidant and good friend. When The Beatles split and Klein purged Apple, Evans survived as an A&R man for Apple Records (he brought Badfinger to Apple's attention). He eventually had a hand in producing. He produced the Badfinger hit 'No Matter What' and helped with John Lennon's 'God Save Us' (released under the name Bill Elliot and The Elastic Oz Band. Elliot would go on to be one half of Splinter, who signed to Dark Horse. Evans co-wrote a song for them too, 'Lonely Man').

On 17 August 1973, Starr had returned from England with the tracks the McCartneys had played on and was ready to finish the album. It was agreed by all that 'I'm The Greatest' was the only way to open the album, and now a suitable closing song was needed. At this time, Evans was staying with Harrison, and according to Kenneth Womack in his book *Living The Beatles Legend - The Untold Story Of Mal Evans*, Evans had the beginning of a song titled 'I'm Not Going To Move' that he had started in Rishikesh five years earlier.

"I had this song going round my head," Evans is quoted. "I asked George if he would help me out with the chords...He started playing on the piano...Ringo was surprised by it, I suppose.' Ringo and Perry loved the song and the recording took place with the ever reliable Voormann on bass, Harrison on electric guitars, Poncia on acoustic guitar, Nicky Hopkins on electric piano, Milt Holland on marimba, and Ringo on drums. Tom Scott, once again, provided the saxophone and horn arrangements, while Jack Nitszche provided a beautiful string arrangement.

Perry said, in 1974, "George began singing it as we drove to Palm Springs, but it was more of a rocker with cynical lyrics." Perry reportedly asked Harrison to make the song less rocky and write some new lyrics. Harrison then worked with Evans and the end result is a remarkable song, custom made to end an album. It bookends the album beautifully with 'I'm The Greatest' opening *Ringo*.

When the song was done, it was felt that something was missing. At Voormann's encouragement, Starr provided a spoken word ending for the album thanking everyone, by name, for working on it. Ringo ends with the beautiful and sentimental "So it's a big good night from your friends and mine, Ringo Starr". It is a sensational way to close an album: bold and original and one of the best album endings.

Bill Schnee made the cut for Starr to 'thank'. He also makes an appearance on the album cover. "It was only cool after I heard the vocal alone and realized he wasn't saying 'Never smiling, Never welcomed'. Back then, I think it is fair to say I didn't smile a lot. I was a very black and white, very serious guy, especially in the studio, well I could be. So the 'never smiling' fit but the 'never welcome' worried me."

According to Bill Schnee, there were no songs left in the can, as there had been with Starr's first two albums. "I'm 90 percent sure there were no songs left over. Richard always knew how to spend money and go over budget." And, although Ringo was hesitant to spend several months on the album, Schnee said "*Ringo* was recorded over six months, with two trips to England."

Ringo was released in North America on 2 November 1973, and one week later in Europe and the UK. The album was to have been released on 29 September 1973, but, according to an article in *Billboard* magazine, was delayed due to problems with the packaging. The album was packaged beautifully with a lyric booklet featuring Klaus Voormann drawings to accompany each song. The cover featured a very interesting painting, done in the same style as *Sgt. Pepper's Lonely Hearts Club Band*, with people involved with the album depicted on the sleeve. The sleeve was painted by Tim Bruckner, a jeweller who dabbled in art.

In 1973 Bruckner was interviewed by Barry Feinstein of Camouflage Productions, who had been designing covers for many artists. He was introduced to Richard Perry and soon he was flying with Feinstein to London to work on the sleeve. He worked out of Ringo or Robin's studio and had a great deal of freedom for the sleeve design. In a 2015 interview with *The Beatles Bible.com* he stated that there was only one directive. "The only directive I got was their desire to have the musicians who played on the album represented on the cover in some way." But he was also clear that he did not see a connection with *Sgt. Pepper's Lonely Hearts Club Band.*

With 'Photograph' already a massive hit, there were big expectations for the album. Or maybe apprehensions. Could Ringo maintain that quality for his rock album? Not surprisingly, the album was greeted with very good reviews. In the 3 November 1973 issue of *Billboard* ('Top Album Picks'), the reviewer is full of praise for "the best Ringo album ever. Rich Perry and his cadre of superstar session helpers have created another stunning production package." When this review was published, 'Photograph' was one week from reaching the top ten. Elsewhere, *Cash Box* were also very complimentary with their assessment of the album. "Ringo continues to develop his own identity in this fascinating Richard Perry produced LP which features the sensational hit single 'Photograph'. The artistry on this album is the most unique in the history of pop music. In fact, every cut on the LP is distinguished by the individual genius of Ringo and the collective talents of his friends." *Record World* also agreed with the others and gave the album two thumbs up, stating that the friends helping out do not overshadow the man himself: "...will give way to greater appreciation of Mr. Starkey's own talents. Ringo's warmly plaintive singing shines in front of all those HEAVY sidemen."

Ben Gerson, in writing for *Rolling Stone*, offered some backhanded compliments, but overall a positive review. Of course he had to run McCartney down, but he seemed to like the album. "It is not surprising, then, that in atmosphere *Ringo* is the most successful record by an ex-Beatle. The album is the document of the good time he had in its making." In the *New York Times,* rock critic Loraine Alterman compliments Perry and in comparing it to Lennon's *Mind Games,* makes it the clear winner. "Producer Richard Perry has worked so hard to achieve a masterpiece that it's on the verge of being overdone. Luckily Ringo's sense of humor saves it from crossing the line." She also has much praise for his writing, stating: "this is a sensational album and it contains the rock song of 1973, 'Oh My My' written by Ringo and a talented guy named Vini Poncia."

Ringo charted for 37 weeks and peaked at number two on *Billboard* (Elton John's *Goodbye Yellow Brick Road* kept it from number one. As noted, *Cash Box* had it reach number one). The album hit the number one spot in Canada on the national RPM charts, while in the UK it only managed to reach number seven and stayed on the charts for nine weeks.

Although *Ringo* was Ringo's biggest success and one of the best selling albums of 1973, it has, to date, not received the 'Deluxe' treatment that other albums from that year have enjoyed. Schnee also questions this development. "There was talk about a 50 year reissue and I think they were thinking. So I asked, 'I heard there was going to be a 50 year reissue, what happened?' I really don't know. I thought there would be one. It is amazing, as big as it was at the time, that record is not overlooked but it is underloved."

Schnee also looks at the album as a whole, and says that it came together quite well given the amount of people who worked on it. "It was all over the place, but the songs came from every direction. Obviously the other Beatles on *Ringo*, with a lot of help from his friends. They were always giving him a leg up. George had more to do with bringing songs on the *Ringo* album than anyone. Any of the Beatles who wrote the song co-produced their song. It was all about seeing it through to completion. Paul was co-producing with Richard his song. And they couldn't have been nicer, Paul and Linda. Ringo is not not nice, he is just Ringo. Paul is genuinely warm and inviting, more than anyone else."

As *Ringo* was being released, Starr got involved with a very interesting and progressive project. In England, in 1973, radio licences were available. Pirate radio stations, as well as European radio, were still threats to the UK, so the Independent Broadcasting Authority was accepting proposals for radio stations across the UK. In the November 4 issue of *Variety*, an article appeared stating that "a talent consortium including Ringo Starr has submitted a bid for the single station that will be assigned to Liverpool." Cilla Black and music hall comic Arthur Askey were also part of the group putting in a bid. Sadly, they never got the licence.

In an interview with John Halsall, for the *Daily Post* (Merseyside Ed.) on 15 November 1973 Starr stated a case for commercial radio in the UK. "Well, I'm hoping it will get more exciting now that commercial radios are coming out 'cause when Caroline and London were going, and all that scene it was just a fantastic time for music...all the different stations would have their own specials. And when that all closed down, the music just fell apart again, and you get into that BBC rut again...it's getting very segregated again."

Starr also contributed to two very interesting and unexpected projects during 1973. The first was an album titled *Get Off*. The double album was a promotional record that was sent to radio stations from the National Association of Progressive Radio Announcers (NAPRA). It was part of their anti-drug campaign, and it featured short clips from a variety of artists, including Ravi Shankar, Phil Ochs, Grand Funk, Frank Zappa and Ringo Starr, to name just a few. Starr was actually recorded in his hotel room at The Beverly Hills Hotel (room 396) on 10 March 1973. His segment is short (30 seconds) and features his drum solo from 'The End' in the background. These segments were intended to be public service announcements to be played between songs on the radio.

The second project was helping Lulu's brother establish a solo career. Billy Lawrie, who had worked with Lulu in the past, was in the process of putting together an album in 1973. Starr co-wrote two songs with him, only one of which has been released ('Rock And Roller'). No doubt Starr met Lawrie through Maurice Gibb, who lived across the street from Starr, and the two became quite good friends. Gibb was married to Lulu at the time, and Gibb and Lulu both contributed to the album, which was recorded at Starr's Startling Studios at his Tittenhurst Park Estate.

Startling Studios, as Starr renamed the studio, was the same studio Lennon (when he owned the property) used to record *Imagine*. Starr would open the studio up for rental for the latter part of the 1970s and much of the 1980s. The studio was also very important for Starr's label Ring O' Records. Although he co-wrote the song, Starr does not play on it. The other song, 'Where Are You Going', has never been released by either artist, although Starr reportedly recorded a version of it during the *Rotogravure* sessions. Starr has never recorded 'Rock And Roller' and to date there are no demos featuring Starr.

The song was released as a single in the UK, and the album, *Ship Imagination,* was released only in the UK. Both the single and the album were scheduled for release in November of 1973. However, according to an article in *Record Mirror* (22 December 1973), the album was to be released in January. The article reads, in part: "Billy is a rocker in style, and a single cut from the LP called 'Rock and Roller', which he wrote with Ringo Starr, was released recently. His LP debuted during the first week of next month when RCA released his album entitled *Ship Imagination*." Neither the album nor the single charted and both are quite collectible. Lawrie and his album received next to no press, with the exception of his sister Lulu discussing the album at length while promoting her then current single, 'The Man Who Sold The World'. She makes no mention of Ringo but she does talk about the songs and RCA's involvement.

Although Starr could not help Lawrie with his career, 1973 proved to be a very successful year for Starr. He was in the spotlight and, quite justifiably, he enjoyed every minute of it. However, his home life was not as rosy, as his marriage to Maureen was falling apart and Apple and The Beatles kept him busy with lawyers and meetings. But artistically, Ringo was making great music and creating a great deal of art. He was writing at the time, recording, and keeping very busy.

Starr, in talking with John Halsall, was also very open about the work he did with others. "I still do a lot of sessions for pals." He also talked about his desire to continue making films, "I don't think I will ever decide to do just films for two years or just records for two years. I always think of myself as a record artist making films, though, and not the other way around."

5

1974

The success of *Ringo* carried well into 1974. Starr continued to experience a great deal of success with the album and the third single to be released. 1974 was a pivotal year for all The Beatles. George Harrison would be the first solo Beatle to tour the US and start Dark Horse Records, John Lennon would have his second solo number one album and his first number one single (while helping David Bowie do the same). Paul McCartney, with a smaller Wings, dominated the charts and the year with the blockbuster *Band On The Run*, and Starr continued to make films and music.

In Starr's world, there was no break between 1973 and 1974 and it was business as usual. In November 1973, as the year was winding into Christmas, Starr helped George Harrison with recording some songs at Harrison's home studio, F.P.S.H.O.T., in Henley-On-Thames. Starr drummed on 'Ding Dong, Ding Dong ' and an early take of 'Dark Horse'. He also drummed on 'So Sad', but the exact recording date of that song is unknown. There is some speculation that it was recorded during Harrison's *Living In The Material World* sessions. The tracks 'Ding Dong, Ding Dong ' and 'So Sad ' would appear later in 1974 when Harrison released his album *Dark Horse*.

Ringo was still in the top ten on the US *Billboard* album charts and on 26 January 1974 Starr's cover of 'You're Sixteen' knocked Al Wilson's 'Show And Tell' out of the number one spot in the *Billboard* singles chart. Ringo was number one again. 'You're Sixteen' also hit number one with *Cash Box* and even charted to number two in *Billboard*'s Easy Listening chart. The single would get to number two in Canada and Ireland, and number four in the UK. It also sparked new interest in the album and Starr was once again at saturation level on the radio.

The single was released early in the year in the UK, where it became a hit. Ringo, it seemed, had the Midas touch. Even Lennon commented to *Rolling Stone*'s Pete Hamil, "I think it's great. Perry's great, Ringo's great, I think the combination was great and look how well they did together. There's no complaints if you're Number One."

With *Ringo* still in the charts, and 'You're Sixteen' having peaked at number one and now slowly declining in the charts, Capitol/Apple decided to release a third and final single from the album. This was an unusual move for Apple; in fact it was the first time Apple released a third single from an album. But due to radio play, there was a demand for the song 'Oh My My' to be released. In the US it was already playlisted on many radio stations, both AM and FM. The song was written by Starr and Vini Poncia and proved to be a smart choice for a single. It was released worldwide, but the UK would have to wait until 1976 to buy it as a single, when it was released to promote Starr's greatest hits collection, *Blast From Your Past*. The flipside was Starr's 'Step Lightly'. Unlike 'Photograph' and 'You're Sixteen', 'Oh My My' was released without a picture sleeve; it was just in the standard Apple sleeve. As with the other two singles, it was released with the customised label of Starr in a star. However, as with the other singles, that would be replaced by the standard Apple at some point.

The song was edited down for radio play. With the album version clocking in at four minutes and sixteen seconds, the single was edited down to three minutes and thirty-nine seconds in North America and Japan. The European release featured the full length version. A special promotional single was released to radio stations in North America, featuring the edited version on both sides, one in stereo and the other a mono mix, which was the industry standard at the time. The single's official release date in North America was 18 February 1974. The 2 March 1974 issue of *Billboard* had a full page ad, using the Klaus Voormann drawing from the lyric booklet in the *Ringo* album. "Soon to be Ringo's third #1 single," the ad proclaimed. "From his platinum album, *Ringo!*"

The same issue of *Billboard* contained a short review for the single in its Top Singles Pick, declaring that the song had a "happy mood both in the bouncy instrumental sound and in Ringo's voice. The song is more an instrumental achievement than it is a lyric." In the 2 March 1974 issue of *Cash Box*, the reviewer wrote: "this barrel-house rocker from the *Ringo* LP is bound to carry him back up to the top again." The reviewer noted Perry's expert production and referred to the song as an "amusing little ditty that's got top ten written all over it." *Record World* made it unanimous, and wrote (in the 2 March 1974 issue): "this latest gleaning should follow 'You're Sixteen' to numero uno. Starr co-wrote this tune, and the superb Perry production is the super-solid stuff from which gold records are made." Starr, it seemed, could do no wrong at this point.

The single became an instant hit. On 9 March 1974, 'Oh My My' entered the *Billboard* top 100 at number 65. Starr's 'You're Sixteen' was still in the top 20. It reached its peak of number five on 27 April 1974, with Grand Funk's cover of 'The Loco-Motion' sitting at number one. It peaked at number three in the Canadian *RPM* charts and number 34 in

Germany. Although Ringo is not known as a songwriter, the song would be covered by Ike and Tina Turner, Bette Midler and Maggie Bell. A snippet of the song can be heard in the comedy novelty record 'Mr President' by Dickie Goodman. Starr performed it live with his All Starr Band on several tours, and live versions can be found on *Live At The Greek Theatre 2008*.

The single's success prompted a telegram from John Lennon. "Congratulations. How dare you? And please write me a hit song."

Another album was released at the beginning of the year, *Presence Of The Lord* by The All Occasion Brass Band, with which Starr was involved. One might not instantly associate a religious album by a brass ensemble as something that Starr would appear on, yet he did. The band consisted of Dave McDaniels, C.B., Rev. D. S. Poncher, Jake The Rake, Jim Price, Jock Ellis, and Stu Blumberg. *Presence Of The Lord* was released in January 1974 on the MCA label. The album also featured help from Chris Spedding, Peter Frampton and Ringo Starr. Chris Spedding recalled that the album "might have been recorded at the same time of Harry Nilsson sessions in 1972 or so." Interestingly, the album contained covers of two Harrison tracks, 'My Sweet Lord' and 'Isn't it A Pity'.

Starr also found time to help a country artist record his debut album. Guthrie Thomas's life would make an incredible book if not film. Born Andrew Lynn Herring, he adopted the name Guthrie from Woody Guthrie and Thomas from Dylan Thomas. Thomas recorded his debut solo album, *Sitting Crooked*, in Los Angeles. Perhaps Jim Keltner introduced him to Starr, who drummed on the album. It was released on Guthrie's label Singing Folks Records and did not attract much attention. It is a solid, traditional country album with a number of famed session players on it, including David Foster, who would turn up on Dark Horse Records with Attitudes, Keltner, Douglas Dillard, Nicolette Larson and Jim Hartford. Ringo would work with Thomas again in 1976.

The film *Son Of Dracula* was finally released on 19 April 1974, with its premiere at the famed Loew's Grand Theater in Atlanta, Georgia. This is the theatre where *Gone With The Wind* had its noted premiere. In North America the film received a PG rating, which meant there were no age restrictions to see the film. The 10 April 1974 issue of *Variety* reported that for the opening, RCA would partner with a local radio station. The label and station "will toss a party in a 7,000-car parking lot to hype the *Son of Dracula* preem. RCA will combine with Cinemation in promoting pic's playoff in other parts of the country." RCA distributed the soundtrack for the film. Cinemation would promote the film as, quote, "the first rock-and-roll Dracula movie." Further, according to *Variety*, there would be "heavy concentration on its musical and comedic elements, with a radio spot developed by Cinemation that goes 'see Nilsson bite Ringo on the neck'."

Perhaps to stir up interest, or perhaps because it was true, Cinemation released a press release stating that John Lennon would be attending the premiere with Ringo Starr and Harry Nilsson. Lennon did not make it to the launch of the film.

Son Of Dracula should have been a hit, given the rock star power in the film: Starr, Keith Moon, Leon Russell, Harry Nilsson, and Led Zeppelin's John Bonham. It was initially filmed in 1972, but it was delayed due to concerns with the overall quality of the film. During 1973, efforts were made to make it slightly more commercial and give it a stronger plot. By the time of its premiere, it had lost all of its appeal with rock music fans. *Son Of Dracula* disappeared quickly, and was destined for midnight showings. However, in Canada (where the film was distributed by Prima Films), it was a little different. It was released a week prior, and was shown at the Coronet in Vancouver. It was not the official world premiere. Canada's *RPM* magazine noted that "The film, starring Ringo Starr and Harry Nilsson, is being distributed here by Primo Films. The opening was attended by local on-air personalities. RCA is now shipping 'Music from the film *Son of Dracula*' on Rappie Records. CKLG-FM co-operated in the promotion of the premiere by give-aways of tickets to the film and albums."

Son Of Dracula does have a plot, but more importantly, it has great music. There is not a lot of footage of Nilsson, so it is great to see him sing 'Without You'. Some of the performances are either stiff or over the top. Nilsson playing a vampire who yearns to be mortal, and fights dark forces, should have been interesting. However, the opposite is true. It is not a terrible film by any standards, but it is not very good either. It is, however, fascinating to watch. Given the director, who had made his fair share of horror films, it should have been more than just fascinating, it should have been brilliant.

Given too the success of the musical *The Rocky Horror Picture Show*, the film should have achieved more success than it did. Again, with the star power and music, and the level of Starr's popularity at the time, it should have done better. Even without social media, perhaps word spread about the film, and killed any chances it had. However, even the film *The Rocky Horror Picture Show* was a flop when it was first released in 1975 and it did not attract an audience until the midnight showings started in 1976. *Son Of Dracula* never achieved the same cult status.

Perhaps because the film had no distribution and seemingly everyone involved with it wanted to divorce themselves from it as quickly as possible, the film has almost disappeared. Only bootleg copies are available, on streaming services and through bootleggers, and the film has become almost mythical. Fans start to question if it was ever even released.

While the soundtrack is quite wonderful and full of great songs, the same can be said for the film. Although it has issues, and is not a cinema classic, it does have its comedic moments and no one can argue with the soundtrack.

Following the premiere (Starr later joked that "12,000 people turned up for the opening and then everyone left the next day without seeing the movie"), Starr hired Graham Chapman of *Monty Python's Flying Circus* to write and record some dialogue for the film. However, it didn't help. Starr lamented that with the additional dialogue, "It made even less sense."

In 2001, speaking with Paul Du Noyer in *Mojo*, Starr was clear about the problem with the film. According to him, he was spending "one thousand pounds a day for booze. They (the cast) were all gone by noon. It was funny. It was fun." However, the fun times also meant that not a lot of work was getting done, and at times crews were kept late. Starr later said, "I didn't know that if you didn't get the crew home and in their beds by midnight, you couldn't work them the next day."

Undeterred by the failure of *Son Of Dracula*, Nilsson and Starr began writing a new film in January 1974, *Harry and Ringo's Night Out*, starring Harry Nilsson and Ringo Starr. It was to be a mix of live-action and animation based on Harry and Ringo taking in the nightlife of LA. It was influenced by Frank Zappa's *200 Motels*, in which Starr appeared. According to Michael Seth Starr in his book *Ringo: With A Little Help*, the film was to be co-financed by Michael Viner, from Pride Records. Viner even reported to *Billboard* that there would be a soundtrack, presumably on Pride Records. Viner is perhaps best known for the song 'Apache' by the Incredible Bongo Band, a group he assembled and produced.

Filming began in October 1974 of the semi-documentary. *Harry and Ringo's Night Out* was intended to be a comical documentary about Starr, Nilsson and Keith Moon in Los Angeles, showing them recording and having fun. The animation would serve to show the 'craziness' of their lifestyle. It would have been a timely film, given that all three were working on albums in Los Angeles at the time. However, the film was never completed or released. A very short clip does exist on Youtube.

Billboard magazine, in reviewing the soundtrack to *Son Of Dracula* on 6 April 1974, seemed very hopeful for the success of the album and movie. They even noted that the album is on Rapple Records (a combination of RCA and Apple), stating: "someone deserves a pat on the back for the one shot label art." The reviewer does note "this freewheeling aural precis a bit confusing and rather disappointing for its lack of new material." Then it is noted that one should "listen closer, and the premium Nilsson favorites included derive a new spunk from often funny new intros, notably when 'Without You' becomes a lament for a vampire's lost fangs. Of the few new musical moments, 'Daybreak' is the finest." High praise for an album that features disjointed dialogue and old Nilsson songs, with one new track, 'Daybreak'.

As indicated in the review, the soundtrack album was a collection of older Harry Nilsson songs, some very big hits ('Without You'), tied in with dialogue from the film. It makes for an entertaining listening experience. Although Starr is given a co-credit on the sleeve, he does not contribute any music. He does play on several tracks, and he can be heard on segments from the film, but he did not contribute any new music to the film or the soundtrack.

Variety reviewed the album as well, noting that the it includes "enough spoken parts to get the full story of their Apple film." The review also makes note of "stellar support as Peter Frampton, Klaus Voormann, Jim Price, Gary Wright. Chris Spedding and others." It also highlights the songs 'Daybreak', 'Remember Christmas', 'Jump Into the Fire' and 'Without You.'

Although the single 'Daybreak' was a minor hit in the US, peaking at number 21 (it got to number 15 in Canada's *RPM* Top 100 and number 17 on *RPM* Adult Pop Charts) the soundtrack reached a dismal 112 on the album charts. Nilsson was having difficulty finding an audience at this point in his career. He was well known, but just not selling records or getting much radio play. His second album for 1974, *Pussy Cats*, would fare better. *Son Of Dracula* sank like a stone - or rather took a stake in the heart - in the UK. The film and the album were ignored. It failed to chart or attract an audience to a movie house. The film distributor, Cinemation Industries, went bankrupt in 1975, and according to one author, "it was not to be a major hit anywhere, and would be cited as the film that would seal the company's fate, especially with a film that featured known musicians."

Son Of Dracula was re-released in 1975, under the title *Young Dracula*, given the success of *Young Frankenstein*. It didn't help the film at all and it flopped again. There is no documentation about how well the film did financially, but given it was credited with causing a film company to declare bankruptcy, one can assume it did not make back any significant money.

Although *Son Of Dracula* was not the classic or comedy that Starr (or Nilsson) had imagined, during this time *That'll Be The Day* was finally released in North America and earned Starr some rave reviews. It led to a full page ad in *Variety* on 31 October 1974. In preparation for nominations for the Academy Awards, the advertisement read: "For your consideration, Ringo Starr best supporting actor for *That'll Be The Day*". Although he deserved a nomination, he did not receive one. *Son Of Dracula* was never considered for any awards.

By this point, Starr was spending a great deal of time in LA and he had become part of a group that became known as the 'Hollywood Vampires'. Nilsson and Lennon would be part of the same gang. The Hollywood Vampires consisted of an exclusive club of famous rock stars living in LA and other members included Alice Cooper, Keith Moon and Micky Dolenz. The group were well known for their all-night parties. Although the spotlight was on Lennon, Starr was part of the party scene, having split from his first wife, Maureen. Ringo and Maureen would officially be divorced in 1975, but they were separated at this point. Interestingly, the Hollywood Vampires fizzled out but Alice Cooper would resurrect the name in 2015 and release an album featuring Paul McCartney singing and playing bass on his composition 'Come And Get It'.

Through his friendship with Nilsson, Starr struck up friendships with artists such as Jimmy Webb. "Yeah. I met them when they were working on *The White Album* at Trident [Studios]. I've run into them occasionally for years," Webb recalled. "Off and on. Odd ones of them. I spent more time with Ringo than anybody else because of Harry [Nilsson]." He eventually got Starr to play drums on an album he was recording. The album, *Land's End*, would be the only album Webb recorded for Asylum Records (he had been on Reprise up to this point), and although he wrote countless hits for other artists, Webb never found success as an artist.

Recording this album proved to be very important to Starr. In an attempt to reach a new audience, Webb decided to work with Robin Cable, an engineer who had worked with Elton John. Webb co-produced the album, and along with Starr, he brought in members of Elton John's band, Joni Mitchell, Tom Scott and other session players. He also brought in David Hentschel, who was well known for his ability to play synthesiser. Hentschel had an impressive resumé, having recorded with Genesis, Elton John and Queen. Starr met Hentschel and was impressed with his playing. Starr appreciated how melodic he made the synthesiser sound. Hentschel would be the first artist to sign to Starr's Ring O' Records.

Land's End was recorded during the summer of 1973, but not released until June of 1974 (July in the UK). Starr would appear on the entire album. Two singles were released from it, 'Crying In My Sleep' (with 'Ocean In His Eyes' on the flipside), and 'Feet In The Sunshine'. 'Feet In The Sunshine' was the only single released in the UK, with 'Lady Fits Her Blue Jeans' on the B-side. The album received very positive reviews. *Billboard,* in the 8 June 1974 issue, said: "This collection of songs was recorded in London working with musicians such as Ringo Starr, Joni Mitchell and Elton John's band. The words are as strong as ever and the instrumental backing complements his ever improving vocals." However, the album and the singles failed to chart.

Besides meeting Hentschel, the recording of the album also led to some unintended consequences for Starr. In speaking with Scott K. Fish, Webb recounted how the recording of one song ended with Starr retiring the drum kit he had used on *Sgt. Pepper's Lonely Hearts Club Band.*

Webb said, "We had an engineer, I won't mention his name, who was having some trouble with his hearing. He had Ringo tuning his drums, I think, for two days. [Ringo] just kept hitting the drums and hitting the drums. He just seemed to get tired and more frustrated with the fact that he couldn't play. We weren't playing anything! [Ringo] just kept hitting these drums. I think, the third day or something we finally got around to playing. Ringo was playing great. He was playing wonderfully. He was playing with him and Nigel Olsson. And it sounded really great. The engineer/producer kept complaining about the drum sound. I think finally we got a take." But due to this situation, Webb later heard from Nilsson that "he put them in the back of a garage somewhere, and he didn't play for, like, a year. I've always felt really terrible about that. That I was involved in that much frustration for the guy [Ringo] that he would actually retire a drum set. Even temporarily." Ringo would team up with Webb again in 1978 for a television show.

While Lennon was in LA he began work on what would become his 1975 album, *Rock 'N' Roll*. He became part of the LA scene and was seen at many clubs. But he did want to record an album and not have to write songs and produce it; he wanted to make a simple rock and roll album, and let someone else take over. Who else was more qualified to produce a rock and roll oldies album than Phil Spector, who was there when the songs were first recorded?

Things did not turn out as planned for Lennon. Quite frankly, an entire book could be written about that project. Realising that the rock and roll album project was not going the way he had hoped, Lennon tried to help his old friend Nilsson to get his career back on solid ground. Lennon also hoped to turn around the negative press he was getting at the time, mostly due to drunken nights out with Nilsson. First, Lennon helped Nilsson sign a new contract with RCA. He advocated on Nilsson's behalf and got him a great deal. Lennon also agreed to not only produce the next album but also to contribute a song. Although Starr did not help Lennon with *Rock'N' Roll* or his 1974 release, *Walls And Bridges*, Starr did help out on what would become *Pussy Cats* by Harry Nilsson.

Although Lennon was in the midst of his "lost weekend" in Los Angeles, he called on some friends and session players, including Ringo Starr, who drums on most of the songs, Keith Moon, Danny Kortchmar, Jesse Ed Davis, Jane Getz, Ken Ascher and good friend Klaus Voormann. Recording started in March of 1974 and would conclude in May. In August, Moon would begin recording his first and only solo album, which would be released in 1975. But first, Nilsson had an album to complete.

Lennon booked Burbank Studios in Los Angeles, and in March of 1974 recording began. Although the album is fine, it seemed doomed from the start. Nilsson, reportedly, ruptured one of his vocal cords but chose to keep this from Lennon. Nilsson decided to push through the sessions, which caused even more issues for his voice. One listen to the album and it's clear that Nilsson's voice is not what it had been just two years earlier. Although it was still Nilsson and he had a great sound for the album, his voice had changed quite dramatically. Several musicians who worked on the album, such as former member of The Monkees, Micky Dolenz, was quoted as saying the recording "caused him permanent damage".

Starr drummed on six of the album's ten tracks and played percussion (maracas) on a seventh track. Four singles were released off the album in total, with Starr drumming on all but one. The first single released, a cover of Jimmy Cliff's 'Many Rivers To Cross' (8 July 1974, released 13 September 1974 in the UK) failed to reset Nilsson's career and was his biggest failure up to that point, peaking in the US singles chart at 109 (the 'Bubbling Under' portion of *Billboard*), while it did much better in Canada, peaking at number 43. *Billboard* did list the song as a 'recommended' single in their Top Picks in the 13 July 1974 issue. *Cash Box* was much kinder, noting that it was produced by Lennon, and that Nilsson "sounds more like John Lennon than Lennon sometimes does himself. A ballad that's one of the best we've heard in years, this one just won't miss." They also note that "the arrangement here is tops." The single did not chart in the UK.

On an interesting side note, on 19 June 1974, a copyright was registered for a new song, 'Where Are You Going?' The song was a co-write between Starr and Billy Lawrie. Starr wrote 'Rock and Roller' with Lawrie, which appeared on his 1973 album, *Ship Imagination*. Perhaps Starr was planning on giving it to Moon, or using it for *Goodnight Vienna*. Starr returned to 'Where Are You Going?' in 1976, suggesting that it was a song he liked and perhaps thought could be a hit.

By August 1974, Starr was eager to begin work on his next solo album. The album would become *Goodnight Vienna*, and unlike *Ringo*, only one former Beatle would help out. With the success of the *Ringo* album, there was a lot riding on this one. *Ringo* had been a huge worldwide success, propelling Starr to the top of the charts and the top of the rock and roll world. People - critics and fans - wondered if he could do it again. He did not have these expectations and pressures when recording *Ringo*. Once again, he teamed up with Richard Perry and he returned to Sunset Studios in Los Angeles (with some overdubs being completed at Producer's Workshop).

In an odd turn of events, given Starr's social activities, he announced in Los Angeles on 17 September 1974 that he was to campaign against young people using drugs for the next twelve months. Starr had participated in the National Association of Progressive Radio Announcers (NAPRA) anti-drug campaign in 1973, and he contributed a track to the album *Get Off*, which was sent out to radio stations. It was not made clear as to what he planned to do during the twelve months, and following the announcement, very little was written about what happened next.

Starr did call upon his friend, John Lennon, with whom he had been spending a great deal of time in Los Angeles, to maybe write him a song. According to May Pang, while Lennon was writing and recording his album *Walls And Bridges*, he wrote the song 'Goodnight Vienna 'and decided to give it to Ringo. He was in New York, but returned to Los Angeles to help with the recording of the song. Richard Perry later said, "I made sure that the band remained as close to John's demo as possible. John played acoustic rhythm guitar on two tracks and piano."

Engineer Bill Schnee agreed. "He wrote that for Ringo. 'I'm The Greatest', from *Ringo*, was written for himself and he changed the lyrics for Ringo."

Although comparisons to *Ringo* can be made, in many ways, this was much more a Ringo Starr album than *Ringo*. His superstar friends were all there, such as John Lennon, Harry Nilsson, Robbie Robertson, Elton John, Billy Preston, Gary Wright and Dr. John. Also there were well known session players, Bobby Keyes (who would be releasing his own music in 1975 on Ringo's label), Jim Keltner and Jesse Ed Davis. But the album does have more of an overall Ringo Starr feel rather than *Ringo* and friends. With *Goodnight Vienna*, the guests did not overshadow Starr, and the absence of Beatle reunions helped focus the spotlight more on Starr himself.

Bill Schnee, who engineered both *Ringo* and *Goodnight Vienna*, reflected on both albums and working with Richard Perry, "I would describe it, on both albums that Richard Perry did, Starr came in ready to be produced. If there is anything Richard was good at, it was producing. He was extremely compliant and he was definitely Ringo. What you see is what you get, light hearted and jovial and always in a good mood.

"On *Ringo* I went in scared to death, needless to say. Every session, you do your best. Back in those days, especially. I did a good bit of work on *Goodnight Vienna* in the Producer's Workshop studio. *Goodnight Vienna* was quicker for sure than recording *Ringo*. It was three months, half the time than *Ringo*."

The sleeve caused a bit of controversy. Using the famous still from the 1954 film *The Day The Earth Stood Still,* Ringo assumed the role of Klaatu, the intergalactic police officer who comes to Earth to warn humans that their behaviour will not be tolerated any longer by the peaceful planets. Behind Ringo stands Gort. Two years after the album was released, a Canadian band named Klaatu released their self-titled debut album. They did not get the name for their band from Ringo, but from the film. However, because their debut album was released sans credits, and they were certainly influenced by The Beatles (and other bands as well), some thought they *could* be The Beatles under a clever pseudonym. The cover of *Goodnight Vienna* was one of the many clues fans cited to prove their point. The band Klaatu were actually three musicians from Canada, Dee Long, Terry Draper and John Woloschuk, who had been making records in Canada as Klaatu since 1974.

In 1974, Starr discussed the sleeve design with Rob Partridge from *Melody Maker*. "We were sitting around the office one day talking about the new album and this good friend of mine suggested an elaborate space set up because he knows I am a science fiction freak, like all the weird stuff from the 50s, and he said he had a designer friend who could create the whole thing. It sounded great until we found out how much it would cost. That ended that. Until I was at my friend Harry Nilsson's house in LA and he had some pictures from *The Day The Earth Stood Still*...and I took one look and said 'That's the stuff.' It fits right with the title."

The other controversy was the credit for the album design. In an email to this author, John Kosh explained what happened. For the record, Kosh would design the next three studio albums by Starr. But Kosh, who had worked with Starr on the wonderful *Beaucoups Of Blues* sleeve, had a hand in designing *Goodnight Vienna*. "I'd like to set the record straight regarding *Goodnight Vienna*. It was my idea to have Ringo standing on the saucer, a parody of the famous scene with Michael Rennie in 1951's *The Day The Earth Stood Still*. I drew it up and presented it to Ringo, the title as yet unknown. It ended up at Capitol where someone added that horrible, ill conceived lettering. Of course I am not credited and that's perhaps just as well." Roy Kohara is credited for the sleeve design.

Even though *Goodnight Vienna* does have many special guests, Starr seemed to be more front and centre. He wrote one song, 'Call Me', for the album, and co-wrote two additional songs with Vini Poncia, 'Oo-Wee' and 'All By Myself'. Perhaps due to this being the second album he had worked on with Perry, they were able to create a very cohesive and strong pop album. Given that the three biggest selling albums in North America in 1974 were 'greatest hits' and 'best of' packages by pop artists (*Elton John's Greatest Hits*, *Santana's Greatest Hits* and *So Far*, a compilation by Crosby, Stills, Nash & Young), nostalgia seemed to be getting a grip on US record buyers. Starr's *Goodnight Vienna* was a breath of fresh air, some brilliant new music from an established artist.

And even though he did not write the majority of the songs, the songs he recorded seemed to reflect his current life at the time. The song 'Snookeroo', for example, was not biographical but it did sum up Starr's youth. In many ways, this sense of the album being more personal for Starr gives the album its charm. It really is more of a cohesive album, and one that does not feel like a collection of singles. This is not a slight against *Ringo*, which is a classic and iconic album. But with *Goodnight Vienna* the sum is greater than its individual parts.

The album kicks off with the title track, written by Lennon. The term 'Goodnight Vienna' is, according to Starr, an expression used in Northern England meaning "I'm getting out of here." The song, which features Lennon on piano, is the perfect opener. A reprise also ends the album in style, with the same players as the opening track. This is custom made for Starr and, again, sets the stage for the rest of the album. Lennon's count in and the pounding piano add a great deal to the proceedings.

Although Lennon's track would introduce the album, it would not be the first single from it. The first single was the last song recorded. 'Only You (And You Alone)' (credited as just 'Only You' on the single), was released four days prior to the album's release date in North America, while it was released the same day as the album in the UK (14 November 1974). In his book, *Cloud Nine: Memoirs Of A Record Producer*, Perry recalled that while they were in the process of recording, Starr and Perry were talking to Lennon and said they were one song short to complete the album. Lennon suggested 'Only You (And You Alone)'.

Bill Schnee, who engineered *Goodnight Vienna,* recalled, "Lennon was in the booth at Sunset Studios and he began strumming 'Only You (And You Alone)'. Richard Perry was in a doo-wop band once, and he was a big fan of the song." The song was written by Buck Ram (who wrote many classic songs including 'I'll Be Home For Christmas') and The Platters took their 1954 recording of the song to number five on the *Billboard* Pop Singles chart, although it went to number one on the R&B charts.

Schnee expanded on what happened in the studio. "On the second album, we didn't have anyone but John. I know one of the great moments was when we were sitting there getting ready to do a cut, and you know how musicians will just sit down and start playing songs, then they work up a groove with the other guys. John was sitting in the iso booth, and he just started singing 'Only You' out of nowhere. And Richard being the astute producer that he was said, 'That's a great one. Ringo, how would you like to do that?' 'I guess so.' And from there we cut one of the hits on the record."

According to Schnee, Lennon was very involved with the arrangement of the song (and others) and could almost be considered a co-producer. "The best thing about *Goodnight Vienna* was spending so much time with John. Richard was credited as the producer, but when John came in, just like *Ringo*, when he came in he was not credited, but he was producing the sessions. John was much more involved."

Matthew Trzcinski wrote that Lennon later said that he was not a fan of Richard Perry. "But on the other hand I think my criticism of somebody like Richard Perry would be that he's great but he's too painstaking," Lennon said. "It gets too slick and somewhere in between that is where I'd like to go."

In her book, *Loving John - The Untold Story*, May Pang stated that Lennon suggested to Ringo to record 'Only You (And You Alone)', even though Lennon had wanted to record it for himself. He reportedly said to Ringo, "This is one I wanted to do, but I will give it to you." Lennon worked closely with Perry and helped arrange the song. Lennon went so far as to record a demo of it, featuring Billy Preston (organ), Jesse Ed Davies (guitar), Steve Cropper (guitar), Klaus Voormann (bass), and Jim Keltner (drums). Lennon played acoustic and it served as a guide for Ringo. Harry Nilsson would later add backing vocals. Lennon's demo would be released in 1998 as part of the *John Lennon Anthology.*

In the 16 November 1974 issue of *Billboard,* in Singles Picks, the writer predicted another hit for Ringo, and commented: "with his distinctive vocals and odd but catchy arrangement, could well be the biggest thing he's came up with since 'Photograph'." The writer also predicted big things for the B-side, the Starr composition 'Call Me'. The single debuted at number 63 in the same issue, the second highest debut for that week (Stevie Wonder's 'Boogie On Reggae Woman' came in at number 62).

Cash Box was equally positive about the single. In the 16 November 1974 issue, the writer states the "1955 Platters classic has been updated superstar style. With Ringo singing lead and John doing some background harmonies the tempo has been upped from the original." The writer predicted that the single would go to number one. It is interesting to note that the number one single on *Billboard* and *Cash Box* was John Lennon's only number one single during his lifetime, 'Whatever Gets You Thru The Night'. *Record World* also predicted big things for the single, saying: "Another Ringo remake for number one." Further, 'Only You' was chosen as 'Smash of the Week' in *Variety* on 26 November 1974 and a "Top Prospect" the week before.

The UK press was supportive of the single. *Record Mirror* (23 November 1974) said Ringo sings it "straight" with "a dash of let's speak a couple of lines" and refers to it as "a pleasant single". But at the same time, the writer is clear that Starr is jumping on a trend of covers, started by Bryan Ferry.

Although the song received saturation level airplay on American radio, it was not the hit the trade magazines had predicted. The song is a faithful adaptation, maybe too faithful, and the vocal arrangement and production are flawless. Starr's voice is strong and he delivers the song without a hint of humour. The B-side, 'Call Me', although also pegged for radio play, didn't help the song's chart position. It did not receive much airtime and was seen as an album cut.

'Call Me' is very much an underrated song for Starr. It is one of his most honest, and he is at his most vulnerable, singing about the end of a relationship; in this case, with his then wife, Maureen. The song features David Foster on piano, which is the foundation of the song. Starr drums alone on this one, with Klaus Voormann on bass. The two provide the perfect rhythm section. Steve Cropper provides very tasteful electric guitar throughout and is remarkably restrained. Former Apple artists Lon and Derrek Van Eaton (at the time they were signed to A&M) provide stellar backing vocals along with Harry Nilsson, Richard Perry, Vini Poncia, Voormann and Cynthia Webb (credited on the album as 'Sweet Cynthia Webb'). Starr provides an emotional vocal and the song is near perfect.

A promo film was made for 'Only You', featuring Ringo and Harry Nilsson (in his trademark bathrobe) on top of the Capitol Building in Los Angeles, with the spaceship from the front cover. It was directed by Stanley Dorfman, the co-creator of the UK's *Top Of The Pops*, where the clip was shown. Ringo is dressed similarly to the cover of *Goodnight Vienna*, wearing star sunglasses. It is a fun film (complete with a spaceship landing in the beginning). It would later be included in the compilation *Photograph:The Very Best Of Ringo Starr* on the bonus DVD. Capitol-EMI did put a lot into promoting the single. A promo copy was sent out to North American radio featuring the song in mono and stereo, and full page advertisements were taken out in magazines.

'Only You' peaked in America on *Billboard* at number six on 11 January 1975. It did go to number one on *Billboard's* Adult Contemporary chart. The number one record on the pop charts that week was Elton John's cover of 'Lucy In The Sky With Diamonds'; Paul McCartney and Wings leapfrogged over Ringo and were sitting at number three with 'Junior's Farm'. Rounding out the top five were: Barry Manilow's 'Mandy' (number five), Neil Sedaka with 'Laughter In The Rain' at number four, and Barry White's 'You're The First, The Last, My Everything' at number two. Starr could not nudge into the top five. 'Only You' peaked at number six on *Cash Box* as well. In the UK, 'Only You' entered the *Record Mirror* top 50 at number 33 in the 30 November 1974 chart, and peaked at a disappointing 29 on 28 December 1974.

In Canada, where Starr had been very successful, with some of his singles charting higher than in the US, 'Only You' failed to register with radio and the fans. It entered the Canadian Top 100 (*RPM* magazine) on 14 November 1974 at number 93. It peaked on 25 January 1975 at number 17. It did make it to number one on Canada's radio playlist chart. On a personal note, I never heard the song on the radio at the time of its release. In the Toronto area, the song seemed to go unnoticed.

The single was released with a picture sleeve, and a special universe label, rather than the standard Apple. The picture sleeve was the same in North America and UK. For the first time it was also the standard sleeve around the world. Later pressings of the single in North America would have the standard Apple.

Bill Schnee noted that Nilsson's backing vocals on the song are incredible and add a great deal to the song. "Just how unbelievably talented that guy was. And one of the poster children, in my mind, for why you don't do drugs because his life ended far too early. He and Ringo were really good mates. To watch Nilsson in the studio come up with background parts was just unbelievable."

Perhaps the song was not the best choice from the album to release as the first single. Elton John's 'Snookeroo' may have been a better choice for a lead-off single. Starr had already covered an oldies standard, and releasing another cover seemed formulaic. The choice may have had more to do with Lennon than Starr. Both George Harrison and Paul McCartney had participated in number one singles for Starr, and perhaps it was felt it was Lennon's turn, and this song, not only featuring Lennon but also suggested by Lennon, would have all three Beatles helping to put Ringo on top again. Sadly, although a sizeable hit, it did not turn out that way.

Although the single 'Only You' did not perform as well as expected on the singles chart, there was still a great deal of excitement for *Goodnight Vienna*. Starr finished recording in August 1974. It was his fourth solo album. And initially reviews were very positive. Tom Nolan noted, in *Rolling Stone*, that it was a pleasant album, which "follows in the winning tradition of *Ringo*". He also noted that the "guest stars perform with easy excellence and Ringo supplies that unalloyed sincerity which is his trademark and trump card." Comparisons to *Ringo* were inevitable.

The 23 November 1974 issue of *Billboard* magazine noted that *Goodnight Vienna* features a "wide variety of songs." The writer went on to say: "As a singer Ringo is not going to set the world on fire, but as a stylist he grows impressibly with each LP." Making it the album pick of the week, the writer predicted that there was some "assurance of several solid singles." The writer also referred to the numerous guests on the album, and yet "Ringo still manages to keep the album his." *Variety* reviewed the album, and stated that "Ringo Starr has an imaginative new set with his original as title." (*Variety* 18 December 1974)

Cash Box (23 November 1974) was also very positive about the album and predicted another hit for Mr Starr. "With much fanfare the new Ringo LP descends upon us much as did his flying saucer promotional effort in Hollywood," the reviewer wrote. "Much fanfare and excitement. Those words key to the entire feel of the LP which has a lot to live up to if it's to match the three gold singles that came from *Ringo* and achieve platinum status as did the aforementioned disk." The reviewer also noted that "Ringo goes into a number of different bags on this LP and with Perry orchestrating, comes up with some intriguing combinations." The track 'Easy For Me' is singled out.

This review says a great deal, as *Goodnight Vienna* does not feel like *Ringo* Part II. It is, in some ways, a very different album, with a different overall sound and flow. There are, of course, similarities, especially with the guest star aspect, but a song like 'Occapella' is as different as anything Starr recorded. The horn arrangement and use of backing vocals make for a very New Orleans jazzy sound. Of course, the aid of Dr. John (on piano and vocals) certainly helped. But it is Starr's willingness to tackle the Allen Toussaint original.

Later, Starr returns to his love of country music, tackling the Roger Miller hurting song 'Husbands And Wives'. The sparse arrangement built around Tom Hensley's electric piano is astounding, and the subtle addition of Carl Fortina's accordion is breathtaking. Vini Poncia's reticent backing vocals fill in all the gaps. Again, given that Starr's first marriage was falling apart at the time, this song must have been difficult for Starr. It may not have the sound of traditional country, but Miller was a respected Nashville writer and the song is closer to country than pop.

Even though a television commercial was produced for the album, featuring John Lennon's voiceover (Starr returned the favour for Lennon's television commercial for *Walls And Bridges*), the album did not do as well as *Ringo*. *Ringo* sold close to two million copies worldwide at the time (it has sold over three million at the time of this writing), while *Goodnight Vienna* sold 1.5 million worldwide in 1974/75 (now close to two million worldwide). That is not a flop.

Seeing the album as not doing well is not surprising, given the album was constantly being compared to *Ringo*, and with only one Beatle helping out, there was much less hype. Engineer Bill Schnee added his thoughts on the album's sales. "It was not the jovial, happy go lucky time that the first record was. Ringo was involved, but he was also along for the ride on both albums. He would have opinions, but Richard Perry was guiding the ship. We had a lot of great people on it, Elton John wrote a song for him, it was the same kind of idea, but somehow didn't work quite as well."

Schnee further added: "I didn't have the same feeling at the time, but I had already been through one with these heavy hitters, the heaviest of heavies. I know there were some great moments, like when he called Elton. He called Elton and asked him to write a song, and Elton comes in and does that very fun song, 'Snookeroo'. That was a great session."

It is also important to consider the 'second album syndrome'. Although *Ringo* was not his first album (it was his third), it was his first huge hit. In some ways, nothing could live up to the expectations of fans and critics. This is quite common. For example, Fleetwood Mac's *Tusk* was seen as a failure when it was released as the follow-up to *Rumours*. This is just one example. While *Tusk* was far from a flop, the same can be said for *Goodnight Vienna*.

Billboard and *Cash Box* both had *Goodnight Vienna* peak at number eight in January 1975, while George Harrison, Ohio Players, Elton John and Joni Mitchell were in the upper regions of the charts. In Canada, the album did not even reach the top ten, making *Ringo* Starr's only top ten album in that country. *Goodnight Vienna* peaked at 12, and in the UK, it did not go higher than 30 after only two weeks on the chart. In the UK, the album chart was dominated by greatest hits packages (Elton John, Elvis Presley, Hits Explosion), Roxy Music, Paul McCartney & Wings, and Queen.

Schnee recalled that Starr was disappointed with the success of *Goodnight Vienna*. "Of course it was, it is always disappointing. It wasn't as fun as a cover as *Ringo*. Although, everything in Hollywood has an effect. In Hollywood, they had a big billboard for *Ringo*, and the 'I' would spin around and it would be *Ringo*. And for *Goodnight Vienna*, they had this thing on top of the Capitol building, which you couldn't see really. It didn't have the same impact. It seemed that as the stars were aligning, nothing aligned quite as well. It was not stiff or anything, just not as big."

Starr and Poncia wrote two songs for the album, 'All By Myself' and 'Oo-Wee'. 'All By Myself' features John Lennon on guitar and Richard Perry providing his trademark bass vocals. Again, taken in the context of Starr's life at the time, it is yet another break-up song, although this one is more of a survivor anthem than a 'poor me'. The song also benefits from the top notch playing of Dr. John (piano), Voormann (bass), Jim Keltner (who joined Starr on drums), Alvin Robinson (a member of Dr. John's band on additional guitar) and a tasteful trumpet solo by Steve Madio. In fact, the entire horn section (Bobby Keyes, Lew McCreary and Trevor Lawrence) add a great deal to the song, as do the backing vocals from Clydie King, Joe Greene, Linda Lawrence, and Vini Poncia.

Nancy Lee Andrews confirmed that Starr was very upset about his divorce from Maureen. In her book *A Dose of Rock 'n' Roll*, she wrote about going out with Starr, Lennon, and May Pang. After recording vocals for *Goodnight Vienna*, the four wound up at The Fiddler, a popular nightspot in Los Angeles. As the night wore on, Andrews wrote that Starr became more and more melancholy, playing Charlie Rich's 'The Most Beautiful Girl In The World' repeatedly on a jukebox. Lee said to Lennon and Pang that he thought "he's still in love with his wife. Look at him, his heart is broken." This sentiment is reflected throughout *Goodnight Vienna*.

An almost identical line-up recorded the other Starr/Poncia song, 'Oo-Wee'. Lennon is not part of the session and guitar is provided by Dennis Coffey. However, with the addition of The Blackberries on backing vocals, the song becomes another glam/disco thumper, somewhat in the same vein as 'Oh My My'. Perhaps sensing another hit with 'Oo-Wee', Capitol-EMI included it on the B-side of the next single in the UK. It would be the third single released in North America. The fact that in North America a promo single of 'Oo-Wee' was provided to radio (Apple P-1882) with mono and stereo versions clearly supports this idea. The song is certainly an earworm, and is very catchy.

The next single released in the UK and Europe was the Elton John/Bernie Taupin song 'Snookeroo', written especially for Starr. As a single it was released 15 February 1975. In fact, beyond a demo, Elton John never recorded the song for himself. In many ways this song is more suited for Starr than 'I'm The Greatest' from *Ringo*. Featuring Elton John on piano and vocals (including John's trademark count-in), this song is the perfect pop song from its time. It also features Robbie Robertson on guitar (which is energetic and flawless) and future Academy Award winner James Newton Howard on synthesiser.

One would think that a song written by Elton John and performed by Ringo Starr, both coming off of massive hits at the time, would be a surefire hit in the UK, but this was not the case. Although *Record Mirror* listed it in their Star Breakers section, it failed to register with listeners and the record buying public. The single appeared on the *Music Week* chart for one week, where it peaked at the very disappointing number 51.

Although Starr was interviewed for *Melody Maker*, he did not do a great deal of promotion for the single or album in the UK. There was no promo film/video for the song, and in reviewing the trade magazines of the time, it did not receive a great deal of radio play.

The title, 'Snookeroo', refers to a person who doesn't work, but spends his day playing the billiard game of snooker. And the song 'Snookeroo' appeared on the B-side of the second single release from the album in North America. 'No No Song' was released as a single on 27 January 1975 and it became the biggest hit from the album. It also created new interest in *Goodnight Vienna* and the album began to go back up the charts, reaching its peak of number eight in the US *Billboard* album charts. Again, as with 'Snookeroo', 'No No Song' seemed to be custom made for Ringo. It was written by Hoyt Axton (who had written hits for Three Dog Night and Linda Rondstadt, and his mother co-wrote 'Heartbreak Hotel' in 1956) and bassist David Jackson.

Old pal Nicky Hopkins was on hand to provide the piano for the song, and Harry Nilsson sang back-up for Starr. Once again Jim Keltner joined Ringo on drums, with Klaus Voormann on bass. Jesse Ed Davis played guitar, while Bobby Keys and Trevor Lawrence supplied the wonderful trademark horns for the song. The song was written by Axton after a night of excessive partying and waking up in a hotel room. He didn't know what town he was in nor how he got there.

"I was afraid if I looked around I'd see the devil sittin' in the chair across the room, sayin' 'I got'cha, boy. You finally overdid it'...That was the day before I wrote the 'No No Song'," said Axton. Ironically, Starr (and Nilsson) were not sober at the time of the recording, and it would be many years before Starr could sing that song being totally clean. Bill Schnee later said that "Harry Nilsson was more involved with this record, part of me doesn't like saying this but part of me will go ahead and say this, that perhaps there were more drugs involved than on the first album [*Ringo*]."

Regardless of Starr's behaviour, the song became a monster hit in 1975. It made it to number three on the *Billboard* charts, while it peaked at number one in Canada and on the *Cash Box* charts. *Record World* reviewed the single on 1 February 1975, but as the B-side to 'Snookeroo'. The writer also compares it to McCartney's 'Junior's Farm' single, which was a double A-side, with 'Sally G' on the flipside. "Expect similar reaction to both this Elton John-Bernie Taupin tune and Hoyt Axton's 'No No Song' on Ringo's latest. It's working class hero saga time, with an 'Ob-la-di Ob-la-da'-type flip." *Cash Box* (1 February 1975) was clear that 'No No Song' was the A-side: "Hoyt Axton wrote this friendly, tongue-in-cheek temperance tune and Ringo delivers it like he really means it!! Flip: 'Snookeroo'...shares their usual hit qualities. If it wasn't backed by the delightful 'No No Song' this couldn't miss."

Billboard, in the singles picks for 1 February 1975, was clear that the A-side was 'Snookeroo', stating: "Ringo follows the ballad 'Only You' with an uptempo, happy song which seems better suited, both commercially and artistically to him. Most of all it's a perfect Ringo type cut, with a title that acts as a perfect hook and a tune that is instantly memorable." The writer does note that the "Flip side of 'Snookeroo' is also likely to get a lot of play, with a number of stations already on it. The drug references, even though the singer is saying that he no longer uses drugs, could hurt airplay some. Still, the song is another good, fun Ringo cut."

Starr himself was under the impression that 'Snookeroo' was the A-side in North America due to the controversial nature of 'No No Song'. Speaking in the *New Musical Express*, Starr said, "It's interesting because last year in America we checked out all the stations, and they said they wouldn't play it there either. So we put our 'Snookeroo' as the A-side, but everyone played 'No No Song', which freaked us all out. I mean, there's been no problems at all. Anyway, it's an anti-drug song. You know me – I'm so nice." He was also clear as to why the song was not released as a single in the UK: "We don't think they'd play it over here. I asked at Capital, and they said no, and I don't think the BBC would play it. I've never heard it on the radio, and it's on the album, so they could play it if they wanted to."

According to Matt Axton (Hoyt Axton's son), the song came directly to Ringo through Hoyt Axton. "My dad was such a big character in the Laurel Canyon scene in those days, I know he was good friends with Ringo and they shared tunes often."

Many of the chart publications listed both songs on their respective singles charts, but in the end 'No No Song' was the clear radio favourite, and is still heard on radio at the time of this book. Starr did a lot to promote the single, even appearing on *The Smothers Brothers* television show on 28 April 1975, keeping the song in the public's consciousness, as the single was beginning its decline down the charts. He also appeared with Axton on Axton's *The Hoyt Axton Country Western Boogie Woogie Gospel Rock and Roll Show*, which was telecast on NBC Network in North America on 22 March 1975.

As *Goodnight Vienna* and Harrison's *Dark Horse* were both ascending the charts, Starr's name appeared on one other album in 1974, Ravi Shankar's *Shankar Family And Friends*. The album was recorded in Los Angeles in 1973, during the sessions for *Ringo*, but not released until 20 September 1974 on Harrison's newly formed label, Dark Horse Records (his *Dark Horse* album was actually released on Apple, as Harrison was still under contract to Capitol-EMI). Although the album is quite beautiful, and Shankar toured with Harrison in 1974, the album did not chart in the UK, and peaked at number 176. A dismal showing for such a great album, and one that was heavily promoted. One can hear Starr's drumming on the only single released from it, the pop-oriented 'I Am Missing You'.

As 1974 was winding down and Christmas was around the corner, Starr made an announcement that no one was expecting. Perhaps it was the most surprising news of the year for Starr. As Apple was winding down, and his contract with Capitol-EMI was coming to an end in 1975, Starr announced the formation of a new label. All the music trade magazines carried the story with a photo of Ringo and the head of Capitol Records. The announcement in *Billboard* magazine read, in part: "Ring O Records has been formed by Ringo Starr and will be distributed in the United States and Canada by Capitol Records. Initial product to be released in February includes the debut LP *Startling Music* featuring material from Starr's *Ringo* LP performed by David Hentschel on the ARP synthesizer. Ringo's own records will continue to be released on Apple, distributed by Capitol. Starr is the first of the ex-Beatles to form his own label for distribution by Capitol and he joins a growing list of performers who have their own logos which are distributed by a major label, such as the Osmonds Kolob which MGM handles. George Harrison's Dark Horse is, of course, going through A&M."

In the UK, the story was slightly different. On 12 April 1975, *Music Week* announced that "Ringo Starr this week launched his new Ring O' Records label with an album, *Startling Music*, by ARP synthesiser exponent David Hentschel, plus a single, 'Oh My My', from the same album. Ring O' Records is being pressed and distributed by Polydor for the world, except the US and Canada, where the distribution is handled by Capitol. Starr said the idea of forming his own label started a year ago when he first played some Hentschel tapes. 'I wanted a new company, with a fresh name, which would reflect my own ideas of talent and music.' But the original Beatles deal with Parlophone at EMI, and the set-up with Apple, he says, remains unaltered - through the EMI contracts are up later this year. Starr owns the Ring O' label, which is managed by Barry Anthony. Starr added that he hoped one day that all the small independent record companies, like Ring O', would get together and form a similar kind of industry organisation as United Artists was originally for the film industry. And he added: 'Ring O' will not be signing new acts willy-nilly. The idea is to find first the talent, and I'll be very involved in that, and if necessary find the right producers to project that talent. But there will be no long roster of new artists'."

There was another change for Ringo Starr. On 27 May 1974, he met supermodel Nancy Andrews. As she said, "I met him in 1974 and we started living together in 1975. The beginning of 1975. I met him when he was recording *Goodnight Vienna*."

Nancy Lee Andrews (as she is known today) would have a huge role in Ringo's private and professional life for the rest of the 1970s. Andrews recalled, "He was a very very busy guy, and we were traversing the globe so much in 1975."

Given this news, 1975 would be be an interesting year.

Starr filming *200 Motels*, 1971

Ringo Starr, Nancy Lee Andrews and Hilary Gerrard (Polydor) (1976) *(photo courtesy of Mike Hales)*

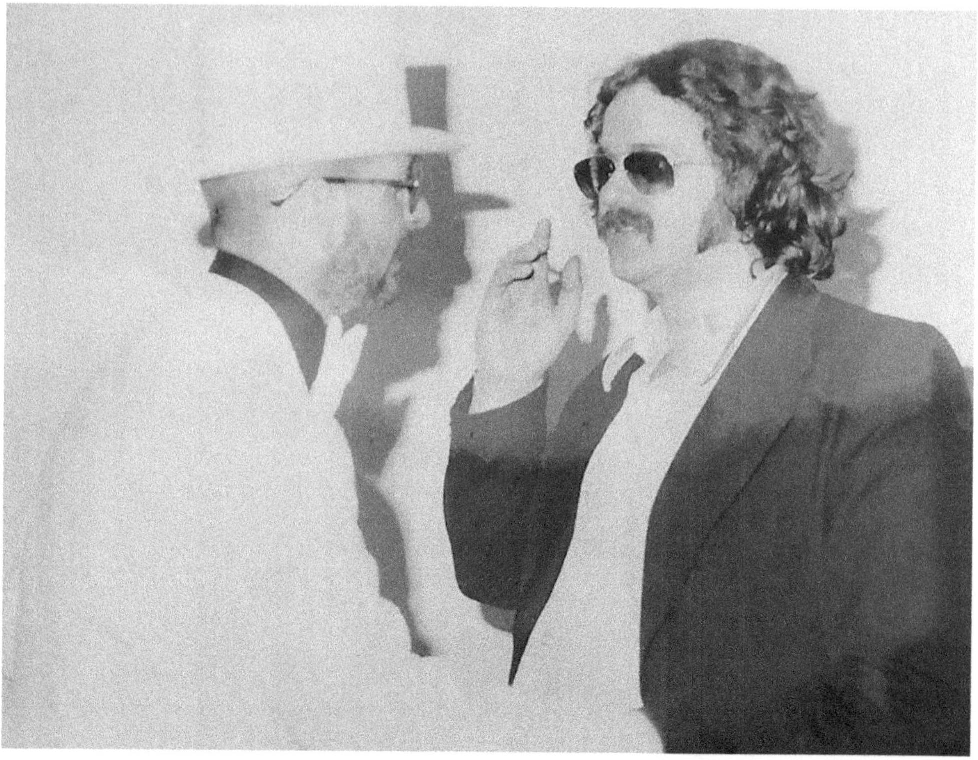

Ringo Starr and Mike Hales landing in Tokyo to promote *Ringo's Rotogravure* (1976)
(photo courtesy of Mike Hales)

Ringo Starr and Jacques Volcouve taken by Jean-Pierre Gamet on Thursday, September 16, 1976, at Charles de Gaulle Airport. *(Photo courtesy of Jacques Volcouve)*

Mike Hales, Ringo Starr and Phonogram executive Flora Brocchetti.
(Photo courtesy of Mike Hales)

Doug Bogie (aka Colonel), or Colonel Doug Bogie, who released his debut single On Ring O'Records in the U.K. in 1975 *(Photo courtesy Doug Bogie)*

Sunset Studios, where Starr recorded songs for *Ringo*, *Goodnight Vienna* and *Ringo's Rotogravure*
(photo by Emily Badgley)

Ring O'Records patch
(courtesy of Ron Kelly)

Ring O'Records watch, still owned by Ron Kelly of *Stormer*.

Stormer single released on Ring O' Records (1978) *(Courtesy of Ron Kelly)*

Stormer at Startling Studios, having some fun while recording their single and unreleased album (1978) *(photo courtesy of Ron Kelly)*

Ringo Starr's Startling studio in 1978 *(Courtesy of Ron Kelly)*

Stormer signing to Ring O'Records with Ringo Starr *(courtesy Ron Kelly)*

Trade ad for the single *'No No Song'*, (1974)

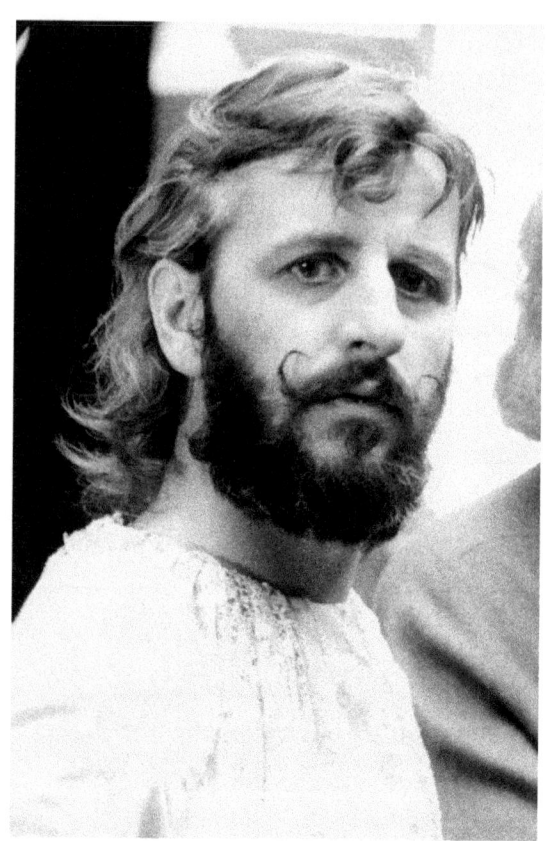

Ringo on the set of *Lisztomania* (1975)

A very sad Ringo Starr looks on his home burning, 1979.

6

1975

One could be forgiven for feeling like the start of 1975 was a repeat of 1974. Starr released singles from the album *Goodnight Vienna* to maintain an interest in the album as it slid down the charts. Not that *Goodnight Vienna* was a flop, at least not in North America, far from it, but it peaked at number eight, which in comparison to *Ringo,* which reached number two on *Billboard* (number one on *Cash Box*), was less successful. *Goodnight Vienna* stayed in the top 200 for 25 weeks, compared to *Ringo,* which stayed on the *Billboard* album charts for 37 weeks. In 1975, when *Goodnight Vienna* reached its peak on *Billboard's* Top 200 (11 January 1975), singles were being played on AM radio in North America.

However, there were big differences in store for Starr in 1975. Fans and the public at large would have to wait until 1976 for any new music by Mr Starkey. In the 1970s, two years without new music was a very long time in the pop world. But Starr had no intention to record a new album or single in 1975; he was busy with other things. This didn't mean he stayed away from recording studios, quite the opposite. He did record with his friends, and he kept busy with acting in films, and with his new label, Ring O' Records. According to Nancy Lee Andrews, Starr was very busy in 1975.

Apple Records, by 1975, was winding down. Harrison and Starr were the last two Beatles to sign artists and by all accounts wanted to keep the label up and running. McCartney and Lennon did not agree and wanted Apple to close. McCartney had established MPL (McCartney Productions Limited, or McCartney Paul Linda) and Lennon was stepping away from all music contracts. There was the option of Starr and Harrison buying Lennon and McCartney out, but that was not entirely viable for many legal reasons.

Once Harrison and Starr decided not to buy Lennon and McCartney out of their shares of Apple and decided to start their own new labels, Starr was very open about his intentions with Ring O' Records. "I wanted a new company, with a fresh name, which would reflect my own ideas of talent and music," he told *Music Week*. In the 12 April 1975 issue of *New Music Express,* Starr confirmed, "It's gonna be a good company. We're talking to several people at the moment. I mean, lots of people have sent in tapes." Starr was very optimistic and had brilliant ideas for the label. "I'd like it to be like United Artists. My aim in the end is to get all the independents together, so that we all can run our own business. As it is, we're all being run by people whose only qualification is as an accountant." He also took a moment to take a swipe at Harrison's Dark Horse Records: "Now, George has these really crazy freaks coming in for his label. 'Hey, man, I've just written this new mantra'; but we just get the rock 'n' roll people."

Starr further explained to Peter Jones of *Billboard* magazine: "I want my own label to stress the creative side and I want it to reflect my own attitudes to music. As for my own recording future, the Beatles' contract with Parlophone at EMI is up later this year, and we'll have to see what happens after that. At Ring O' we want to spend a lot of time picking the right artists, then finding the right producers and so on, so that it is a whole creative package."

Author Axel Korinth stated in his book for the *Stormer Unreleased Album - Deluxe Edition* that Starr was quoted as saying "I thought, 'we'll form a label', no one will have to beg", almost quoting John Lennon when he (along with Paul McCartney) announced the launch of Apple Records. Korinth also states that Lennon came up with the name Ring O' Records. One thing is certain: it was never developed to be a vanity label for Starr.

Starr addressed the issue of him recording for his own label. "I don't know whether I'll put myself on the label. Right now I can't, 'cos I'm with EMI, but that finishes next year. After that, we'll see if it's a good idea. Maybe we'll do it how we did Apple, whereby we were only on Apple courtesy of EMI." Starr never released his own music on Ring O' Records.

In addition to the start of his new record label, music that Starr had been helping his friends with was set to be released in 1975. One of the first albums released in 1975 to feature Starr was Harry Nilsson's *Duit On Mon Dei* (a play on words from the Royal Family's motto "*Dieu et mon droit*". *Duit On Mon Dei* can originally be found on the front sleeve of Starr's *Ringo* LP. Starr drums on one song on the album, 'Kojak Columbo', a song about North American television detectives, and provided vocals on the closing track, 'Good For God'. This was Nilsson's first self-produced album, and although there were positive notices, the album failed to make *Billboard's* Top 100 albums (it peaked at 141), and did not chart in the UK. In the US, it was Nilsson's lowest charting album since 1970's *Nilsson Sings Newman*. 'Kojak Columbo' was the only single taken from the album, and it did not make any impact. *Billboard* did list it as a recommended single in their pop picks (Lennon's

'Stand By Me' was the main pick that week). Airplay was nil, and the song did not chart.

The presence of Ringo Starr and other well known rockers/musicians (such as Gloria Jones, Dr. John, Jane Getz and Klaus Voormann to name a few) was not enough to interest people in a new album by Nilsson. *Billboard* did note, in one of the most positive reviews of Nilsson's album, "Harry has come up with his most listenable album in several years". It didn't help airplay, or sales. This was the beginning of Nilsson's popularity decline, which he was not able to steer away from in his lifetime. *Duit On Mon Dei* would also be the last album by Nilsson that Starr appeared on in the 1970s, although he is thanked on ...*That's The Way It Is* (1976). There is speculation he worked on that album but to date there is no recording documentation to suggest he played on it.

Also during March, another album featuring Starr was released. Like *Duit On Mon Dei*, Keith Moon's *Two Sides Of The Moon* was recorded in 1974 and was released in March 1975. It was a failure, critically and commercially. Moon recorded his debut album with help from his friends in Los Angeles, including Starr. Other well known musicians on the album include Joe Walsh, Dick Dale, Flo and Eddie and David Foster. John Lennon even contributed a song, 'Move Over Ms. L', which Lennon would later record and release on the B-side of 'Stand By Me'. Starr provides vocals for 'Solid Gold' and even earned a co-writer credit for his chat with Moon on 'Together'. Starr does not drum on the album but he was credited for the album title.

Moon's album received a particularly negative review from Dave Marsh in *Rolling Stone* magazine, who wrote "Moon's fatal flaws are several. But the biggest problem with *Two Sides of the Moon* is that there isn't any legitimate reason for its existence." Marsh is being a little harsh, as the album is not that bad and does have its moments. It is also very reflective of the times and the status of artists such as Moon, who was supported by a major label (Polydor in the UK and Tracks/MCA in the US) - major labels were still investing in rock stars, especially with a 'name' that would attract radio play and record buyers. The star power of the album helped Moon and provided him with the support that he needed. Three singles were released from the album in the US: 'Don't Worry Baby' with 'Together' on the flipside, 'Solid Gold' with 'Move Over Ms. L' and 'Crazy As A Fox' with 'In My Life' on the B-side. Only 'Don't Worry Baby' was released in the UK. Moon did not have any chart success with any of the singles on either side of the ocean.

In April 1975, Carly Simon released her fifth studio album, *Playing Possum*. As with her previous two albums, it was produced by Richard Perry. Perry called in a favour from Starr, who drummed on one track, the Dr. John composition, 'More And More'. Simon and Perry began recording the album in 1974, and no doubt 'More And More' was recorded following the sessions for *Goodnight Vienna*. *Playing Possum* was a success: it made the top ten on the album charts in North America, and 'More and More' was selected as the third and final single from the album. The album was released in April, while the single appeared in September. *Billboard* deemed it "recommended" in their Top Single Picks, while *Cash Box* reviewed the single and referred to it as a "a hard blues vocal over barrelhouse piano, with Memphis style horns and a soulful female chorus... This disk should turn a lot of ears her way." Sadly, the single, although a great recording, failed to hit the ears of the record buying public and it peaked at number 94 on the *Billboard* Top 100 singles chart.

By April, however, Starr was back in the UK, busy promoting the first single and album released worldwide for Ring O' Records. David Hentschel's *Startling Music* was released on 17 February 1975 on Ring O' Records in the US (ST-11372) and on 18 April 1975 in the UK (2320 101). The delay in the UK had to do with Starr signing with Polydor Records, while he was still technically signed to Capitol in the US, who had entered into an agreement to distribute Ring O' Records in North America.

Hentschel had worked on many albums in the early 1970s, three of which Starr had contributed to. Hentschel's credits include George Harrison's *All Things Must Pass*, Harry Nilsson's *Nilsson Schmilsson* and Jimmy Webb's *Land's End*. He had also worked with Genesis, Renaissance, Queen, Nazareth and Mike Oldfield, to name just a few. There is no doubt that Starr knew of Hentschel and his talented style of playing the synthesiser. However, in an interview in April 1975's *New Musical Express*, Starr maintained that he heard of Hentschel through Hentschel's manager, John Gilbert.

"John Gilbert brought me a tape of this music, and it was all on an ARP – the best ARP music I'd ever 'eard. I was thinking of starting a label, and we thought it would be good if he did something for the label, and we thought it would be good if he copied the *Ringo* album."

Hentschel later said, "I wanted to do more freelance work. My manager John Gilbert knew Neil Aspinall and this led to the *Startling Music* project because Ringo was looking for something for his new record label. Ringo had bought a new ARP 2500 synthesiser for his home studio specifically for the album. He was around for most of the recording, so he had to appear on it." Starr appeared on one song.

According to Hentschel, they even spent a night writing music together, which apparently did not go anywhere. This was Starr's second time trying to write using a synthesiser (the first time was with Maurice Gibb), and the second time nothing came of it. The ARP 2500 cost approximately £5000 (which is about $35,000 US in today's money). As Ringo said, "That is a lot of money for a lot of plugs."

Hentschel, a classically trained musician, best known for his work with Rick Wakeman, Elton John, The Nice and Paul McCartney seemed, in some ways, an unlikely signing for the label. Starr said at the time of the album's release: "At first we were a bit strict, trying to get him to do exact copies of the songs; then he played us one he'd arranged himself, 'Devil Woman', and it 'worked.' So we sent him back to do a few more how he wanted them, rather than following the basic pattern that I'd laid down."

It seemed to be an intriguing idea, a synthesiser interpretation of Starr's *Ringo* album. Even more interesting, as it was Hentschel's debut album. "I mean, he really wanted to do a symphony, but I forced him into it," Ringo said, perhaps jokingly. Hentschel recorded the album between June and August 1974 at Starr's studio in his home. Starr had purchased Lennon's home, Tittenhurst Park, and turned Lennon's home studio into a state of the art studio, which many artists would use well into the 1980s. It also became very convenient for artists who signed to Starr's record label.

Keep in mind that synthesiser albums were not all that common in 1974. Kraftwerk made a mark with their classic *Autobahn* album, and artists like Tangerine Dream, Brian Eno, David Bowie and Can were experimenting with the instrument, but although these artists were critically acclaimed, they were not hugely successful in terms of sales. They were, however, incredibly influential. But other than for Bowie and Kraftwerk, the synthesiser was still an instrument to augment music rather than being the star attraction.

As for *Startling Music*, Starr pointed out: "It took about a year to get together. We started it in June last year (1974). 'Course I didn't know at the time that he was Elton John's engineer and ARP player." In other words, Hentschel was busy with his session work, while working on his debut album.

The fact that it was released a full three months earlier in the US than in the UK may have had more to do with Capitol (the distributor in the US) feeling they needed to strike while the iron was hot (*Goodnight Vienna* on Apple via Capitol was peaking on the charts) than any other reason. Starr's contract was about to end with Capitol/EMI, so perhaps there was a sense of urgency to release the album, promote it, and keep Starr happy, so he would re-sign to the label. Keep in mind that he had just had two very successful albums, and all four Beatles were still producing hits, so it stands to reason that Capitol wanted to keep Starr. One way to keep him signed was to keep him happy.

A single lifted from the album, 'Oh My My' with 'Devil Woman' on the B-side, was released on 17 February 1975 (4030) in North America. The same single was released in the UK on 21 March 1975 (2017101). *Record Mirror* reviewed the single in their 17 April 1975 issue: "Doesn't really sound too like the original, more a jolly little electronic exercise, but if that's what they want to do…" It wasn't a negative review, but nor was it positive. It did earn radio play in London, as it was listed on 5 March 1975 of David Carter's Radio London Playlist. The review also sums up the music quite well. Hentschel was not making Eno ambient music, or Kraftwerk synthesised music. *Startling Music* was closer to middle of the road (MOR) music than anything experimental. It was still somewhat forward thinking in the rock world.

In the US, a promo single was released with a mono mix on one side and stereo mix on the other (P-4030). In the 20 February 1975 issue of *Cash Box*, a full page ad advertising the album was quite hard to miss. In the same issue, *Cash Box* gave the single a positive review. "David Hentschel… reworks it into a whole new sound with synthesizers flying. Pumping and bumping along, this song's happy little melody is infectious and you're bound to catch it." Even *Variety* seemed to like the album and gave it a very positive review.

The critic for *Cash Box* had this to say about the album: "An interesting instrumental treatment of Ringo's #1 LP, *Ringo*, is presented on Starr's new Capitol distributed Ring O' label by capable David Hentschel. Hentschel's arrangements of such tunes as 'Photograph', 'Oh My My', 'Have You Seen My Baby', 'You're 16', and 'I'm The Greatest' are excellent, offering a whole new and lively set of interpretations of these great tunes. The production is clear as a bell and we can only add that we feel optimistic about the success of this LP" (20 February 1975).

Starr was very enthusiastic about Hentschel and his playing of the synthesiser. "I think he's probably the greatest player of that machine in the world. I mean [Stevie] Wonder, of course, is amazing – but he uses it on a freak-out level, whereas David uses it to take the place of an orchestra. He gets such a natural sound."

Because of his past work experience and Starr's name, Hentschel was able to enlist Phil Collins on drums for most of the album, Ronnie Caryl (Flaming Youth) on guitar and Starr himself with 'finger clicks' on 'Step Lightly' (he is joined by the co-producer of the album, John Gilbert). Starr did not repeat his tap dancing for this cover version. Even with the special guests, the album did not attract record buyers. The major music magazines did not review it, but local newspapers in the US and the UK did review the album.

In the US, for example, the *Bangor Daily News* noted that the album is "sassy and direct and should delight the teen set." The critic also refers to Hentschel as an "effective pianist" (24 June 1975, Pg. 6). The critic for *The Buffalo Herald* noted that the album "comes across as weak and dull" (28 Feb 1975 p 10). *The Boston Globe* (21 February 1975) said that the album "provides pleasant enough background music for a trip to the dentist." It refers to the album as "plodding" and adds is only saved by "real drums and guitars". The critic for *Dayton Daily News* stated "save your money" as there is "nothing Startling about this album" (28 February 1975).

The press in the UK was not entirely complimentary. "Personally, I find it a lot more monotonous than the original album that at least had words to listen to" wrote the critic for *Bracknell and Ascot Times* (01 May 1975). The critic for the *Acton Gazette* (19 June 1975) wrote that the original album was "ordinary" and this new version of it "did little for me". The writer also advises Hentschel to join up with other musicians before he enters a studio.

Not surprisingly, the album failed to chart and it would be the first and last Ring O' Records album released via Capitol and the only album released in North America. Ring O' Records released one more single in the US before Capitol dropped the label. There were probably a number of reasons for Capitol deciding to part ways with Ring O' Records so quickly, but one reason was due to poor record sales. Hentschel's album and single did not sell (exact sales figures were not made available); and the Bobby Keys single was not successful either.

The other reason had to do with Starr's contract with Capitol coming to an end, and he made it known that he was looking for a new label. Before Starr had signed to WEA, he was openly being courted by record companies, most notably ABC Records. When Starr's contract came to end, he eventually signed with Atlantic (WEA) in North America. When the next Ring O' Records single released in the US, it seemed that Capitol did not put a great deal of effort into promoting it. The single, by Bobby Keys, 'Gimmie The Key', would be released in August 1975. Meanwhile, Starr had other projects on the go.

During an interview with Bob Woffinden, Starr reveals some information and plans. He does make a note of saying that "Yes, I'm still designing furniture with Robin Cruikshank. We do mirrors as well, and we have the franchise on the Disney characters. That all goes tumbling along – it goes on without me. We design things together, and then Robin runs all the business side." And as for recording, Starr talked about wanting to do a second country album (which he would do in 2025) but there were no clear recording plans at the time. "I don't know whether the third album will be with Richard Perry. Maybe he's busy – maybe I'm busy, we haven't talked about it yet. I'm just going back to LA next week to try to get some things together for it."

It is important to note that he refers to his next album as his 'third', seemingly discounting his first two albums. This issue will come back in 1977 with the album title *Ringo The 4th*.

Starr also talked about starring in a science fiction/comedy television series written by Graham Chapman (of *Monty Python's Flying Circus* fame, who also tried to assist with *Son Of Dracula*), and co-starring with Burt Reynolds in a comedy, playing, of all things, Reynolds' somewhat dull servant. Neither of these projects got off the ground, although Starr would revisit the television idea in the 1980s, with a slightly different plot.

In May, Starr was still in promotion mode for the single 'No No Song'. On 2 May 1975, he made a brief appearance on Hoyt Axton's television show, The *Hoyt Axton Country Western Boogie Woogie Gospel Rock and Roll Show*. According to an article in *Variety*, the show aired on KNXT and Starr came on during the finale of 'No No Song'. NBC picked up the show and aired it at a later date.

As the spring turned into summer, a decision was made to release a third single from *Goodnight Vienna*. On 2 June 1975, the title track of the album was released in a slightly different form. The song, now titled '(It's All Down To) Goodnight Vienna' was a medley of the two versions from the album. The reprise of the song was mixed to the opening track and it produced a whole new song, not available on any album until 2007 when it was included on the compilation *Photograph - The Very Best Of Ringo Starr*. In fact, that was the first time the song was available outside of North America. The song was released as a single in other countries, but the single featured the album cut without the reprise mix. The single was also released as 'Goodnight Vienna', not using the North American single title.

By the time the single was released, the album had left the Top 200 album charts, so perhaps it was hoped that the single would spark interest in the album. It didn't work. However, once again, reviews in the trades were very positive for the single. *Billboard* went so far as to review both sides (the flip being 'Oo-Wee') and treated it as a double A-side. "First side of what appears to be another two-sided hit for Ringo," wrote the critic, "is title cut from most recent LP. Good, upbeat sing-a-long type song." For 'Oo-Wee', it is noted that it is a "Strong, rhythm oriented song in quite a different vein from the first side of the single."

Cash Box was equally enthusiastic, maybe even more so. "Ringo releases the title track of his #1 LP, a rousing rocker by Mr Lennon, with super rhythm, piano, and... accordion tracks! Also equally strong for programming is flip, 'Oo-Wee'." *Record World* agreed that the single would be yet another hit, and referred to it as being a return to rock and roll for Starr.

Besides full page ads in the trade magazines, Apple/Capitol/Starr did very little to promote the single. It was released in a nice picture sleeve, which was in tune with the original album sleeve (Starr sitting on a star). Promo copies were sent out to radio; in fact two were sent out, one with the stereo and mono mixes of '(It's All Down To) Goodnight Vienna' (on a standard Apple label), and the other being a separate promo single for the B-side, 'Oo-Wee', once again featuring mono and stereo mixes of the song. But it did not help airplay. Initially radio programmed it, but within weeks interest had waned and the single received scant airplay for the most part.

The single did not do as well as hoped or expected, as on 19 July 1975, it peaked at number 31 on *Billboard's* Top 100 (Paul McCartney and Wings held the number one spot with 'Listen To What The Man Said') after being on the chart for six weeks. Given the success of the album, and the first two singles, not to mention the three top five singles from *Ringo*, the lack of success was something of a mystery. The album had been out for almost a year, so perhaps the excitement of a new single by Ringo Starr may have waned, especially since it really was not new. Having said that, the song had everything going for it to be a huge hit.

It would have one more week on the top 100 and then it was gone. It did not spark any renewed interest in the album. It peaked at number 31 on the *Cash Box* chart. In Canada, it was a much bigger hit, just missing the top ten when it peaked at number 13 on the *RPM* Top 100 Singles chart, charting higher than 'Only You'.

'(It's All Down To) Goodnight Vienna' was Starr's last single on the Apple label in North America.

Meanwhile, Ring O' Records was quite serious about establishing itself as a viable record label. Starr decided to help an old friend and released a single by the session player Bobby Keys. Starr had played on Keys' debut solo album, and Keys had worked on Starr's records. After hearing 'Gimmie The Key', Starr and label manager Barry Anthony must have thought that they had a hit on their hands. Not only would he be helping a friend, but the song would help Ring O' Records with establishing itself with a potential hit.

Thinking that 'Gimmie The Key', a jazzy pop (with a touch of disco) instrumental, might become a hit was not so far fetched. Given the success of Average White Band's 'Pick Up The Pieces' (which featured future Ringo Starr and The All Starrs bassist Hamish Stuart. Stuart also played with McCartney from 1989 through to 1993), which topped the charts in 1974, it was easy to see how 'Gimmie The Key' was a surefire hit. 'Gimmie The Key' was a song cut from the same cloth, a thumping jazzy instrumental dance hit, complete with a chant chorus ("Gimmie the key…Gimmie that key").

When the single was released on 25 August 1975, the trades seemed to agree. *Cash Box*, in their singles review of 30 August 1975, said "This record's got it from the first groove — funky lead guitar work, clean production and sax trax from one of rockdom's most respected purveyors of jazz-sax. Must be super big in the disco market, watch for it to break out like crazy AM pop. Fine work." The writer for *Cash Box* also adds that this is the first release for Ring O' Records (it wasn't) and that there was "Big Capitol push." *Billboard* also listed it as a single pick for the week of 30 August 1975.

Record World (30 August 1975) was equally enthusiastic, stating: "Longtime rock arranger to the stars gets his solo debut shot via Ringo's label. An AWB-type instrumental that could break with black radio and discos locked up!" Since there were no singles from Keys' debut album in 1972, 'Gimmie The Key' was certainly his debut single. An extended version was released in North America with the word 'DISCO' over the Ring O' Records label. The single received no coverage in the UK, when it was released on 5th September 1975.

The flipside of the single, 'Honkey Tonk (Parts 1 & 2)', and 'Gimmie The Key' are products of their time. 'Honkey Tonk (Parts 1 & 2)' tries to incorporate jazz, country and western swing and a bit of dance music. It is an interesting experiment and, in some ways, it's more interesting than the A-side.

As noted above, in 1975, it was not uncommon for jazz/funk instrumentals to catch on and become hits, especially in the burgeoning dance/disco clubs. Thinking that the song had potential was very sound. However, one scan of the music trades at the time indicates that the single received little airplay. Perhaps being a one off single, with no album to support, hurt its chances. Keys himself seemed to dismiss the single as if it did not even warrant a mention in his memoir, *Every Night's A Saturday Night: The Rock And Roll Life Of Legendary Sax Man, Bobby Keys*. Certainly, the Disco version, which is curiously not on 12 inch vinyl as was the style at the time, did not help the single and it disappeared from the public's consciousness.

A promo of the single exists, with the song in mono and stereo. It was released throughout Europe with a picture sleeve, and in the US it had a special Bobby Keys sleeve. But, again, the single did not draw any attention and failed to chart. 'Gimmie The Key' was the last single and last record released in North America on the Ring O' Records label.

At the time of the Bobby Keys single release, an article appeared in *Variety* magazine (20 August 1975) stating that Carl Groszmann had signed to Ring O' Records. It was added that the Australian born singer/songwriter was a protege of Harry Nilsson. It is important to note that Groszmann's name is spelled differently in many articles, and even on record sleeves. However, for the purposes of this book, the spelling on the Ring O' Records label is the spelling that is used.

Earlier in the year, on 5 February 1975 to be exact, a small article appeared in *Variety* stating that Ken Russell would be directing a film about Franz Liszt. Russell had written the script based on the book *Nélida* written by Marie d'Agoult, and it was announced that Roger Daltrey would star, playing Liszt. Ringo Starr had also signed on to be part of the film, playing The Pope (Pope Pius IX). At this stage, the film was titled *Liszt*. This was changed to *Lisztomania* when it premiered on 10 October 1975. *Lisztomania* began filming in London at Shepperton Studios in February. While Ringo was in England setting up Ring O' Records, he took time out to shoot the film. Nancy Lee Andrews has written that Starr was very happy to play tour guide for her and show her around London and other areas of England.

The film, released on 10 October 1975 in the UK and a day later in the US, garnered some positive reviews. The *Los Angeles Times* critic Kevin Thomas, in the 17 October 1975 edition, gave the film a good review, and mentioned Starr as a "Cowboy boot wearing Pope". The *Boston Globe* critic was positive about the film and Starr's performance got a mention. The critic for *Variety* complimented the art direction and costumes. He was also clear that "The overall result is either pleasing to some-one, or it's not; that's the way with Russell's pictures." He also mentioned that the "Casting of Ringo Starr as the Pope is further evidence of Russell's showmanship" (10 October 1975).

Not all reviews were positive. Gene Siskell of *The Chicago Tribune* referred to the movie as just "Boring", while Leonard Maltin referred to it as a "dog". The moviegoing audience didn't know what to make of it. The marketing teams tried to tie it in to Russell's successful film *Tommy*, released earlier in 1975. To be clear, it had nothing to do with *Tommy*, but it also had star power and a fantastic soundtrack. But all of that was not enough, and the film barely broke even. It is not a film one finds on the late show, but has gone on to be a cult classic.

Starr continued to work with his Ring O' Records label well into 1975, and in November, an artist that he signed on 5 July 1975 finally released his Ring O' Records debut single. According to *Cash Box*, "Ringo Starr recently announced his first signing to Ring O' Records, singer-composer Carl Groszmann. Groszmann, who has been with several companies and has written material for Status Quo and other groups, will release his first single under the deal later this summer with an LP expected at the end of the year."

Groszmann did release a single in 1970 on Decca Records ('Thunderbird'), and had some success with his first band, Steve And The Board. When Status Quo took his 'Down The Dustpipe', he established himself in the UK. 'I've Had It' with 'C'mon Rock And Roll' made its appearance in the UK on 14 November 1975. It is interesting that in the 12th April 1975 issue of *Music Week* in the UK (the same issue announcing the launch of Ring O' Records), it is noted that Carl Groszmann had signed with Pinnacle records, a label in the UK known for children's music that was now branching out to the adult market. Sue Welbourne (sales and promotion manager) said: "We have a lot of confidence in Carl Groszmann and feel that he could be another talent in the vein of Leo Sayer." Groszmann did not release any music on Pinnacle and it is not clear how he got out of that contract to sign with Ring O' Records.

Music Week did not review Groszmann's single but it did get a mention in the new releases for the week of 15 November 1975. The single was not reviewed in any other publications in the UK or Europe. However, Andy Gray, in the *Evening Chronicle of Newcastle Upon Tyne*, referred to it as a "fast, brisk, disco record" with a steady beat. He also referred to Groszmann's vocals as "strident" and said that the song "is drilled into you until it stays in your head" (27 December 1975). Interestingly, in the same article he reviewed a Dark Horse single by Splinter ('Green Line Bus').

The single was not released in the US, nor was it released in Europe. It was not released anywhere outside of the UK, making it the first Ring O' Records release to be UK-only. In some ways the record got lost in the shuffle as Ring O' Records was beginning to reorganise itself. But, unlike the next release, Anthony Barry could not secure a licensing deal with any other labels to release the single. It is a shame, as both sides are quite good and both songs have all but disappeared.

The same can be said about the next single on Ring O'Records. Musician and record engineer/mixer Doug Bogie (he was an original member of Queen) released his debut single on Ring O' Records in the UK. Under the name Colonel, the single 'Cokey Cokey' b/w 'Away In A Manger' was released on 21 November 1975 (it was released in North America on 8 December 1975 on the ABC Records label and credited to

Colonel Doug Bogie). Ring O' Records licensed the single to ABC Records in Europe and North America. In speaking with this author, Bogie said of the single: "It was just a bit of fun, you know. But it came about in a very off the wall way."

According to Bogie, who had a job at CBS records as an engineer, he was still working on his music. "I had been working on a sci-fi based story album. As an 18 or 19 year old, you are a little bit arrogant about what you do, you think what you do is important, you know? 'I can make a concept album, why not? Other people do.' It was called *House Up In The Stars*. And I had made it, with other people's help, I was quite proud of it."

Ring O' Records was just starting up, so Bogie contacted the label. "I made an appointment at Ring O' Records. I thought it was worth a try. CBS wouldn't be interested because I was a staff engineer. The only person I got through to was a nice lady at Ring O' Records. Which was quite new at the time, this was early 1975. And they gave me the address, made an appointment, got my bag, put my reel in, and a few bits and pieces, and walked there."

Interestingly, Bogie almost missed his appointment with Starr due to the fact that the Ring O' Records office was difficult to find. "I walked to the posh part of town, London, where his office was. In Soho. It was a similar address to Jack Barkly's Rolls Royce showroom. So, I am in the middle of this very posh square, everything looks to be a million dollars, everywhere you look, and I can't find this bloody office. I am expecting to see something like McCartney Productions in the square. My eye catches a brass plate, no logo or anything. It just said Ring O' Records, like a doctor's plate, and it was literally beside the showroom. I open the door, up about six flights of stairs and there is a white painted door, with a glass partition."

Bogie described meeting Starr and getting signed to the label. When Bogie made it to the office, "I knock on the door, 'Come in', expecting to find the receptionist to be put in my place and sit to see Mr Starkey. But it is just a room, a table, a bit of audio gear, a couple of chairs and on the table is a tea set. Sitting at the table is Ringo Starr. No workers, just Ringo and Harry Nilsson sitting. When you are that age and a bit full of yourself and you are working in the business, you are not freaked out by superstars, because you see them as part of your work day week. 'Hello, you Doug? You want a cup of tea?' 'Yeah that would be great, thank you very much.'

"He is very charming, a really nice man. I did my pitch, put my demo on the Revox, you know the open reel tape recorder, did a bit of chat…and I could see it was not going well. They are very nice but they say, it isn't really their kind of deal. 'Good luck with it.' I thought ok, I had a cup of tea with Ringo Starr, that can't be bad. Harry Nilsson says, 'it was interesting ...got anything else in your bag?' Well actually I do, I have this little novelty thing I had been doing, a tatty tape, plopped it on and played them the two songs. And they are bouncing away, having a good old laugh and a good old time. And I walked out with a cheque for 400 quid, and a promise of a release."

Bogie himself did not know the single was released until he received a letter from Ring O' Records. "I did get a letter saying the single is out in Germany, out in the UK and in the States." The interesting and novelty single received very good reviews at the time of its release. In the US, in the 13 December 1975 issue of *Record World*, the reviewer was very kind. "A traditional tune scored in a hard rock vein is heavy on the guitars and synthesizer. This anonymous group of musicians makes a mighty impression." *Cash Box* agreed and stated "effectively electrified the 'Manger'. Steady bass and drum rhythm pumping away underneath the traditional lyrics interspersed with heavy guitar riffs. The break is rock and roll and the intent is AM pop, which should be a cinch. Also look for disco action."

In the UK, *Record Mirror* mentioned it in conjunction with a review of another version of the song by Old Bill. They sum up Bogie's version with one line: "Oddly, there's also a less inventive pop-reggae version out, by Colonel" (*Record Mirror* 29 November 1975). Clearly the single's A-sides were different in the UK from the rest of the world. The favoured A-side in the US and Europe was 'Away In A Manager'. This makes total sense given the closeness to Christmas for the release of the single. The single was also listed in new releases in the 22 November 1975 issue of *Music Week*.

Although the single received airplay, it was not particularly well promoted. According to Bogie, "I was simply not interesting or important enough. In all fairness, I don't think I saw any promotion of any of their stuff by anybody." The single was released in Europe and Australia, but once again it was on the ABC Records label. This single was the last Ring O' Records single released until 1977.

Starr ended the year with a contractual obligation album, *Blast From Your Past*. It was released in North America on 20 November 1975, and almost a month later in the UK (12 December 1975). It was his last album on Apple and the last album through EMI until 1990, when EMI released the first live album from Ringo And The All Starrs (titled *Ringo Starr And His All Starr Band*) in the UK. It is not clear as to how much Starr was involved with the overall package, song selection and promotion. One thing *was* clear: this ended his relationship with Capitol-EMI, and his lack of involvement in promoting the album says a great deal. Again, this may be the reason for Capitol dropping Ring O' Records mid 1975.

The album is a collection of all but one of his singles, not placed in chronological order. Sadly, nothing from *Sentimental Journey* is included, but the argument could be made that there were no singles released from the album. Two songs on the album, 'No No Song' and 'Oh My My', were pulled from the album to form a single in the UK when *Blast From Your Past* was released. Neither song had been released as a single there, and the double A-side seemed like a good idea to promote the album. The single was released in the UK on 9 January 1976, with very little fanfare or promotion. There were no singles released in North America, although some consideration should have been given to 'I'm The Greatest'. It could have been a chart hit and helped sell the album. As it was, the album underperformed with sales in most countries.

In the UK, the album did not bother the charts. In North America, it entered *Billboard*'s Top 200 album chart on 6 December 1975 and peaked at number 30 on 17 January 1976. On *Cash Box*'s charts, it peaked at number 40 on 24 January 1975. And *Record World* charted it to number 64 on 17 January 1975. In Canada's *RPM* top 100 album chart, it peaked at 45 on 17 January 1975.

Although the album featured a number of hits (in North America), it is not overly surprising that it did not do well. Although greatest hits albums by Carly Simon, America and Elton John soared to the top of the charts, this one didn't. It may have been that there was nothing new on the album, and all but three songs were already on large selling albums. Radio play was scant and promotion for the album was scarce as well. The sleeve design by Capitol's Roy Kohara was not up to Starr's standards and it was far too early to rely on nostalgia.

It was a great idea to do a 'best of' for Christmas, but there has to be a reason for people to purchase an album. *Ringo* and *Goodnight Vienna* both sold well, so perhaps the public did not see reason enough to buy the album. Perhaps adding more tracks, and a couple of 'new' songs, would have created more of a buzz for the record. The album is remarkably short, clocking in at just under 32 minutes. Even by 1975's standards, this is very short; and there are only ten songs. It was simply a contractual obligation and ended Starr's relationship with EMI.

Bill Schnee, in talking with this author, was clear that he did not mix nor engineer the compilation. Nor did he help assemble it. He was under the impression that Starr let EMI assemble the album, and their in-house sleeve designers handled the packaging and putting the album together. Three of the ten tracks made their debut on an album. The inclusion of the B-side 'Early 1970' is interesting, in that it is one of three songs on the collection that were not hits. However, the top 40 single '(It's All Down To) Goodnight Vienna' is nowhere to be seen. Given the short tracklist, several other songs could have been included without difficulty.

Rosalind Russell, writing for *Record Mirror* in the 3 January 1976 issue, noted in her review that she was almost run over by Ringo's car, but she does not hold a grudge. In fact she writes that the collection is " jolly nice" and "It's a compilation of his best known songs, about three of which were hits. The others, although not smash successes, must have been a personal boost for him, because they all worked quite well." She even notes "I like 'Only You'. It's old fashioned and quaint, the way love songs ought to be."

In the US, where Starr had had more hit singles than in the UK, *Billboard* magazine, in the Album Picks for the 29 November 1975 issue, was very enthusiastic about the album and saw it as the perfect album for Christmas. The writer says: "Ringo can handle a wide variety of material, from rockers to ballads to oldies to originals. A far better than average voice." Further, the writer adds: "Here we have a collection of 10 fun-filled singles, and we don't find many collections like that anymore." Finally, it is noted that the album "contains several hits new fans may be missing."

Cash Box, in the 29 November 1975 issue, started the review with somewhat of a backhanded compliment: "Ringo Starr's post Beatles musical attempts have been a decidedly mixed bag. In his hands the strains of pop, rock and country were injected with an unheard of dimension and life." Later the reviewer adds: "On *Blast From Your Past* all of these forces, in their finest commercial and creative light are showcased."

Record World was complimentary of Starr and the album. "Ringo's solo work has consistently been the happy-go-luckiest of all the former Beatles. (Isn't it good to know some people just have fun making rock and roll music?)" (29 November 1975).

In 1975, Starr said during an interview, accompanied by Ring O' Records general manager, Barry Anthony, "I've done quite a lot on the production side. Apple Films was there, and nobody was doing anything with it, and I worked on it and we did two feature films and two documentaries." Those documentaries had not yet been released, but that would change in 1976. Starr added, "What worries me about the business side is that the record industry is being taken over by lawyers and accountants, often at the expense of the creative people."

As the album was slowly climbing the charts, on 13 December 1975, an article appeared in *Record World* about a court judgement in the ABKCO-Apple lawsuit. It was reported that "ABKCO Industries, Inc.

has announced that in its action to recover loans and advances, it had obtained Summary Judgment against Apple Records, Inc. (Calif.) for the full amount of such loans and advances, together with certain interest and costs." This spelled the end of Apple Records, and in fact many articles at the time indicated that for all intents and purposes, Apple was shutting its doors. There was no word on the studio at this time. But, with the exception of Lennon, each Beatle had their own studio and Harrison and Starr their own labels.

Starr would have one more release on Apple in 1976. However, much like 1975, 1976 was shaping up to be a very busy year for Mr. Starkey.

7

1976

By 1976, Ringo Starr had firmly established himself as a solo artist and a popular music success. He continued to work, and because he continued to release his music and albums near Christmas, fans were still buying his records. For the third year in a row, he started the new year with an album climbing the charts (*Blast From Your Past*) and a new single, 'Oh My My' b/w 'No No Song'. That single was released into the UK market to promote *Blast From Your Past* on 9 January 1976. Unlike in the previous two years, this single did not have any impact as a promotional tool or a single; it did not chart and *Blast From Your Past* continued to decline in sales in the UK. 'Oh My My' would be Starr's last single on Apple Records and the second last Apple single; Harrison would have the distinction of the last Apple single when 'This Guitar (Can't Keep From Crying)' was released almost a month later.

But Starr would be shaking things up very soon. As of January 26, 1976, his contract with EMI was done, and he was looking for a new label. It was no secret that all the major labels were interested in him, and it was reported in 1975 that ABC Records were offering him five million dollars for five years. Remember, ABC did handle the Colonel Doug Bogie single for the world excluding the UK. But Starr did not sign with them. In March, everything would be made clear.

In the 21 February 1976 issue of *Record World*, it was reported that Vera Lynn was releasing a new single, 'Don't You Remember When'. The song was written and produced by Lynsey De Paul. Lynsey De Paul was a very successful singer/songwriter who had had two top ten singles in the UK and a number one hit in Europe ('Sugar Me' made number five in the UK and number one throughout Europe). The short article mentioned that Ringo Starr played tambourine on the song. The single was actually written by De Paul and Barry Blue, and it was recorded in 1975, when Starr had been romantically linked to De Paul. The single was released on 20 February 1976 on the EMI label, and although it received positive reviews, it failed to register with record buyers and did not chart.

Not only was Starr helping Vera Lynn, Ringo also sat behind his drum kit for the band The Manhattan Transfer when they were recording their second album for Atlantic Records, which was produced by Richard Perry. Starr and Jim Keltner drummed on two songs, 'Zindy Lou' and

'S.O.S.'. At that period, The Manhattan Transfer consisted of Tim Hauser, Laurel Massé, Alan Paul, and Janis Siegel. The album peaked at number 48 in the US and produced a number one single in the UK ('Chanson D'Amour'). The sessions were held in Los Angeles early in 1976.

The Manhattan Transfer was a band that focused on vocals and pop music from the 1940s and 1950s. They had just signed to Atlantic and were looking for a hit and a big album. Richard Perry assembled great musicians to assist the band in achieving their goal.

Laurel Massé, one time member of The Manhattan Transfer, spoke with this author. She stated that although their first album for Atlantic Records had done well, especially in the UK, the label was eager for the band to have a more pop sound for their second release. "We grumbled at this, but we managed to slip a little jazz in there, but it was more pop oriented and Motown kind of stuff," said Massé. "Richard Perry was selected as producer because he had produced a lot of pop records. Leo Sayer, The Pointer Sisters were some of his artists. He had a really good track record that way, so we had him. And because we had him, we had access to calling musicians for the record that we might not have even thought of. I don't know that we would have thought of having Ringo Starr. And I am pretty certain we would not have the thought of having Ringo Starr and Jimmy Keltner on drums on the same track. Dr. John is on that particular track ('Zindy Lou'). And all of that, I think, is because of the connections with Richard."

Massé and the band were certainly excited to have Ringo Starr on the album. "That is how I got to meet somebody who was a God. He wasn't very chatty but he was friendly and he just knew exactly what to play and how to play it. And he and Keltner playing together knew exactly how to play together. It was really masterful. That was Ringo, that was really exciting. Part of my favourite memory was just the watching of this person, being life-sized. I saw them on their first television show in the UK, where we were living at the time. And that was it! I was ten. I saw them at Shea Stadium, we were back in the states. To record with Ringo, he was life-size and he was a human, and two drummers could play together, intuitively, the way those two drummers did. And it was the first time I had met Ringo in person. That was special, to have, for even a brief moment, a sideman who was a Beatle. It was pretty astounding."

The album, *Coming Out*, not only received some very good reviews, but also proved to be a bigger album than their first for Atlantic. The album even went gold in Australia. Although Starr was not credited for the success, Perry did receive a great deal of credit for their transition from a nostalgic act to a modern pop combo.

Starr then moved from pop to country for his next session work. According to Harry Castleman and Walter J. Podrazik, Starr participated in the recording of Guthrie Thomas's album *Lies And Alibis* in early 1976. The album was released on 3 May 1976, and was recorded at Cherokee Studios in Los Angeles. Starr actually did more than participate. He gave Thomas a song he had written and never recorded, 'Band Of Steel'. It is a straight ahead country song that would not have been out of place on Starr's own *Beaucoups Of Blues* album, released in 1970. Besides playing drums on the song (alongside Jim Keltner), Ringo provides vocals as well. He also drummed on 'Good Days Are Rollin' In' and 'Ramblin' Cocaine Blues'. Starr had drummed on Guthrie's debut album, and he was obviously a fan.

Thomas produced the album, and one look at the credits shows that Thomas was deep in the LA music scene, and had a lot of session players as friends. Besides Starr, David Foster (who was signed to Dark Horse Records at the time as part of the Attitudes), David Paich (Toto), Jim Hartford, and Steve Cropper (Booker T And The M.G.'s) all joined Guthrie for the recording.

The album's official release date is 3 May 1976, which is odd given the album was not reviewed until the 10 July 1976 issue of Canada's *RPM* magazine. The review is quite complimentary towards the album and highlights Starr's contribution, saying: "One cut fun for country is 'Band Of Steel', written by Ringo Starr, who plays drums and swaps verses with Thomas on the cut. It's the only pure country format song on the LP." There were no singles released from the album, and *Lies And Alibis* failed to chart. The album was a clear indication that Starr had not forgotten or lost his love of country music.

Further adventures awaited Thomas and his connection with Starr. In June, Guthrie was arrested and charged with kidnapping his ex-girlfriend. In the 25 July 1976 issue of *Austin-American Statesman*, it is claimed that Starr was going to participate in a benefit concert for Thomas. The concert went ahead without Starr, and Thomas later denied ever suggesting that Starr would be participating.

Thomas passed away on 13 July 2016. He never achieved the success he deserved, possibly due to his life choices and situations in which he was involved. He also refused to 'play the game' and be part of the recording establishment. He was a Nashville outlaw, but unlike Willie Nelson and Waylon Jennings, for example, he could not develop the fanbase and support. Sadly, although he made some very impressive albums, he is largely forgotten. It is interesting that of all the country artists with whom Starr could work, he contributed to an up and coming, independent artist. Once again, this is an example of Starr trying to assist artists.

Starr also provided a cameo vocal for another Nashville outlaw artist, Kinky Friedman. Born Richard Samet 'Kinky' Friedman, he was a singer, songwriter, novelist, humorist, politician, and columnist for *Texas Monthly*. He created some of the most original and brilliant country/folk/Americana albums and his mystery/detective novels were always a treat. He once said that he based his career on satirists Will Rogers and Mark Twain.

Starr met Friedman through Bob Dylan, when Starr performed with the Bob Dylan Rolling Thunder Revue tour, in a show at the Astrodome in Houston, Texas. It was a benefit concert to assist in the defence of Rubin 'Hurricane' Carter, titled The Night Of The Hurricane II (the first Night Of The Hurricane happened on 8 December 1975 at Madison Square Garden in New York City). Carter had been falsely imprisoned for murders he did not commit. Dylan had written a song, 'Hurricane', about Carter. The song appeared on his number one album, *Desire*, and was a top 40 hit for Dylan.

According to Ruth Buzzi, "Ringo said he loved The Kinkster, mentioned how much he respected his songwriting, and said he always has a great time when he and Kinky were together, on stage and off. The most famous drummer of the most famous band to ever appear on earth told me Kinky was one of the smartest guys he ever knew."

Friedman's album, *Lasso From El Paso*, was a star studded event, with artists like Ronnie Wood, The Band, Lowell George (Little Feat) and Eric Clapton all contributing. One track, 'Sold American', was recorded at Ft. Collins, Colorado, as part of Bob Dylan's Rolling Thunder Revue. Other recording sessions took place at Sugar Hill Studios, Houston, Texas, Shangri-La Studios, Malibu, California, and Haji Sound in Hollywood. It was released in November 1976. The album was meant to capitalise on Friedman's appearance on the Rolling Thunder Revue, so virtually every member of the tour is credited on the LP jacket.

Starr made a brief appearance on the song 'Men's Room, L.A.' as the voice of Jesus Christ. Not surprisingly, the song about Friedman's dilemma over using a picture of Jesus for toilet paper was not released as a single, nor did it receive much airplay. The album did not chart but received good reviews at the time. According to *Cash Box* and *Record World*, the album was a favourite at colleges and universities in the US.

Record World acknowledged his part in the Rolling Thunder Revue in their review. "His stint with the Rolling Thunder Revue has planted a certain familiarity for him as well as providing the core of the back-up musicians and vocalists used. There are even ballads to balance the humor" (27 November 1976). *Cash Box*, in reviewing the album, wrote: "humorous ones like 'Ahab The Arab', and 'Men's Room, L.A.', there are the lovely ballads 'Dear Abbie' and 'Lady Yesterday'."(11 December 1976). *Billboard* reviewed the album and stated: "Kinky and his posse of big name guest stars (Ringo, Clapton, etc) are equally as convincing in love songs or social commentary as in off-color jokes" (27 November 1976).

One look at the albums with which Starr was associated and one can see that he was very comfortable within many different genres. From jazz/pop/nostalgia to country to outlaw country to rock, Starr was able to go from genre to genre with a great deal of ease. Friedman's was an interesting album with which Starr was involved, given the role he gladly took.

Friedman passed away in 2024. Like Guthrie Thomas, Kinky Friedman was another country artist who did not fit any mould. At times he was folk and at times he was pure country. Starr's one contribution to Friedman's album is amusing and a little out of character for Starr. It is not usual for Starr to take on the role of Jesus. Sadly, it was the only time the two worked together, even though Friedman recorded and released albums until his death.

By March 1976, Starr was shaking things up with his career. He was also ready to record and release his own music.

According to the music trade papers, Ringo Starr signed to Polydor Records worldwide, except Canada and the United States. In those countries he signed to Atlantic Records. On 20 March 1976, *Cash Box* ran an article announcing: "Atlantic Records has signed Ringo Starr to a long-term recording contract. Under an agreement between WEA Records B.V. of Holland and Ringo Starr, Atlantic will be the sole distributor of Starr's recordings in the U.S. and Canada."

The deal was signed in the Netherlands. Polydor's Mike Hales was present for the signing. Mike Hales was vice president of popular music in Hamburg in the head office. The article further pointed out that "Also present at the signing ceremony in the Presidential Suite of the Hilton Hotel in Amsterdam were Ben Bunders, managing director of WEA Holland, Jerry Greenberg, president of Atlantic/ Atco Records, Hillary Gerard, friend and business associate of Ringo Starr, Bruce Grakal, Starr's attorney, Earl McGrath, director of artist development of Atlantic/Atco, Bob Kornheiser, vice-president of Atlantic/Atco and Phil Carson, Atlantic's international chief."

One week later, *Cash Box* reported that "Ringo Starr has signed an exclusive long-term recording contract with Polydor International, covering the world excluding the U.S. and Canada. He thus becomes the second former Beatle to sever a 12 year relationship with EMI. The agreement calls for the delivery of seven albums for the next five years. Recording of the first begins in April, due for release in June. Polydor president Mike Hales commented, 'We are delighted to have Ringo in the Polydor family, to greatly strengthen our growing roster of international stars'."

In a conversation with this author, Mike Hales confirms the reasoning behind signing Starr. "We were keen to sign him, because, despite the fact that Polydor was a major international label, and we distributed a lot of labels, like Atlantic and and Elektra, Buddha and MGM, we didn't have a great many marquee names on the label. Probably The Bee Gees were the biggest and at that point in time, they were going through a fairly deep trough of lack of success prior to *Saturday Night Fever*. I felt the label as a whole needed some more glamour, it needed some marquee names. Becoming aware that Ringo was becoming available was a great interest. I pitched in and got talking to Hilary (Gerrard). It all came together rather well."

In 1976, Atlantic was part of the WEA (which stood for Warners/Elektra/Atlantic) umbrella, meaning that in 1976, Warner Brothers (WEA) had two solo Beatles, as George Harrison signed to Warners in 1976. Atlantic Records was one of the biggest and most respected labels at the time. Atlantic Records began in 1947, and was formed by Ahmet Ertegun and Herb Abramson. It began as a rhythm and blues label, but things changed in 1967 when it was sold to Warner Brothers-Seven Arts. Once Warner Brothers acquired Elektra Records, it became known as WEA, with each label having their own autonomy within the bigger organisation. In 1969, Atlantic expanded its roster beyond rhythm and blues when it signed Led Zeppelin. Atlantic became a rock label, signing Crosby, Stills, Nash and Young, Yes, Genesis, and many other major rock acts. Ringo seemed to be in good company.

Record World, in reporting Starr signing to Atlantic Records, made a note in their publication that "Ahmet Ertegun, chairman of Atlantic/Atco Records, has announced in Amsterdam that Atlantic has signed Ringo Starr to a long-term recording contract." But the article also stated that "Under an agreement between WEA Records B.V. of Holland and Ringo Starr, Atlantic will be the sole distributor of Starr's recordings in the U.S. and Canada" (20 March 1976). Although Ring O' Records resumed production in 1977, during Starr's time with Atlantic Records, none of the Ring O' Records were released in North America.

According to an article in *Variety* from 3 March 1976, "The Polydor deal calls for seven LPs over five years, with first release due in June.

Presumably the Atlantic contract covers the same product, though details there were not available at press time."

Polydor, on the other hand, had an even longer history. Polydor Records was founded on 2 April 1913 by German Polyphon-Musikwerke AG in Leipzig and registered on 25 July 1914, although the actual company dates back to 1897. By the 1960s the label had become known for both classical and pop music, and in fact, it was Polydor that signed The Beatles to their first recording contract on 21 June 1961. Their main job was to provide backing for British singer Tony Sheridan, who was based in Germany. Polydor eventually signed artists such as The Who, Cream, Bee Gees, Eric Clapton and Jimi Hendrix, to name just a few. Again, Starr was in good company.

Hales also recalls that Starr received a great deal of attention given the history of The Beatles and Hamburg, Germany. "When he came over to Hamburg to sign, I suppose, to sign the contract, because he was at that point one of the first Beatles to come back to Germany and caused a great stir in Hamburg. We would tend to be together during the day and half the night because he was very keen to look up Bettina, the barmaid, and various other people who figured in the lives of The Beatles when they first went to the Star Club. So we were out and about all night and he would go back to his hotel and go back to bed, of course. I would go to my office and sleep for a couple of hours before the next day's work began."

It is interesting to note that ABC had been in the running to sign Starr to a worldwide deal. It was reported in the 10 January 1976 issue of *Record World* that "Ringo Starr has not signed his reported five million dollar contract with ABC Records, and he may never put pen to paper. The deal, once reported as firm, is now shaky and may never come off." No reason is given for the change of heart. However, it may well be due to the poor reception of the one Ring O' Records single which they distributed in Europe and North America by Doug Bogie. By 1975, Ring O' Records had yet to prove itself, and it may be that companies were not willing to take the label just to get Starr, especially since he was not releasing any of his music on the label.

Starr said, in an interview with Paul Gambaccini in 1976: "Atlantic is very good in America, not in Europe. Polydor is very good in Europe, not in America. I've got the best of both worlds. No sense in my going with one if I don't think they're going to do the business." Atlantic made the decision, very early on, to not distribute Ring O' Records in Canada and the US. Starr was serious about his label and he was looking for distribution for the records being issued on that label.

As Starr was signing his new record deals, The Beatles were making an unusual comeback. Unusual in that they had been apart for six years. In 1976, a revised Beatlemania was getting ready to explode worldwide. Perhaps due to the numerous proposals to bring The Beatles back together, there was a great deal of revived interest in the band. Rumours of the four getting back together were an almost daily news story.

In the 13 March 1976 issue of *Billboard*, it was reported that "EMI has issued the Beatles' original version of 'Yesterday' as a single for the first time, almost six years since the group's last single, 'Let it Be'. But EMI is not disclosing whether the move signals a newly acquired freedom on its part to work the Beatles' old repertoire in previously untried ways, or whether it means that various restrictions upon issuing and repackaging the material, certainly contained in past Beatle contracts with EMI, have expired." The single would go to number eight in the UK and number four in Ireland. The then eleven-year-old song was successfully competing with the current disco and pop records. In fact, the week that 'Yesterday' peaked at number eight, The Beatles had four other titles in the top 50!

While The Beatles began world domination in 1976, a couple of film projects of Ringo Starr surfaced in different ways in the US. According to *Variety* (3 March 1976), under the heading 'Ringo Starr, Producer', it is stated that: "Two one-hour films produced by former Beatle Ringo Starr for Apple Films will be distributed non-theatrically in the U.S. through Wavehill Productions Inc. Lome Blair, formerly with the BBC in London, has arrived in this country to handle the distribution. Blair directed both films, each concerned with a voyage through the Spice Islands of Indonesia. Another former Beatle, George Harrison, scored the pics." The films *Wow* and *Monsoon* would eventually premiere at Wilshire Ebell in Los Angeles, on 9th May 1976.

Dr Lawrence Blair, who co-produced the films with his brother Lorne Blair and wrote the script, said that he "first met him [Starr] in 1971, at the Apple headquarters in London." He says that "Apple was searching for interesting film projects to back. Ringo had heard about John Michel (a close friend of mine) who awakened Britain to the 'sacred geometry' behind churches and cathedrals, and the convergence of Ley Lines on which many of these were built. It was John who introduced Prince Charles (now the King) to these concepts, which still fascinate him. Apple wanted to produce a film of John's work but John told Ringo that he was more interested in furthering his research at that stage than having it 'popularised' and he suggested that the Blair brothers' expeditions might be a more suitable project for Apple to invest in. So it was through John that my late brother Lorne and I were invited to pitch Apple with our idea of filming in Indonesia."

Although the advertisement and article stated that Harrison had scored the film, Dr Blair is clear that Harrison had nothing to do with the film, although later in life the two became quite friendly. According to Dr Blair: "Our project was specifically Ringo's baby at Apple. It was Ringo (and his business advisor Hilary Gerard) who we met on a number of occasions at the Apple office, but by the time we brought the raw footage back, nine months later, Apple had disbanded and chaos reigned. But my brother Lorne subsequently edited the first cuts under Ringo's auspices. He had initially provided 2000 pounds, and a bit more to edit the two films, but we failed to sell them, as they were too, shall we say, revolutionary for the BBC at the time. Many films later we managed to sell *Ring of Fire*, which included much of the footage Ringo had originally underwritten for us."

As for the premieres in Los Angeles, Dr Blair had little memory of the event except to note that "We would have shown our footage in LA, long before it appeared in the *Ring of Fire* version." By 1976, Apple was in the process of dissolving and Apple Films did not seem to exist. However, the films were shown. Dr Blair remembers that Starr had little to do with the film. "He watched all the rushes with us, and the edits, and was intrigued and somewhat bewildered. We had told him, before departing for Indonesia, that we planned to film the Toraja tribe, who believe their ancestors came from the Pleiades in sky ships, and the historically very piratical Bugis seafaring tribe, and he said he thought [he] was investing in movies about flying saucers and pirates." He had nothing to do with the *Ring of Fire* series, edited many years later in Boston for PBS and the BBC, except for financing some of the early, valuable footage in it.

During an interview to launch Ring O' Records, Starr did mention that he had recently produced two short movies for Apple Films, and said he was the only one working at Apple Films. These two films were clearly important to him: as Dr Blair stated, Starr enjoyed the films, with his bewildered enthusiasm. The films did not sell at the time, and did not surface again for many years, when, as Dr Blair points out, footage was incorporated into the BBC/PBS documentary *Ring Of Fire*. It was a five part documentary which debuted on 6 June 1988. A digital transfer was completed in 2021. The documentary was nominated for an Emmy in 1999. Dr Blair would appear with Ringo in another documentary titled *Oh My God*, released in 2009, a film that looked at celebrities' views of God and religion.

There was other film news in March 1976. In the 26 March 1976 issue of *Variety* an article appeared stating that the court was proceeding in Bankruptcy No. 75 B 1661, In the Matter of Cinemation Industries, Inc., the film company which distributed *Son Of Dracula* just two years before. Cinemation Industries had declared bankruptcy. "Simon Rosenbach, Auctioneer. Will sell at public auction on behalf of Sellers, the interest of Cinemation Industries, Inc., if any, in and to the following motion pictures and pre-print materials, prints, and advertising materials therefore (collectively the 'Pictures'), which will be sold individually or in bulk."

When Starr stated in an interview with *Q* magazine that no one wanted it, he was not joking. By all accounts, the film was not purchased and the rights for the film in 2025 are somewhat in limbo. However, Starr made it quite clear: "It is not the best film ever made, but I've seen worse." As of 2025, the film is not available in any format, although it has been bootlegged several times.

In April, it was time for Starr to record his next studio album, *Ringo's Rotogravure*.

For the record, the word 'rotogravure' is not one used often in 1976, and was an unlikely name for an album. A 'rotogravure' is a type of printing method for photographs that uses a metal cylinder and an engraving to imprint the image using ink. At one time it was the standard for newspapers, and is still used today, though it is not as common. The word is used in the classic song, 'Easter Parade' by Irving Berlin, first heard in the 1942 film *Holiday Inn*.

During an interview on Dutch TV, Starr talked about the origin of the title of the album. "It came from the movie, *Easter Parade*, Judy Garland said it, and I was freaked out, What's she saying? You'll find your picture in the rotogravure. Then I found out what it was, it's a machine that prints pictures very fast and was the first name for a New York colour supplement. The tracks themselves are pictures."

Starr recorded the album from April 1976 through to July 1976. Initially he had planned to work with Richard Perry again, but since he had recently signed to Atlantic Records, a suggestion was made that he could use their 'in-house' producer, Arif Mardin. Starr told Lisa Robinson of the *New Musical Express*, "since we were trying another label, we'd try another producer."

In 1977, Starr said: "It's time for a change, I think, you know. You can't get Arif [Mardin] to produce you unless you sign to Atlantic, which is not the reason why we signed. We met Arif, he came to London for five hours to have a chat, and at the end I said, 'I'd like to work with you,' and he said, 'Well, I'd like to work with you.' I made him come to

LA and we were still getting to know each other in a way, in a way, and he didn't know the players. It turned out fine."

Nancy Lee Andrews recalled that Atlantic Records was the one behind the change of producers. "Wexler [Jerry Wexler, CEO of Atlantic Records, and an original partner] and Ertegun wanted Arif." In her view, Arif Mardin was not the right producer for Starr. "Arif was coming in from Aretha and a blues background, basically. It was very difficult for these guys to get together. Richie at this point was writing a lot of songs with Vini Poncia and Vini was Perry's right hand man. He did so much with The Pointer Sisters and Melissa Manchester. They had been writing songs together, and it just didn't meld. It was very frustrating for both of them. Another thing that happened was that Arif was New York, but LA was Ringo's type of town. They had their core players, Jim Keltner, and all those 1970s guys. Then we went to New York and Arif was picking the band. So for *Ringo The 4th*, they didn't have his core group that he was used to playing with. It was so frustrating for Ringo."

Mardin was a musician, and one of the most famous record producers in the music world. He had scored hits with The Bee Gees (*Main Course*, 1975) and had produced artists such as Cher, Carly Simon, Bette Midler and many more. He was well known and in terms of getting hits, he was well established. Although Mardin typically recorded in New York, Starr had requested that the album be recorded in Los Angeles. Starr had certainly settled in LA and wanted to be near his friends.

By August, music trade papers were starting to write about the forthcoming album. There was a great deal of excitement, as expectations were very high, given the success of his previous two studio albums. Ron McCreight in *Record World* (28 August 1976) wrote "Ringo Starr's first album for Polydor will be issued mid-September on both sides of the Atlantic. *Ringo's Rotogravure (a Passing Picture Show)* includes songs by his three former colleagues being aided by several world renowned jammers, including Dr. John, Nilsson, Frampton, Melissa, Lennon, and Paul & Linda McCartney. It was all put together under the expert supervision of Arif Mardin." The subtitle 'A Passing Picture Show' did not last long as a subtitle. For the purposes of this book, *Ringo's Rotogravure* is, at times, referred to simply as *Rotogravure*.

Once again, Ringo had some help from his old bandmates. Even though Paul McCartney and George Harrison did not help with *Goodnight Vienna,* they were more than willing to help with *Ringo's Rotogravure*. "Well, Paul asked to write a song. I asked John and... eventually he came up with 'You Got Me Cooking' [which became 'Cookin' (In The Kitchen Of Love)']," Starr said. "I also asked George to write one, but there was an old one of his that was never released by anybody that I always loved... I asked him if instead of writing one, could I have that old one? He said 'fine'; it saved him a job. It's called 'I Still Love You,' a big ballady thing." In the end, although Harrison agreed, he was not happy with the outcome of the song.

According to Nancy Lee Andrews, McCartney said his song, 'Pure Gold', was about her and Starr. "We were strolling down 5th Avenue back to the Plaza Hotel and we heard someone calling Ringo's name. I turned and saw Paul and Linda across the street. I mean what is the chance of that? Paul had a photographer following him so when he caught up with us the photographer snapped away. Paul and Linda came back to the hotel with us and we ordered some tea up to the suite. I found Paul very charming and down to earth. He and Linda were a real couple; you know, they were a unit. Linda had a wonderful sense of humour. We never hung out with them. They were always on the farm and Paul had his own music. He did write a song for *Ringo's Rotogravure*, 'Pure Gold'. Paul said it was about me for Ringo, so he recorded it."

Joining Starr (who played drums along with Jim Keltner) on 'Pure Gold' are Lon Van Eaton (guitar), Jane Getz and John Jarvis (piano) and Voormann on bass, with George Devens on congas. Starr and Poncia sang, while the McCartneys provided backing vocals. Paul and Linda recorded their vocals during the famous *Wings Over America* tour in between dates in California. They recorded their part on 17 June 1976. Paul McCartney and Wings did three shows in Los Angeles beginning 21 June 1976, ending the North American leg of the tour. The strings on the song were recorded later in June, in New York City.

Starr has been quoted as saying: "Him and Linda came down, and I'm the hustler, I said, 'Do you want to sing?' At that time of the night – it was about eight o'clock – they said, 'No, no...' So we went out for dinner and ate, and they had a few drinks. Then we came back and wandered round to the studio, and they decided they were ready to sing! The three of us were out there, and I was a bit tipsy, as they say, so I'm shouting along with them, and Arif's saying, 'We've got you, you know, we've got your vocal down, so back off.' So, we let the stars take over. We love each other and there they are."

The song is pure McCartney and a beautiful love song. Mardin gives the song a lush treatment, and Starr's vocals are quite strong with the McCartneys supporting him.

During a television interview on Dutch TV, Starr addressed any Beatle reunion questions by being very clear: "We are friendly, no we are not getting together and a couple of them play on my record, and that doesn't mean we are getting together. That is the end of it. There's no George, just John and Paul."

Unlike the other three Beatles, John Lennon, in 1976, had not signed to any record label, and although no one knew it at the time, was starting his five year break from recording and performing. However, he (and reportedly Yoko Ono) took some time out of their break to fly to Los Angeles to participate on a song Lennon had written for Ringo. 'Cookin' (In The Kitchen Of Love)' seemed more apt for Lennon, as he later reported that he discovered his talent in the kitchen during his musical break. It is a jaunty number, with Lennon on piano (and uncredited vocals), and Dr. John on guitar and organ. Melissa Manchester and Duitch Helmer sing back-up with Will Lee on bass.

Nancy Lee Andrews remembered that Lennon basically produced the song. "John was in the booth producing the song. It was great."

The song was recorded on 27 May 1976. It was the last time Lennon was, reportedly, in a recording studio until August 1980 when he started work on *Double Fantasy*. During his interview with David Scheff in 1980, Lennon stated that he contributed the song and playing purely out of friendship to Starr. However, Lennon also added that he was not really happy with the song.

"I was cooking at the time. I just sort of knocked it off for him. The Arif Mardin… no fault of Arif's, but just the vibes in the studio were not good that day. And I'd come all the way from New York with Yoko. I didn't really wanna go down there and do the session. And Ringo had asked, so we went down there and did it, but the feeling in the studio wasn't good and the track didn't come alive at all. And I'm thinking what the hell am I doing down here, you know, being taken for granted, I felt."

George Harrison was even less happy with Starr's arrangement of an old Harrison song, 'I'll Still Love You'. Harrison attempted his own version for *All Things Must Pass*, in 1970, but it didn't turn out to his satisfaction. He later offered it to Ronnie Spector, and old Liverpool friend Cilla Black (her version did come out in 2003 on her compilation *Cilla: The Best of 1963–78*. On the CD it is titled 'I'll Still Love You (When Every Song Is Sung)'). But the song lingered in the archives for many years. Starr was a fan of the song, and although Harrison was not available to help with it, Starr went ahead with his version. Harrison was struck with hepatitis while he was recording his 1976 Dark Horse debut album, *33 and ⅓*.

Harrison later stated: "When I wrote 'When Every Song Is Sung' I had it titled 'Whenever'. I got the chord sequence and 'when every song is sung' were the first words to come out of my mouth and it developed from there. It was one of those that I tried several times to record: Ronnie Spector, Phil's wife, had a go at it; Cilla Black also – in fact I started to produce it for Cilla as a single but we didn't finish it. We also did it with

Leon Russell and his wife Mary and in the end Ringo recorded it. As Shirley Bassey once suggested in a newspaper, after having a 'hit' with 'Something', that she and I could be like Dionne Warwick and Burt Bacharach, if we got together, I thought this would be a good one for her..."

At the time of *Ringo's Rotogravure*'s release, Starr recalled: "I also asked George to write one, but there was an old one of his that was never released by anybody that I always loved – I was on the session when it was recorded."

Helping Ringo with the song are Lon Van Eaton, who provided a very Harrison-inspired solo and guitar throughout the song, while Jane Getz added wonderful piano. Arif Mardin played the ARP, which adds a great deal and fills out the song. Klaus Voormann played bass, doing his usual quality work. Gene Orloff orchestrated strings. Starr and Keltner drummed on the song and David Lasley (famous for singing with James Taylor) sang back-up. However, when the song was done, Harrison did not like it. Harrison went so far as to threaten a lawsuit to prevent the song from being released. Said Ringo: "Sue me if you want, but I'll always love you." Very clearly, Harrison's threat upset Ringo, as in 1988 he joked about it during an appearance on the show *Aspel & Company* with George. When asked about any arguments between the two, Starr responded, "Well, the last time we were cross was when George was suing me."

Starr and Polydor must have thought highly of the song, as a promo film was made. This suggests that it was considered for a single release. Quite possibly it might have done very well as a single, but it did not seem to get beyond the planning stages. Perhaps the threat of the lawsuit caused all concerned to pause for thought. It is a shame: the film is simple, but well done, and the song is one of the strongest on the album.

If *Goodnight Vienna* was Starr's break-up album, *Rotogravure* was a rebirth for him. New labels, a new producer (Arif Mardin), and he was in a very serious new relationship with Nancy Andrews. This new love and his new chapter is certainly reflected in the album. While the old formula of superstar friends (including two former Beatles) helping out was the same, the album was different from his previous two.

Starr first met Nancy Lee Andrews on 27 May 1974 in Los Angeles during a party for Harry Nilsson's *Pussycats* release party, hosted by John Lennon. By 1974 Andrews was an established supermodel quite well known in the fashion world. Through May Pang, Andrews had met John Lennon, and Lennon was playing matchmaker for Starr. However, the relationship took time to take off. Andrews said, "Three months went by and John had said, come meet us at the Wilshire. Of course I went up to the suite, and it's Ringo's suite. I thought to myself, 'I'm being set up.' Later May told me that for 'three months he had been asking about you'." They began living together in 1975. As Andrews says, "He was a very very busy guy, and we were traversing the globe so much."

The album opens with the first single from it, which was released three days after the album hit the stores. 'A Dose of Rock 'n' Roll' appeared on Atlantic Records on 20 September 1976 in America and Canada. Polydor waited a month to couple 'A Dose Of Rock 'n' Roll' and the country flavoured 'Cryin' for the UK and Europe. By 3 October 1976, according to *Billboard*, 'A Dose Of Rock 'n' Roll' was one of the top radio added songs across America and it was noted as a breakout. This means that most Rock and Top 40 radio stations were playing the new Ringo Starr song.

Cash Box, in their 2 October 1976 Single Reviews, wrote: "Starr's first single for Atlantic...Gone are the Apple days." The reviewer pointed out that the song "Starts off slow and bluesy. Before you know it, the song takes off with a spotless production from Arif Mardin. Good rock music, with a beat you can dance to." *Record World* made it unanimous, writing in the 2 October 1976 issue: "Ringo's first single in well over a year marks a return to the goodtime, sing-along style he popularized with the *Ringo* album. Peter Frampton adds some spicy guitar licks to keep it moving along."

'A Dose Of Rock 'n' Roll' was written by Carl Groszmann (although it is spelt Grossman on the North American single label, in Europe and the UK it was the correct spelling of his name) with old friend Klaus Voormann on bass, Jim Keltner joining Starr on drums, Dr. John on keyboards, a horn section featuring The Brecker Brothers, and three guitarists: Jesse Ed Davies, Danny Kortchmar and Peter Frampton. George Young, Alan Rubin and Lewis Delgatto were also part of the horn section. Vini Poncia, Melissa Manchester, Joe Bean and Duitch Helmer sing the back-up. Melissa Manchester provides wonderful vocals that fit perfectly with Starr. In 1976 Peter Frampton was probably the biggest rock star in North America (*Frampton Comes Alive* was number one), and his playing on the song should have guaranteed Starr with a hit. It is a great rock-pop song with a very catchy and strong melody. Starr's drumming and vocals fit the song perfectly and it does pack a great deal of energy.

Groszmann, as noted, was signed to Ring O' Records. Later, in reflection of both the song and the label, Starr stated: "That song was from Carl Groszmann who was on Ring O' Records. I started a label in England and I had these five or six acts. We did it the old school way where I supported them all while they wrote their songs and they all ended up with an album. But then I couldn't go to any more board meetings, so I decided to close down Ringo O' Records – and every artist sued me. I didn't learn anything from Apple Records. I was still into it for the love and the music."

The American promo single and the UK stock copy cut off the intro and the song begins with the slow bluesy opening. The burst of music with Ringo's "All right" was edited from those versions. Starr did not film a promotional clip for the song, and did not appear on American television to promote the single. Perhaps he thought his first new music in over a year and a half would be immediately welcomed, but times had changed since 1974.

The single peaked on the *Billboard* charts on 6 November 1976 at number 26, after just seven weeks in the top 100. The number one song that week was Rod Stewart's 'Tonight's The Night' with 'Disco Duck' (by Rick Dees and his Cast of Idiots) at number two. Gordon Lightfoot's 'The Wreck Of The Edmund Fitzgerald' rounded out the top three. It peaked at number 26 on *Cash Box* the same week, while *Record World* charted the song just inside the top 40, peaking at number 32. In Canada, the single fared better by getting to number 20 on the national *RPM* charts. It didn't chart in the UK. In North America, 'A Dose of Rock 'n' Roll' was Ringo's last top 40 hit until 1982 ('Wrack My Brain').

In the UK, the single received remarkably little attention. In the 8 October 1976 issue of *Record Mirror,* a small article did appear: "A new Ringo Starr single is released on October 15 'A Dose Of Rock 'n' Roll', from his *Ringo's Rotogravure* album issued this week. Interestingly, the first single scheduled to be released in the UK was the Dave Jordan song, 'You Don't Know Me At All', but changed at the last minute." *Record Mirror* reviewed the single on 22 October 1976 and were far from kind. They referred to Starr as Mr Stubblehead (referring to his head shaven look) and David Brown wrote: "give this one a wide berth. It's a bit of an insult."

The B-side of the single was the country song 'Cryin'. It was written by Ringo and his songwriting partner, Vini Poncia. Ringo taps into the 'hurting' aspect of country music and it could very well be about his break-up with Maureen. Dr. John's piano has a perfect honky tonk sound. Starr and Keltner play drums on the song, old friend Lon Van Eaton is on guitar, Cooker Lo Presti replaces Voormann for this song on bass, 'Sneaky' Pete Klienow (who had worked on Lennon's *Mind Games* album in 1973) is on slide guitar, John Jarvis is on piano and Vini Poncia plays the electric piano.

Nancy Lee Andrews said the song was inspired by her. "My mother is from Alabama, which was another connection we had…country music.

George did 'I'll Still Love You'. Which was an older song that he had for years. But it hurts me to hear Ringo sing it. You can hear a pain in him as he sings it. It always hurts me."

Polydor took a global view of the album, and attempted to market the album and singles to specific markets. In this way, Europe, Mexico, and the UK all had different singles pulled from *Ringo's Rotogravure*. Although it was cancelled in the UK, 'You Don't Know Me At All' was released as a single throughout Europe (it peaked at number 18 in Holland), while the more Spanish flavoured 'Las Brisas' (which he wrote with Nancy Andrews) got the nod as an A-side in Mexico. Even though there were different A-sides, all the singles featured the song 'Cryin' on the flipside. Starr made a promo film for 'You Don't Know Me At All' which no doubt helped promote the single. It was filmed in Hamburg and Monte Carlo.

'You Don't Know Me At All' was written by New Zealand singer/songwriter Dave Jordan, who was based in London. He was best known as a folksinger, and he also worked with Lyndsey De Paul, with whom Starr had had a relationship and worked. It is a mellow, middle of the road song that would have fitted perfectly on Adult Oriented radio stations. Jordan had established himself as a songwriter, providing songs for Roger Whittaker, and he released his own albums as well, although there is no record of him recording his own version of 'You Don't Know Me At All'.

The promo film is well worth watching. It was one of three filmed for the album, and all three were directed by Bruce Gowers (who would later direct episodes of *American Idol*). According to Nancy Lee Andrews, "three days before he shaved his head." As to the reason for shaving his head, according to Andrews: "We were down at the beach in Monte Carlo, and it was the middle of the afternoon, two or three. He said, 'I'm going up to the barber to get a trim and a facial thing done and I will be back in an hour.' But it was getting late, about two hours, you know, where is he? He did have this thing where he would disappear." Andrews had found out that Ringo had made a pit stop at the bar before the barber and when she got to their apartment, Ringo came out and he looked like an alien. "And I asked, 'what have you done to yourself?' And he was on the floor and he said 'I went to the barber'."

You can see people's reactions as Ringo was filmed walking the streets of Monte Carlo and Hamburg. No one expected a solo Beatle to be roaming the streets, and no one expected Starr to look the way he does in the clip. Starr seems completely at his ease as he walks along, acknowledging his fans and genuinely having fun. Promo films were still gaining popularity. This one aired throughout Europe.

'Las Brisas' was a song that Starr wrote with Nancy Lee Andrews. It translates as 'the breezes', and it was the name of a well known hotel at the time.

"We used a mariachi band on ['Las Brisas'] because we were in Mexico when we wrote the song. We recruited one from a Mexican restaurant here in LA," said Starr. Starr joined the Mariachi Los Galleros de Pedro Rey and played maracas, while Vini Poncia sang the backing vocals. Andrews recalled: "We were in Mexico on a junket kind of thing. On the way to Mexico City, he said, let's go to the Las Brisas Hotel in Acapulco for two or three days. We were there, it was so wonderful and we were in a restaurant and Ritchie is, of course, sticking cigarettes in his ear playing to his little group. I'm sitting there enjoying the music, and I am the little girl that used to write poetry and I am writing the lyrics down. We got back to the hotel, and I went into the bathroom and I had a little micro tape recorder and in the morning, we got up and had breakfast and I said, I think I have written a song. I pressed play and he said 'God, that's great! Let's put it on the album!' We got back to LA and it wound up going on the album."

Nancy Lee Andrews spoke to Marshall Terrill of *Daytrippin'* about 'Las Brisas'. "We were in Acapulco, I think it was the first year of our relationship, and it was so romantic at the Las Brisas Hotel. Everything was pink — pink jeeps, pink flowers floating in the pool, etc. I was fascinated with the language and was asking someone to translate words for me and write them down on a napkin in a poem form. A band was playing and Ringo picked up the napkin and started singing the words. We worked on it over the next few days and it became our little song."

According to Lon Van Eaton, Starr was recording in Los Angeles "in Sunset Sound, and I even wrote a song about Ringo and the session at Sunset Sound. We were doing the album, and we played, good musicians, Dr. John, Van Dyke Parks, and Ringo said, 'This is great,' and it really wasn't, and we did another take, and he said, 'Boy, this is great.' We decided to take a break and take a walk to this Mexican restaurant, and this mariachi band was playing and Ringo said, 'Come back to the studio and play, and I will play the drums to keep the beat.' So that is what happened, and that is why they are on the album, I think they were called Los Galleros de Pedro Rey. They were professional musicians, and they played with Ringo and it was fun."

Lon Van Eaton was initially surprised with Starr's happiness with the song, even though in his estimation, it was not working as intended. This experience led Van Eaton to write the (sadly) unreleased song 'It's Great'. He also provides an interesting perspective on Ringo during that time period. "Later I wrote a song called 'It's Great', and it was about that. The thing that happened was, it finally occurred to us that if you have a perspective that 'I'd be shovelling fish in Liverpool if it hadn't been for music and all my breaks', you have to be great and that was a really learning thing."

Although it reportedly received airtime in Mexico, the single failed to make the top 50 on their national charts. The flipside for the single was 'Lady Gaye', an interesting track from *Ringo's Rotogravure*. The song was inspired by, and in reality based on, 'Birmingham' by Clifford T. Ward (from his 1975 album *No More Rock 'N' Roll*). Harry Nilsson provides backing vocals for this song. The single reportedly sold 12,500 copies in Mexico.

'Lady Gaye' is basically a cover version of Ward's 'Birmingham'. Voormann (bass), Dr. John (keyboards), Danny Kortchmar and Jess Ed Davies (guitar) and Keltner and Starr (drums) contribute to the easy listening song. Mardin's arrangement includes a marimba (played by George Devons), and a horn section composed of Michael Brecker, Lou Marini and Lewis Delgatto. Vini Poncia (who co-wrote the song) and Harry Nilsson provide the standard backing vocals. The song is fine, but really nothing special, and may have been put to better use as a B-side.

Eric Clapton contributed a song as well, 'This Be Called A Song'. It is a typical mid 1970s Clapton song, on which he plays guitar. Very little is known about the song as neither Clapton nor Starr have ever discussed it. It is very melodic with a catchy tune and quite possibly could have been a hit for Starr. It was recorded on 17 May 1976, the same day Starr recorded 'Pure Gold'. 'This Be Called A Song' featured Clapton (along with Lon Van Eaton) on guitar, Voormann on bass, Keltner and Starr on drums, Jane Getz on piano and Robert Greenidge on steel drums. Melissa Manchester, Vini Poncia and Joe Bean provide the backing vocals.

The second (and last) single to be released from the album in the UK and North America was the 1962 hit 'Hey Baby'. The song was written by Margaret Cobb and Bruce Channel. Channel had the hit with it in 1962. It is a song that Lennon credited for influencing The Beatles, especially the harmonica playing in the song. Delbert McClinton not only provided the harmonica in the song, but taught Lennon some techniques when he was on a package tour of the UK with The Beatles.

Starr's version was released as a single on 22 November 1976 in Canada and the US. John Jarvis (who played with Leo Sayer) provided the great keyboards, while Cooker Lo Presti played bass. Keltner, once again, joined Starr on drums and Lon Van Eaton was on hand for the guitar. The horn section featured The Brecker Brothers (Randy and Michael) and Lewis Delgatto. 'The Mad Mauries' are credited with backing vocals and handclaps. Starr's version is very similar in nature to his cover of 'You're Sixteen'. Starr keeps elements from the original, while adding some of his own character to the song.

Cash Box referred to Starr's version of the song as a "go-getter" and said: "It's a sizzling remake of Bruce Channel's old hit." The writer of the Singles Review page also notes that "Starr turns out some of his own vibrant power and style. The chorus sings backup throughout the song. Already has heavy FM play —should burst upon the AM stations instantly." In the same review section, George Harrison's 'This Song' is also pegged as a future hit and gets a very good review (*Cash Box* 27 November 1976). Starr's single would stall at 69 on *Cash Box*, while Harrison scraped into the top 30.

In the liner notes for his compilation album *Photograph - The Very Best Of Ringo*, Starr recalled that Mardin wanted him to record the song. "I think Arif Mardin who was producing that album made the call about covering the old Bruce Channel hit. Arif had a difficult time with me because I was difficult at that period of my life. He and Ahmet were two of the best people in the music business ever. Arif was such a gentle man and there are not enough of them in the world. I can't really even tell you if it was a great experience because a lot of it is… gone. The proof is we've got the record – and that's about it."

Record World noted: "Bruce Channel's hit from 1962 is given a singalong treatment as only Ringo can do it. The song, from his *Rotogravure* album, should bring some good time sounds to the top of the charts and end the year on a spirited note." *Record World* charted the single at 93. *Billboard* didn't review the single but listed it in their 'recommended' section of Single Picks. Although the single was released on 22 November 1976, it did not enter the *Billboard* singles chart until 29 January 1977, over two months after the release. It peaked two weeks later on 12 February 1977 at number 74. It did not get reviewed or chart in England.

The promo film soundtrack features a very different version of the song. On the promo film, there is some very nice guitar work from Lon Van Eaton and a count in before the song begins with 'Hey, hey baby'. This version should have been released on record, as it adds a great deal to the song.

In 1977, Starr was very clear that he was not happy about the relative failure of both singles. He spoke with Bill Minkins. "I know! But you see, I had complete faith… You talk about picking singles. I thought 'Dose of Rock 'N' Roll' could not fail, and 'Hey! Baby', I mean, are you kidding? And they did nothing. I'm too crazy now. People beg for things to get to the Top 40. I get annoyed if it's not number one. If I put a single out I want it to be number one." Clearly, Starr was not happy with the commercial success of *Ringo's Rotogravure*.

Starr further clarified the situation: "I want number one because that's the game. I'm not going out there to be forty-ninth. If I wanted to do that I'd do something else. When I put it out I want it to be number one, otherwise there's no point. I'm pleased you liked those two tracks, because I loved them. I could not believe why they didn't do it. Just something which is why I like the rock 'n' roll game, because you don't know. After all these years I don't know what a number one is. I think I know, and I put the records out and it ends up they're not. Something happens. I don't know."

The album ends with an improvised track, 'Spooky Weirdness', the title of which does not appear on the back of the album cover on some pressings (or even on the label). It is a fun minute and a half, and an interesting way to end *Ringo's Rotogravure*. By all accounts it was improvised and demonstrates the players having a bit of fun, with some short but interesting drumming from Ringo. It is weird, but not scary.

It is interesting to note that Starr thanks the Lennons and McCartneys (and Apple) in the thank yous for the album. Harrison is not mentioned. As noted above, besides not appearing on the album, Harrison was very clear about his unhappiness with 'I'll Still Love You'. Starr and Harrison would, in quick order, sort everything out and become close friends again. Harrison would even help Ringo with Starr's television show in 1978.

When the album was released in the UK and Europe, it came with a magnifying glass. The magnifying glass was only released as a promo item in the US. Mike Hales of Polydor said: "We bought half a million magnifying glasses to give away with the album." Ringo was keen on the idea of the magnifying glass, and during the interview on the television show *Voor de Vuist Weg,* he said it was for the back sleeve with a picture of the door of Apple Records, now shut down and covered in graffiti. "So you can see better, you look at the back and see if your name is there."

Some may even consider *Ringo's Rotogravure* as one of his best sleeves in his career. John Kosh designed it. "Ringo loved to constantly roll the printers' term 'rotogravure' around for no other reason than that. So it became the album title," Kosh reported to me via an email. "It was my idea to have David Alexander shoot that stunning studio portrait in black and white. We always had a box of props and toys in the studio. Ringo chose a cheap plastic magnifying glass and there you have it. Atlantic slipped one into the package for the first run in the States. The desecrated Apple door was Ritchie's idea."

The album was a gatefold sleeve, with an accompanying lyric sheet. Each person who played on or worked on the album had their photo in the gatefold, each posing with a piece of food. "I was handed a stack of Polaroids for the gatefold and decided to make a checker board of them," said Kosh. The only exception was a photo of Ringo's three children, although that photo did not appear in the UK pressing, and was replaced with a photo of Ringo.

In the 28 August 1976 issue of *Billboard*, there is an article that makes it clear that Polydor and Starr were ready and willing to promote the album. Once again, they refer to the album as *Ringo's Rotogravure (A Passing Picture Show)*. The article does discuss the magnifying glasses and states they will be included in album and tape copies. However, "Deluxe glasses engraved with the album's title will be distributed to disk jockeys and journalists while special magnifying glasses will be available to the trade for window displays. Additional promotion aids include a poster, silver star giveaway, T-shirts, plus a taped radio interview and tv promotion film featuring three tracks which are regarded as possible singles." The article is also clear that "Starr himself will be actively involved in promoting the album, with tv appearances in France, Italy, Germany, Holland and Scandinavia on a European trek, before flying to Japan."

According to Hales, Starr paid for and produced all three promotional films, and Polydor had no creative input to the album (and future Polydor releases). It was reported that Ringo was making a 45 minute film, *Ringo's Songs*, to be released with the album. The film never materialised.

But he did note that Starr was extremely co-operative with promoting the album. "We got to work on it straight away. I took Ringo on a promotional tour. We flew around Germany, France, Italy and Japan. At some point during the tour, it may have been prior to going to Japan, he shaved his head for some reason and he turned up completely bald. He was wearing a white suit, top hat and all sorts of stuff in Japan, and they went crazy over there for him. From the company's perspective, it put us on the map. A bit more than we were previously."

Japan turned out to be a very interesting experience for Hales and Starr. Hales remembered, "He was the first Beatle to go back to Japan. The reaction was sensational. It was unbelievable. We were at the hotel and walking through the corridors to go to this big press reception. They had done this giant ice carving of his name and all sorts of stuff. A group of us, we were just walking in the corridor, and turned the corner, and there were four teenage girls in front of us who fainted en masse in front of him. It was unbelievable to watch, but Ringo just takes things in his stride." In Japan, the promo albums also included a four page booklet titled 'We Love Ringo Starr'.

While in Japan, Ringo did some unusual recording for a rather unique and unexpected project. Hales remembered that while in Japan, "We were together for a week or so, and he went to Osaka to do a TV commercial and I went on to Australia for business." It was more than one commercial. The television commercials were for a new line of suits from Japan's Simple Life. Ringo filmed four different television commercials and recorded four different songs. The song 'I Love My Suit' features Monkees member Davy Jones and Harry Nilsson. Jones was already in Japan, as he found a great deal of success as a solo artist touring the country. Nilsson was with Ringo. The commercials were never shown outside of Japan and Starr never released the songs on any album. The commercials hit the airwaves in 1977. Jones actually released a version of the song, with Starr on lead vocals, as part of his *Lost And Found Rarities Vol. 2* collection that was available as a download from his website in the 1990s.

Ringo's Rotogravure had a great deal riding on it. The expectations were very high for Starr's first studio album in two years. In the 1970s, two years between albums was not commonplace. It was often thought that fans have a short attention span, so there should not be a lot of time between albums. Not to mention that he had just signed a new record deal. He wanted to provide both labels with a best selling album.

Ringo's Rotogravure received good reviews and *Billboard* seemed to think it was destined to be a very popular album. "At long last, a new LP by this former Beatle. As usual, the wit and wisdom of Starr play the commanding role in the success of this effort. His ability to adapt songs to his whimsical style, especially rock 'n' roll, are what makes him a superstar on his own." The writer noted the special guests and referred to the album as a winner. Mardin received warranted praise as well. "Producer Arif Mardin deserves special mention for his outstanding work in bringing out the talents of this musician. As usual the release of an LP by a former Beatle is a major event. This is Starr's initial album at Atlantic so expect a big push from the label" (*Billboard* 9 October 1976).

Cash Box (9 October 1976) equally thought the album would be very popular. "Ringo's much anticipated debut Atlantic LP is as good as promised." Further, it was noted: "Ringo's right in the middle, his distinctive voice wrapped around some great new pop tunes. He's co-writer on a number of them; old friends Harrison, Lennon, and McCartney wrote him one each. Ringo's always had great success with singles; this LP looks to match or better those achievements. A great package will lend itself to a prominent display."

The other reviews were not bad. Billy Altman, writing in *Rolling Stone*, wrote: "it is a pleasant outing." *Melody Maker's* headline was "Jolly nice, Ringo", calling it a "pleasing album."

But the album did not do as well as hoped. It peaked at number 28 on *Billboard's* Top 200 (it did even worse on *Cash Box*, peaking at number 56), and did not chart in the UK. However, it did well throughout Europe, even making the top ten in Austria. In Canada's *RPM* Top 100, the album peaked at a disappointing number 35.

Mike Hales said, on reflection: "The end result wasn't that great, because the album didn't sell that well but it was at a point that the label needed some big names. Ringo filled the bill very well. But it didn't do well in England. I don't want to put it down, the whole exercise was a huge benefit to both parties. We gave him a huge promotional push which was a huge benefit to him and he helped us by being on the label."

Starr ended the year by participating in *The Last Waltz*, The Band's (unintended) farewell concert. Ringo played drums on one song ('I Shall Be Released', which is on the original album) and participated in the all star jam at the end of the concert. The songs performed were titled 'Jam 1' and 'Jam 2' and later released on later box sets of the album. The show took place on 25 November 1976 (Thanksgiving Day) and artists who performed with The Band during their career took part. Of course, The Band helped Starr on *Ringo* and Robertson guested on *Goodnight Vienna*. The album and film of the concert would not be released until 1978.

8

1977

As 1976 turned over to 1977, Starr was once again in the position of promoting his most recent album with a second single from that release. Starr bridged 1976 to 1977 with a single from his then most recent album, *Ringo's Rotogravure*. However, unlike singles in previous years, 'Hey Baby' was not the success that Starr or Atlantic/Polydor had hoped it would be. *Ringo's Rotogravure* did not achieve the success of *Ringo* or *Goodnight Vienna*, and the single 'Hey Baby' did very little to resurrect interest in the album. Both labels were a bit concerned about their new signing. Starr was concerned as well. For Starr it was a choice between going back to the old formula or trying something new.

There were other changes in the music industry, especially with Polydor Records. The method for promoting albums had changed in Europe and the UK by 1977. This affected the way *Ringo The 4th* would be advertised throughout the continent, the UK and Ireland. Instead of all of the promotion coming out of one head office, as it had been with *Ringo's Rotogravure*, each territory/country was now responsible for promoting records in their areas. This explains the numerous variations of singles from *Ringo The 4th* and even *Bad Boy*, released in 1978. To a certain extent, this was happening in 1976 when different singles were released in different countries, but it was more evident in 1977.

Starr got caught in the crossfire in Europe and the UK when different territories took over promotion. There was not the effort put into *Ringo The 4th* as there was with *Ringo's Rotogravure*. As a result, *Ringo The 4th* never had the same chance as *Ringo's Rotogravure*, which led it to selling fewer copies. This was not due to the quality of the music.

In speaking with the author, Mike Hales remembered: "There was a big push on *Rotogravure*, but then it was up to the individual territories to do what they felt was right for the follow up releases and perhaps they just didn't have quite the same enthusiasm without him being in the country."

Mike Hales, who was responsible for promotion of music with Polydor, explained that each country would be responsible for the promotion of the new releases from an artist, including print ads, and air time on national or regional radio. The idea of regional advertising works much better for artists who are touring. As an artist comes into each territory, they are able to promote the album, and plug their latest single on radio interviews. Because Starr was not touring, he did not have this advantage, so he tried to use interviews, press conferences and promotional films for the singles. To be clear, Starr had no intention of touring. During an interview on Australian television in 1976, to promote *Ringo's Rotogravure*, he did float the idea of what would become his All-Starr tours, where he would bring together a superstar band and share centre stage with others. But by 1977, he was occupied with other artistic endeavours.

Yet 1977 would prove very busy for Starr. Along with *Ringo The 4th*, he appeared in a film, had a big role on a children's album, recorded with friends, resurrected Ring O' Records and made promo films for singles from his forthcoming album. However, with all those projects, none of these releases met with the success and attention of his 1970s commercial peak of 1973 through to 1975. The music world had shifted a great deal since 1975, and a 'name' was no longer enough to sell a record or even guarantee airtime on radio. Starr, and some of his fellow artists from the 1960s and early 1970s, were finding it difficult to successfully keep up with the times. This wasn't because his music was poor, it was simply because the music business was changing.

In December 1976, Ringo Starr started filming *Sextette*, a film that was adapted from a 1961 stage production by Mae West, who also starred in the film. *Variety* wrote many articles about the filming of the movie, which starred West, Timothy Dalton, Dom DeLuise, Tony Curtis, Keith Moon, Alice Cooper, Van McCoy and Ringo Starr. The film was big news, as it was West's 'big comeback'. In the 28 March 1977 issue of *Variety*, it was announced that the film was completed. The problem was, however, the producers could not find a film company to distribute it. The studio originally backing the film withdrew, and it was produced as an independent film. *Sextette* would linger until it was released in March of 1978.

But the fact that he took this role, following his part in *Lisztomania*, demonstrates that Starr was still expanding his acting resumé and trying new things. With *Sextette*, Starr tried something different from previous films. Even though the film would not be as good as anyone hoped, it did give Starr a chance to act in a romantic comedy, something he had never done up to that point. In many ways Starr's film career was similar to his recorded music. From his first solo role in 1968 in the comedy *Candy* (playing an obsessed gardener) and the socio-comedy of *The Magic Christian* (1969), Starr played Frank Zappa (*200 Motels*), a 1950s Teddy Boy (1973's *That'll Be The Day*), Merlin The Magician (*Son Of Dracula*) and the Pope (*Lisztomania*), produced films about nature and directed a documentary about a rock star (*Born To Boogie*). He took great care with his acting and film career.

In August, Starr filmed sequences for another film that would not be released until May 1979. Starr joined Keith Moon in Moon's home near London to film interview sequences for The Who documentary *The Kids Are Alright*. The humorous conversation is spread throughout the film. Starr also took time to record radio commercials and film trailers for the film. The radio ads were pressed on vinyl and sent to radio stations, and are now highly sought after collector items.

Starr had been friends with Moon for many years, and the two had great rapport. Starr's voiceovers and appearances in the trailers were amusing and perfect. It was great seeing Starr with Moon, after he had worked on Moon's solo album.

In the recording world, Starr also found time to help out a couple of old friends, George Harrison and Jim Keltner. Never one to hold a grudge, even though, according to Keith Badman in his book *The Beatles: After the Break-Up 1970-2000 : A Day-By-Day Diary*, Harrison had threatened to sue him over 'I'll Still Love You', Starr made a guest appearance on Attitudes' second and last album, *Good News*. Keltner was the drummer for the band, which included David Foster, Danny Kortchmar and Paul Stallworth. *Good News* was released on Harrison's Dark Horse Records on 5 May 1977 (US) and 3 June 1977 (UK). Even with Starr drumming on the title track, the album did not get much attention and failed to chart on either side of the Atlantic. 'Good News' did appear on the flipside of the single 'In A Stranger's Arms', which also failed to chart. Following the release of this album, Warner Brothers, who distributed Dark Horse Records, dropped the band from their label. They split shortly after the album's release.

Starr also made an appearance with a new group, The Alpha Band, which featured T Bone Burnett. Starr worked on The Alpha Band's second album, *Spark In The Dark*. The pair met during the recording and stayed in touch ever since. Starr is featured on two tracks, 'Born In Captivity' and 'You Angel You'. "We bonded as friends in the 70s. I was a resident in LA for a while and I had a lot of parties and any party I had, he was there. And I did not invite him once," laughed Starr. Starr recalled in 2025: "We got to know each other a little bit, and that's how this album came about. Olivia [Harrison] was reading *Poems For George* at the Sunset Marquis Hotel and I was there, and he was there. I love the man." Burnett would write and produce (for the most part) Starr's very successful country album, *Look Up,* in 2024 (released in 2025).

At this time, Starr was also getting his own label up and running again. It had lain dormant for one year. After failing to secure a distributor, Starr re-signed the label to Polydor Records in the UK and Phonogram for Europe and the world, excluding North America. Starr never made a deal with any record company to distribute Ring O' Records in North America.

According to *Record Mirror*, Ring O' Records had signed a new deal with Polydor Records and the label would be marketing and distributing records. Mike Hales, who at this stage had the title of 'director of popular music for Polydor International', was quoted: "We are delighted to renew our association with Ringo's label, which after a slight false start last year now has a manager in whom we have the greatest confidence." That person was New Zealand born Terry Condon. He had been with Polydor for over ten years at this point, in New Zealand. He was promoted to working in their Hamburg office and eventually, before taking on Ring O' Records, was the A&R manager in Polydor's London office. Hales further added that the label would be "aiming to develop new artists, concentrating on up to five of them in its first year." (*Record Mirror* 28 May 1977)

In an interview with Paul Gambaccini in 1976, while Ring O' Records was on pause, Starr said, "I wound up going to all these meetings. It was exactly like Apple, but it only took me a year to realise I was getting nutsy and there was nothing happening." He also added, "So, we are trying to get a new structure for the record company. It will probably start again next year.

Writing in *Cash Box* in the 27 August 1977 issue, Elizabeth Rod quoted Condon at the time: "Ringo himself is certainly interested in the company's progress, but otherwise has no active participation in it. His record contract is with Polydor - not us. We don't want the reputation of being Ringo's plaything and being held up and sustained by his record sales." It was clear that although this was Starr's label, it was not a vanity project. He also wanted draw a very clear line between Starr's music and the Ring O' Records artists.

In the same interview, Condon also discussed that fact that Ring O' Records was going to focus on the UK. "The label has always been UK-based," said Condon, "and my job is to find UK talent for worldwide exploitation." Condon felt the best plan of action was to sign artists and focus on singles. Condon explained that Ring O' Records could gain a reputation as an artist-oriented label, and this could only be achieved through singles. It was also an easier way for the label to establish itself financially. Condon said at the time: "I'm not anti-album, of course, but one of our artists, Rab Noakes, summed it up very well. He recorded albums for A&M and WEA before coming to us, and I was willing to go straight for an album with him. But, as he said, if you can't break with a single, how can you expect to break with an album? I want to see a flow of good products but not too much. It won't necessarily be limited to singles initially from artists. If we're approached with an album concept which seems to have commercial viability over a few months, we'll do it. That's something that can mean prestige for a label." In many ways, Starr and his advisors were looking at the past for the model of a record company/label.

Condon was very open and honest in the interview for *Cash Box*. He explained that Ring O' Records was intended to be "self-contained, and includes Startling Music and Startling Studio. The latter is a 24-track recording operation being built at Ringo Starr's estate at Ascot in Berkshire, where clients will be able to take extended bookings to work on recording projects in peaceful rural surroundings with accommodations available for up to 14 people." Although the studio had been used, the new Startling Studio was scheduled to officially open in September. Condon was very clear that the facilities are exclusively for Ring O' Records purposes until Christmas, after which it would be open to the general public. Of Startling Publishing, on the other hand, he said: "The publishing company will promote writers signed to it, placing their material, and will not be limited merely to artists recording for the label."

The plan seemed not only feasible but quite well thought out. In many ways, Starr was trying to do what Apple attempted, and what George Harrison had been doing with Dark Horse since 1974. Everything could be done in-house, reducing costs and allowing record sales to fund future projects. It was designed to be a cottage industry of sorts, and the business plan was very sound. This plan and method was evident with the next artist who signed to the new Ring O' Records, Graham Bonnet.

Bonnet was a member of the band Marbles, who had a top five hit in the UK with a song composed by the Bee Gees, 'Only One Woman'. He had released a couple of solo singles on RCA before being signed to Ring O' Records. Although his records were quite good, he did not have any hits. He would go on to have success with Rainbow and with his own band, but in 1977, he was a rock singer, who, coincidently, had once auditioned for Rory Storm And The Hurricanes. He didn't pass that audition, but he did succeed with his demo with Ring O' Records.

"Ringo knew of my earlier stuff with The Marbles," recalled Graham Bonnet. "It was a foot in the door, so to speak. Somebody from the office knew Ringo really well, and all of the guys I worked with all knew him. The deal came up, which was great. So, I went to John Lennon's house to record, which was kind of cool. Ringo had bought that house, and used the studio in it. I got to go into the bathtub where John Lennon had his bath."

His debut single for Ring O' Records, released on 3 June 1977, was a cover of Bob Dylan's 'It's All Over Now, Baby Blue'. However, the single was released on Mercury Records outside of the UK and a few European countries. It was a shame for Ring O' Records, as the single made it to number three on the Australian national charts. Australia was one of the countries where the single was released on Mercury.

Although this debut single did receive airplay in the UK, and a good review in *Record Mirror*, it failed to chart. Brian Kotz, in *Record Mirror*, wrote: "it's a pretty competent version. I doubt if it'll see the light of day in the charts, but it deserves to." There was little promotion, with the exception of being included in full page advertisements for Polydor releases (there is no mention of Ring O' Records in the advertisement).

Bonnet recalled that he did not get a lot of airplay. "They never played my stuff on the radio in the UK. One time I heard 'It's All Over Now, Baby Blue' on Radio One or whatever it was. The DJ was really horrible. 'That was Graham Bonnet with "It's All Over Now, Baby Blue", it certainly is.' It was a real bummer, and the single bombed, no one liked it, no one wanted to listen to it. It never got any airplay at all. It was very different from the r&b stuff I did with The Marbles, because this was straight rock. In Australia, they played all day."

Less than two months later (12 August 1977), Ring O' Records released his second single for the label, 'Danny', with a cover of the classic 'Rock Island Line' on the flipside. The song 'Danny' was written by Ben Weisman and Fred Wise, and was originally intended for Elvis Presley's film *Kid Creole*. It is best known as a hit by Conway Twitty in 1959.

Again, the single met with little success, although there is evidence that it received airplay. *Music Week* (20 August 1977) wrote that it might be a hit. "Previous single, a reworking of the Dylan song, 'It's All Over Now, Baby Blue', gained considerable airplay. The disc sounds rather laboured although there is a pronounced beat." It only charted in Australia (where, once again, it was released on Mercury Records) and peaked at number 79. Both singles would be collected and released on his debut album.

The album, simply titled *Graham Bonnet*, was released in September 1977, and as with the two singles, it was produced by Pip Williams, known for producing The Moody Blues and Status Quo. It is a well produced rock album. Although an original copy is difficult to find, it has been re-released in several box sets of Bonnet's solo work. Ringo did not play on it, and did not seem to have much to do with the album. Although the album failed to reach the charts in the UK, it did make it to number seven in Australia and number 11 in New Zealand.

"I knew him [Pip Williams] because he was producing Sweet at the time," said Bonnet. "He was working with Colin Blunstone as well. Pip was contacted through the office, and he wanted to produce me because he knew all the old stuff I did with my cousin in The Marbles. Pip was a great producer, a great arranger and a great guitar player. All the stuff you hear on the Sweet records is Pip playing."

The album received very positive reviews throughout England, including in the 17 September 1977 issue of *Music Week*. "He has an extraordinary voice, in range if not in quality and is a professional singer who knows how to get the best out of a song. Bonnet is a singer's singer; his vocal elasticity is admirable, but lends distance. He now needs some down-to-earth numbers with lots of guts and warmth, plus a hit single which 'Danny' does not look like being." Barry Cain, writing for *Record Mirror* (10 September 1977) states: "Oh sure, the guy can sing… Stylish production and a bunch of ace session men too but two sides of cover versions ain't gonna impress anybody. A shame because Bonnet has an undoubted talent. Instead of plumbing for a safe bet he should have taken a gamble. He needs to."

"I am very proud of that album," Bonnet said. "It was my very first solo album and I enjoyed it. I am very proud of that album. I met Ringo at the office, he came up when the album was released. It was really nice to meet him. I wanted to talk to him a little more, because I wanted to talk about not getting the gig with Rory Storm and The Hurricanes. Rory had left the band, and they were looking for a singer and my neighbour had heard me singing. I was 14, and living near Butlin's Holiday Camp. My neighbour was working at Butlin's, and he told Ringo about me, and he asked how old I was, and my neighbour said '14'; Ringo said 'Oh God! That's too young.' One of those weird things. I wanted to say something to him in London, but there were too many people there."

A third single was released from the album in November 1977, 'Goodnight and Good Morning'. It was a cover of a Daryl Hall and John Oates song. "They were really big in England. My manager's wife said how much she loved them. I didn't particularly like them, but I listened again and I heard this song that my manager suggested I cover. And it worked very well."

Rosalind Russell, writing in *Record Mirror* (5 November 1977) said: "Close, but not close enough. The hookline was quite thrilling, the rest qualifies for the great melting pot in the sky." The single failed to chart. Bonnet would have one more release, in 1978, that proved to be very successful for him. The reviewer seems to be on to something; this is an interesting take on a fairly obscure Daryl Hall and John Oates song, and once again, Bonnet gives it his all. Bonnet wrote the B-side, 'Wino

Song', which is featured on his debut album. This is a solid slice of British rock/soul/blues and is enjoyable. Perhaps it may have served Bonnet better if it had been the A-side.

Following the Bonnet releases, Ring O' Records was busy with a reissue of *The Whale*, by John Tavener (originally released on Apple), which does feature a cameo from Ringo Starr. The sleeve design was very different from the Apple release. Gone was the painting of the whale, and now it was a blue-tinged photo of the tail of a whale disappearing into the ocean. The re-release attracted positive notices. Starr obviously loved the album, and given that Tavener was debuting a new opera in 1977, *A Gentle Spirit*, the time seemed right to bring the classic album back to the record store. *The Whale* would be re-released again in 1992 (on Apple) and 2010 (again on Apple). *The Whale* is a highly respected classical piece and Tavener was able to bring new classical works to the forefront. He was knighted in 2000 for his service in music. John Tavener passed away in 2013.

Ring O' Records turned their attention back to Carl Groszmann, who released his second and last single for Ring O' Records on 22 October 1977. 'Face Of A Permanent Stranger', backed with 'Your Own Affair', was poorly promoted, and not released outside of the UK. It failed to chart or attract any attention. Both songs were written by Groszmann. It is not known why he disappeared from the label at this point and it could be that the two songs were actually recorded in 1975 and not released until 1977. One critic in the UK (*The Mail –Millom and South Copeland* ed.) did predict great things for the single and thought it would be a hit for Groszmann. Groszmann did not release any more music after this single.

The song itself is an average 1970s rocker. Although quite good, it just does not stand out from the other pop-rock songs of the time. Groszmann has a good voice and the song would not have been out of place on *Ringo's Rotogravure*. The B-side, 'Your Own Affair', is also a standard rocker that is quite good. What his two singles show is that Groszmann was a terrific writer and good performer. One can only wonder what he would have done with an album. It is sad that his last single did not provide him the attention he justly deserved.

Carl Groszmann passed away in 2018. He never achieved the level of success that he deserved, either as a writer or performer. He was a very gifted artist who had the light shine on him for an all-too-brief time. Groszmann will be remembered for his writing (Status Quo and Ringo Starr) but he was also a talented performer.

Ring O' Records was a very busy label during the latter half of 1977. In November, they released the label's debut single from a new signing,

Suzanne Lynch, who went by the name Suzanne. Born in New Zealand, she became very popular with her sister under the name The Chicks. She soon relocated to the UK and released several solo albums. She also became a very much in-demand session singer. Starr met Suzanne while he was working with Cat Stevens on what would become his *Izitso* album. Starr's contributions did not make it on to the finished album, but Suzanne and her husband/producer worked on the album as well, and Suzanne was soon with Ring O' Records.

Her Ring O' Records debut single, 'Born On Halloween' (written by Russ Ballard, who would work with Starr in the future), was released on 22 October 1977. As with Carl Groszmann, the single was not promoted and received very little attention. It was only released in the UK, with a picture sleeve for radio stations. The picture sleeve did not help draw attention to the single or Suzanne, and it did not chart. She would have more success in 1978. The B-side, 'Like No One Else', was written by the famous keyboardist, songwriter and producer, Carson Whitsett.

The single is actually good. Suzanne's voice is quite pleasant and the production and arrangements for both songs are ideal for her. It is a soft country pop song that should have found some fans.

Local newspapers throughout the UK thought that Suzanne was going to make it big. Writing for *The Mail (Millom and South Copeland ed.)* Bob Eborall was very enthusiastic about Suzanne and her potential to be the next big thing. In his article on 5 November 1977 he wrote "Now 'Born On Halloween' sees the birth of a new solo star on our pop scene". In the Singles Review for *Black Country Evening Mail*, the critic compares her to Olivia Newton-John and thinks that the Russ Ballard song will do well for Suzanne.

After getting Ring O' Records up and running, it was time for Starr to get back to music. With his film work on *Sextette* completed, he could now focus on his next album and later another recording project. His next two projects were complete departures for Starr.

According to Nancy Lee Andrews, Starr (and Andrews) flew to New York City on 9 January 1977 to record *Ringo The 4th*. Andrews wrote in her book *A Dose Of Rock 'n' Roll* that Starr found New York City "conducive for making music". She further noted that "Manhattan had a tempo that gave him a new power to express himself." However, it is likely that the time spent in January was to meet with Arif Mardin and plan the release of the album. Also, it could be that Starr and Poncia scheduled time to prepare for the album by writing the songs.

According to other sources, recording of the album began on 5 February 1977. It appears that Mardin and Starr started work on the album in Los Angeles. Starr entered Cherokee Studios for what would be the second and last album Mardin produced for him. Perhaps due to the relative disappointment with the sales of *Ringo's Rotogravure*, Mardin and Starr decided on a very different direction for the new album. First and foremost, Starr and Vini Poncia wrote all but four songs for the album. And although there were some famous friends (Bette Midler, Luther Vandross, David Foster, Melissa Manchester), the album mainly used very respected session players. Some of Starr's old friends were there, such as Lon Van Eaton (guitar), David Bromberg (guitar) and Danny Kortchmar (guitar) but new names appeared on the album inner sleeve such as Cornell Dupree (guitar) and Dick Fegy (acoustic guitar). Jim Keltner did not help on the album; instead Steve Gadd assisted Starr on drums.

Initially the sessions were not that productive, with the first two songs recorded, 'Lover Please' and 'Wild Shining Stars', remaining unreleased. By the end of February, three tracks had been recorded that ended up on the album *Ringo The Fourth*, 'Out On The Streets', 'It's No Secret' and 'Gypsies In Flight'.

Arif Mardin took Starr out of his comfort zone, and in June moved the sessions to New York City. This would mark Starr's first time recording in the city, using mostly New York City based sessions players. It was the first time since *Beaucoups Of Blues* that the majority of the album was recorded with a small band for all the tracks. Joining Starr were David Spinozza (lead guitar), John Tropea and Jeff Mironov (guitars), Tony Levin (bass), Don Grolnick (keyboards) and Steven Gadd (drums). Arif Mardin assembled top New York City session players and set to work on the album.

According to David Spinozza, "We recorded together, there were no rehearsals. We just went into the studio and ran it. No rehearsals. You go into the studio, Arif would come in with the charts, sometimes single notes are written, sometimes it is just a musical sketch. Ringo would sing the song, or play this. Hey, what was that? Let's use it as the intro."

For the most part, Spinozza remembers the sessions as pleasant and quick. "I think it was about a week, maybe a week and a half. We are pretty fast in New York. In a three hour session, we tried to get two or three songs done. You get ten songs done pretty quickly, the basic tracks. The overdubs would come later. But we started with guitar, bass, drums, keyboards. It was pretty smooth. One thing I do remember, when there were playbacks, we didn't go into the booth, control room. We stayed out in the studio."

Spinozza noted that there were overdubs, horns, and other keyboards following the main sessions, although he was not part of those. But still, the album was completed very quickly. The song 'Just A Dream', which was used as a B-side for the two singles released in North America, was also recorded during these sessions.

According to both Spinozza and Nancy Lee Andrews, it seemed Starr was out of his element in New York City, playing with session players. Spinozza remembered that it "felt like he resented playing with studio guys. I thought he felt that we were put upon him. I remember thinking he would be more comfortable with the guys he plays with. None of us really knew him. We were New York guys. I felt he was that uncomfortable. It was a little uncomfortable, he didn't seem to be enjoying it very much. I talked to a couple of guys later and maybe it wasn't the right mix. I think he preferred working with rock and roll stars. Studio guys are a whole different breed. But the studio guys approach it very differently. We are not rock stars."

Andrews agreed, noting that his last three studio albums were recorded (for the most part) in Los Angeles. "From *Ringo* to *Goodnight Vienna* to *Rotogravure*, and we got to New York and it changed. It all changed. I think he felt he was losing control of the content and for what he was trying to do with his music. At one point, Arif even had him doing some disco, and he is not that."

Spinozza had not met Starr prior to the recording. "It was at Atlantic studios. I got the call from Arif, because I worked with Arif a lot. Different records he produced or co-produced. He probably called me, I didn't know Ringo. It was the first time I met him and the first time I worked with him. I had done the [John Lennon] *Mind Games* album and I had done [Paul McCartney] *Ram*, maybe they sent me. They could have sent me. But it was more likely Arif, because I worked with him a lot. But I never met Ringo when I worked on *Mind Games* or *Ram*."

Recording in New York City wrapped up by the end of June. One track known to have been recorded and still unreleased is 'By Your Side'. David Spinozza has no memory of the song. Starr returned to Cherokee Studios for further overdubs and orchestration and recorded more songs that have not seen the light of day: 'Birmingham', 'This Party' and a different version of 'Just a Dream'.

'Wings', the first single from *Ringo The 4th*, was released on 25 August 1977. *Billboard* listed it as a recommended single in their 27 August 1977 issue, but there was no review. *Cash Box*, on the other hand, did review the single and spoke in glowing terms. "This taste of a forthcoming album indicates that things really clicked among Ringo, co-writer Vini Poncia and producer Arif Mardin. The haunting melody is carried by a closely knit ensemble of vocalists, and supported by a richly textured horn section and stabbing guitars...this record definitely has that pop appeal."

Record World (10 September 1977) reviewed 'Wings' and also gave it a very positive nod. "This preview of a new Ringo LP finds him in a more thoughtful mood than usual, but the thumping drums and added horns help build the song's energy to a powerful finish. His voice responds well, too." Very high praise for the single.

In the 17 September 1977 issue of *Record Mirror*, it was announced that Ringo Starr was to release his new single "…'Wings' as his first American single from his upcoming *Ringo The Fourth* album." *Cash Box* announced the single (and an upcoming two hour radio special for *King Biscuit Flower Hour*) on 3 September 1977. That same week, *Cash Box* noted that a few stations across America were adding the single.

Although the single received some healthy airtime upon initial release, the radio play died quickly, and the single did not chart anywhere in the world. Polydor, in the UK, passed on the single, and waited for the second single, 'Drowning In The Sea Of Love'. 'Wings' was released in America, Canada, Japan and Ireland. Japan had a special picture sleeve. In the US, a promo single was released to radio stations, featuring the standard stereo mix and a mono mix for AM radio. But there was little promotion otherwise. Starr didn't appear on any shows, or make himself available to radio stations.

'Wings' is an interesting song and a departure for Ringo. It is a slow burning rocker with stellar playing from the session musicians as well as solid drumming from Ringo (and Gadd). It has a bluesy overtone and great horn arrangement. It is a song that Ringo holds in high regard, as he re-recorded the song for his 2012 album *Ringo 2012*. Starr also released a live version (with The All-Starrs) on the 2012 charity album *Songs After Sandy: Friends of Red Hook for Sandy Relief*, a benefit album in the aftermath of Hurricane Sandy.

The song clearly demonstrates that Starr was trying to adapt and move with the times. This song would not have fitted on any of his previous three albums. It is a song of its time and certainly, in hindsight, deserved a much better fate. The week that 'Wings' was released in North America, Starr had to compete with Elvis Presley's death (he passed away on August 16) and interesting new singles by the likes of Captain and Tennille ('Circles') and a new single from Peter Frampton ('Signed, Sealed and Delivered (I'm Yours)'), and The Spinners ('Heaven On Earth (So Fine)'). While easy listening (James Taylor, Rita Coolidge) and disco dominated the top ten (Andy Gibb, Emotions), 'Wings' did not fit easily into either category, so it can be assumed that radio programmers getting new Captain and Tennile and Peter Frampton might favour those tracks over a slow rocker.

The song features the core studio players for the album, but also features some familiar names singing back-up. Luther Vandross, Lynn Pitney, Marietta Waters, Maxine Anderson, Melissa Manchester, Rebecca Louis, Robin Clark, and Vini Poncia all lent their voices to the song. Playing on the song, and for the majority of the album, are David Spinozza, John Tropea, Jeff Mironov on guitar; Don Grolnick (keyboards) and Ken Bichel (synthesiser); Tony Levin (bass); Starr and Steve Gadd on drums. These players are used throughout *Ringo The 4th*.

The B-side for this single (and 'Drowning In The Sea Of Love') is a non-album song, 'Just A Dream'. It's a remarkably strong song, with one foot in disco and the other in pop. It is melodic and would have fitted nicely on *Ringo The 4th*, although as a non-album bonus cut it is a welcome addition to Starr's discography. It could be argued that the song could have been an A-side. It was his first non-album B-side single since 1973's 'Down And Out'. 'Just A Dream' features the same musicians as 'Wings'.

Variety announced in their 31 August 1977 issue that to coincide with the release of the 'Wings' single and upcoming album, "Some 250 radio stations are airing a DIR Broadcasting two-hour Starr radio special, Sunday (4), to coincide with the album's release…" DIR stood for Designs In Radio and were responsible for such radio shows as *King Biscuit Flower Hour* and *Conversations With*. The show ran on 29 August 1977 as *Innerview*.

During the interview, Starr was quite candid with interviewer Bill Minkin about his desire to be number one as a solo artist and how proud he was of *Ringo The 4th*, given that he had co-written over half of the album. "This new one, *Ringo the 4th*, it's us knowing each other better and me coming to New York, which was most amazing because I hadn't been for four years. To be thrown into the middle of this band where I didn't know any of the players. I hadn't played with any of them… There's a lot of adrenaline in New York. New York is totally different from LA, as everyone knows."

Starr was equally open about his hopes for the two singles from *Ringo The 4th*. "It was a single. We've got other singles on there. One is 'Wings', which stands a good chance, I feel. It's one Vini and I wrote. We had the meeting at Atlantic and they're saying you've got to push the album and all that. The economics of the situation."

'Wings' was one of six songs included on the album *Ringo The 4th* written by Starr and Vini Poncia. They also wrote 'Just A Dream', which was not included on the album but did serve as a B-side twice. The fact that he co-wrote the material indicates that the album was very serious for Starr. This was the first album in which the majority of the songs were co-written by him. He was not relying on other writers, friends or oldies to make an album, and in many ways this was very refreshing. Starr and Poncia's songs are melodic and Mardin did a great job producing and arranging them. If Starr was out of his comfort zone, it does not come across in the music.

Ringo The 4th is often referred to as Ringo's disco album, but this is really not the case. Nor does it do the album justice. There are a couple of disco flavoured songs on the album, but it is much more interesting and diverse than 'just a disco album'. Songs like 'It's Not Secret' are very much middle of the road, easy listening pop rock, as is the lovely 'Gypsies In Flight'. It is another straight ahead pop song. Starr's vocals are robust throughout and the playing is top of the line. Lyrically, these are love songs, no doubt inspired by Nancy Lee Andrews, and pure romantic escape. The songs are catchy and stay with the listener long after the record is over. Songs like 'Simple Love Song', which ends the album, may have a disco flare, especially with the strings, but this song is much more of a pop song, and may have made a better debut single to represent the album.

'Out On The Streets' and 'Gave It All Up' show different musical and lyrical sides to Ringo. He is obviously using his own past to create stories for the songs. 'Out On The Streets' also features a rather odd ending of Starr talking about being mugged. If he was trying to show his tough side, it may not have come off as planned. Still, there is an interesting use of sound effects and Mardin and Starr certainly created a very different sounding Ringo Starr song. Collectors might take note that the first CD issue of *Ringo The 4th* features a noticeably longer ending with more of the street dialogue.

'Gave It All Up' is a rather personal and introspective song from Starr. It is a buried gem that has a great melody, and emotional vocals from Ringo. The choral backing vocals and strings add an element of drama to the song and lyrically it appears to be somewhat autobiographical for Starr (and perhaps Poncia). One thing is certain, Starr was being honest at points throughout the song and it stands as one of his most interesting and underrated. It is also an example of just how great a songwriter Starr had become.

Of the covers, one was a hit from 1972, when Joe Simon took the Kenny Gamble and Leon Huff song 'Drowning In The Sea Of Love' into the top 20 in America. It is a song that must have stuck with Starr or Mardin. But Ringo's version is mighty. It is the song that most people point to as an example of disco songs being on the album. 'Can She Do It Like She Dances', on the other hand, was originally released by King Floyd in 1976 and was written by songwriters Steve Duboff and Gerry

Robinson. It was not a hit upon its original release. Former Monkee Davy Jones (who sang with Starr on his Japanese commercials) recorded a much more disco flavoured version of the song in 1981. He released it as a single in Japan and changed the title to 'Can She Do It (Like She Dances)'.

'Tango All Night' was written by Steve Hague and Tom Seufert. It was originally released in 1976 by La Seine. 'Tango All Night' was released as a single in Argentina (with 'It's Not Secret') on the B-side. As Mike Hales had said, each territory was promoting the album on their own, and in Argentina, it was felt that this Latin flavoured song would be a hit. Finally, the last cover on the album is 'Sneaking Sally Through The Alley', a song written by Allen Toussaint (with whom Ringo worked on *Goodnight Vienna* and whose song 'Occapella' Starr covered). 'Sneaking Sally Through the Alley' had been a minor hit for Robert Palmer in 1974 (although he titled the song 'Sneakin' Sally Through the Alley').

Once again, John Kosh designed the sleeve for *Ringo The 4th*. Starr did like to work with people with whom he had a relationship and who he trusted. He had known Kosh since Kosh worked for The Beatles and Apple, so Starr trusted his sleeve designs to Kosh.

The title itself remains somewhat of a mystery. The 4th could refer to Ringo being the fourth Beatle to join the band, or it could refer to the notion that it was his fourth 'rock' album. Andrews is certain that it is the latter. However, *Ringo The 4th* did have a memorable sleeve. According to John Kosh, "Again, Ringo walked in with a box of slides. We decided which shots should be cropped tight for the front and the back."

Andrews wrote in her book that Starr had said "It sounds medieval! Get me a sword!" Andrews' friend from Tulsa, a model by the name of Rita Wolf, was the woman sitting on Starr's shoulders for the cover. It was Andrews' first album cover, although she had been taking photos for years.

"We were in New York, we were at the Plaza hotel," remembered Nancy Lee Andrews. "I always had time on my own when he was recording. My girlfriend, Rita, from Tulsa, Ringo loved her. We were sitting there having lunch in the room, and I said, 'what do you want to do for the album cover?' I didn't think I was going to take it. And he said 'I don't know, I don't know. It is my fourth album.' And Rita said, why don't you call it *Ringo The 4th*, and he went 'Yeah! Let's go medieval.' I said, 'Chainmail, sword, what are we talking about?' And he said, 'Get me all of it and we will see what happens.'

"So I went down to a prop house, with my girlfriend Cherry Vanilla [Kathy Dorritie], who knew everybody in Manhattan, and I got all the props, chainmail, sword, and we went back to the hotel. There was a huge walk-in closet, which someone would call a bedroom. It was empty. I dressed him up, put him on the waste basket, on top of a pillow. So I said, 'Let's put Rita in some underwear on your shoulders.' He said 'Yeah' and that's how it happened. She is hanging on the bar on his shoulders and he is saying 'Oh my God, my ass is killing me.' This is when it was so much fun, the creativity flowed."

Starr not only had fun when Andrews was behind the camera, but he trusted her, and for three albums they worked together. She assisted him with photos and design.

"He knew my photography, and he trusted me. I had been taking pictures for years. And we were such posers for each other all over the world. He knew I knew my lighting. It worked out."

The album entered the *Billboard* Top 200 on 15 October 1977 at number 179. It would eventually peak four weeks later at number 162 and drop off the charts after only six weeks. On the *Cash Box* Top 200, it peaked at 194 (5 November 1977). It did a bit better in Canada, peaking at 94 on the *RPM* Top 100 (5 November 1977 after only two weeks in the top 100) and in Australia it made it to number 65. The week that *Ringo The 4th* peaked on *Billboard*, the top five albums were Fleetwood Mac (*Rumours*), Linda Ronstadt (*Simple Dreams*), Steely Dan (*Aja*, engineered by Bill Schnee), Foreigner and The Rolling Stones (*Love You Live*).

Ringo The 4th was the only studio album by one of The Beatles in 1977. Paul McCartney and Wings went to number one in 1977 with *Wings Over America*, and The Beatles made it to number two with *Live At The Hollywood Bowl* (it went to number one in the UK). The Beatles would score a second gold album in 1977 with the successful *Love Songs*. The *Live At The Star Club,1962* double album did not do as well, but perhaps the overall sound of that album lost sales. But it serves as an historic document.

In the UK, Wings would score a huge hit with 'Mull Of Kintyre', which would take over from 'She Loves You' as the largest selling single in the UK.

For some reason Starr's album just did not connect with record buyers. Initially it received positive response from radio, but that fell off very quickly. The well produced album certainly deserved a much better fate, and over the years the album has been re-evaluated positively.

The music trade papers were very positive about the album at the time. In the *Billboard* Album Reviews for 1 October 1977, the reviewer noted that *Ringo The 4th* "is a polished exercise in the fundamentals of basic rock 'n' roll. Included are rockers, ballads and even a tango that all reflect Ringo's often comic vocal intonations." The reviewer also noted that six of the ten tracks were co-written by Starr, showcasing "his innate sense for mainstream good time rock." On the same date, *Record World* reviewed the album, stating: "Six of the 10 tracks here are Ringo-Vini Poncia originals, perhaps signalling a move to more independence for the affable Starr. His own 'Wings' and 'Out On The Streets' stand out." They note that it is geared for FM radio play and complimented the covers. *Cash Box*'s review for the album is somewhat less focused but did make it clear that "Ringo is having a great time here as he lends his distinctive vocals and his pounding drum kit to a set that a number of his more instantly recognizable friends contributed substantially toward." Interestingly, the word 'disco' is never mentioned.

Variety even gave the album a good review, predicting great things for it. The critic stated that it "is a bright rock program that should continue the sales success he's had since the Beatles breakup. Excellent support musicians and backup vocalists contribute to the appeal of this Arif Mardin production." Once again, there is no mention of 'disco'.

In the UK, critics were not as kind. In *Music Week* (8 October 1977), the reviewer referred to the album as "funk" but added that "Frankly, it does not come off." The reviewer is quite critical of his cover versions ("just do not sound right") but wrote: "The most successful song is a Starkey composition, which sounds like something like a personal statement, 'Gave It All Up For You'. It is restrained and within his capabilities." Sheila Prophet, writing in *Record Mirror,* is much harsher. "The vocals are as flat and strained as ever, the material as uninspired. A couple of tracks might make it as singles." She notes that his cover of 'Sneaking Sally Through The Alley' might be a hit, and once again, one of his compositions is singled out: " 'Out On The Streets' complete with outside broadcast sound effects is a jolly little romp." But she was clear that there is "not enough to justify a whole album."

Starr later said, "I'm very happy with it. This album, more than *Rotogravure*. I think it's stronger because Vini and I wrote six tracks. I know those songs better." Some critics agreed that this was a chance for Starr to demonstrate his writing abilities. The critic for *Retford, Gainsborough and Worksop Times* (14 October 1977) gave *Ringo The 4th* a positive review and complimented Starr on his writing. The critic for *Widnes Weekly News* (28 October 1977) wrote "an excellent showcase for Ringo's writing abilities." Steve Grimsby, writing for *Grimsby Evening Telegraph* (3 December 1977) wrote "not bad work, with perhaps 'Wings' being the most memorable."

Although the album did not sell very well, it is an album of which Starr should be very proud. The album is full of strong songs, great production and perfect musicianship. Songs such as 'Simple Love Song', 'Gypsies In Flight' and 'It's No Secret' are excellent slices of pop music. One wonders if 'It's No Secret' may have been a better choice for the first single from the album. Elsewhere Starr looks back on his life and constructs creative and imaginative semi-autobiographical songs. And then there is 'Wings', a lost gem. It is no surprise the Starr returned to it years later. It is a brilliant song. Starr had one more album with Poncia, but their songwriting partnership, perhaps, never reached its full potential. Had *Ringo's Rotogravure* been more successful, perhaps *Ringo The 4th* would have been much more embraced by the rock world.

The UK got their first single from the album on 16 September 1977 when 'Drowning In The Seas of Love' was released with 'Just A Dream' on the B-side. The same single was released in North America on 18 October 1977. *Billboard* listed it as a recommended single in their 29 October 1977 issue. *Cash Box* was much kinder and reviewed the single in their Singles Review - Picks Of The Week. The review was simple but positive. "Ringo has long been respected for the strength of his cover versions, and this selection from *Ringo The 4th* continues the tradition. The Gamble & Huff song, previously recorded by Joe Simon, is perfectly complemented by the production talents of Arif Mardin."

The single version of the song released in the UK is the American radio edit. In the US, a promo single was sent out to radio featuring the long (album) version and a radio edit. A twelve inch 'Disco' single was also sent to radio stations, with the album version on both sides.

Once again, the UK music press either ignored the single or gave it a bad review. In the 17 September issue of *Record Mirror*, Rosalind Russell wrote that 'Drowning In The Sea Of Love' is a "naff song" and, in her opinion, it would not be a hit. She also wrote that the single "hasn't made up its mind what it wants to be… starts off like Golden Earring, goes into funk, flirts with disco (with girly backing), wallops through film theme land à la *The Magnificent Seven*... and finally consummates with a string section. It's pretty bad." Colin Gay, writing for *The Bolton News*, said: "I am disappointed with Ringo Starr's new single…Joe Simon's classic is treated badly."

It was the only song on the album for which a promo film was shot. It aired initially in France. The promo film seems to have been filmed in France, complete with shots of Ringo wandering through a casino. One person did achieve a moment of fame from the music video. The *Huddersfield Daily Examiner* wrote an article about a famous resident,

Rowena Michelle (25 August 1977). She had just returned from Monte Carlo where she "played a miming mermaid" for the promotional film.

It should also be noted that two other singles were released from the album. In Australia, 'Sneaking Sally Through The Alley' was issued as a single with 'Tango All Night' on the flip. 'Tango All Night' was given the A-side treatment in Argentina with 'It's No Secret' on the B-side. Neither single charted in their respective countries and, as with 'Drowning In The Sea Of Love', did very little in resurrecting any interest in the album.

As *Ringo The 4th* was trying to find an audience, Polydor was getting set to release an album which featured Starr in a key role. Actor Donald Pleasence wrote a book, which was published in 1977, titled *Scouse The Mouse*. It was illustrated by Gerald Potterton. Pleasence, at the time, was best known as an actor in the UK, usually playing villains. Some of his notable roles up to 1977 included Flight Lieutenant Colin Blythe in *The Great Escape* (1963), the villain Ernst Stavro Blofeld in the James Bond film *You Only Live Twice* (1967), SEN 5241 in *THX 1138* (1971), and the damaged Clarence 'Doc' Tydon in *Wake in Fright* (1971). A cute story about a Liverpool mouse who wants to make it as a singer in New York City seemed odd coming from him.

Pleasance also played the heavy in the 1978 film *Sgt. Pepper's Lonely Hearts Club Band*, as B.D. Hoffler or B.D. Brockhurst, the owner of the evil record company.

The book came from stories he used to tell his daughter at bedtime, and he decided to write the stories down. He told reporter Phillip Key that he named the character Scouse because "Scouse rhymed with mouse, or mouse rhymes with Scouse. I can't remember which, although I have been to Liverpool." The book was published by the New English Library.

The idea was to turn the much loved children's book into an animated children's special with several guests voicing the various parts of the story. Due to a strike at the time, the animation never came about. However, an album was recorded.

In the 3 December 1977 issue of *Music Week*, it was noted that "Polydor is banking on major sales from the under ten audiences to launch its latest children's album, *Scouse The Mouse* (Polydor 2480 429), which features Ringo Starr, Adam Faith, Barbara Dickson and the story's author, Donald Pleasence." The article also noted that there was some fairly intensive advertising for the album. "Advertising for the LP takes the form of half-page spots in *Look And Learn, Look In, Bunty, Debbie, Jack & Jill, Judy, Mandy, Spellbound* and *Playhour*. These draw attention to the colouring/drawing competition featured on the record's inner sleeve."

Gerald Potterton, who illustrated the book, listened to early demos of the songs for the album, and thought Starr was perfect for Scouse. The word Scouse is a slang term for people from Liverpool. He made the suggestion to Pleasence and Pleasence agreed. Pleasence, reportedly, requested a meeting with Starr and flew to Monaco to meet with him and play him the demos. Pleasence reported that Ringo was instantly hooked and wanted to be part of the project. He was happy to play a mouse from Liverpool with aspirations to go to America to be famous.

The album also included Barbara Dickson (who in 1974 appeared in the London play *John, Paul, George, Ringo... & Bert*), Adam Faith (who had taken over the role of Mike for the sequel to *That'll Be The Day*, and whose 1974 album *I Survive* featured backing vocals from Paul and Linda McCartney), Ben Chatterly, Jim Parker, Donald Pleasence and his daughters Lucy and Polly. Brown noted that the album was basically recorded in London, while Starr's vocals were recorded in Paris. The 30 July 1977 issue of *Music Week* also noted that the majority of the album was recorded at Berwick Studies, but Starr was recorded in Paris. However, according to Keith Badman, Starr recorded the vocals in July 1977 at Berwick Street Studios in London. The album was produced by Hugh Murphy (Gerry Rafferty) and featured Henry Spinetti on drums, who not only drummed for George Harrison and would work with Paul McCartney but was also the younger brother of actor Victor Spinetti (who co-starred with The Beatles in *A Hard Day's Night, Help!* and *The Magical Mystery Tour* films).

Roger Brown, who wrote the majority of the songs for the album, recalled meeting Ringo Starr. "Ringo had a suite at The Ritz in London which was actually bigger than any house I've ever owned. I had to go over there with my guitar and knock on the door and play him the songs so that we could find out what keys to put them in. It's very interesting to knock on a door and the door opens, and there's a Beatle standing there."

Brown further added that:" He was very easy to work with, except one night he went out partying with Eric Clapton and didn't show up the next day."

The album was intended to be the soundtrack for an animated television special of the same name. However, due to labour disputes, the television show was shelved. The Grunwick Dispute, which lasted two years in the UK (1976 - 1978) had a huge impact on the film industry due to the film processing plant walking out.

In 2020, storyboards from the animated show were auctioned off on Ebay, being sold by a person whose father had worked on the show. The storyboards were found in an attic. Since there is no footage of the special, these storyboards are the only remains of the unreleased film. It is a pity, as the film would have no doubt boosted sales for the album.

Scouse The Mouse was warmly received by critics and it was quite novel for rock stars to record an album for children. Once again, like Starr's *Sentimental Journey* or *Beaucoups Of Blues*, he was well ahead of the curve. It would be many years before rock artists such as Jewel, Linda Ronstadt, Lisa Loeb or many others tackled that genre. Paul McCartney may have been one of the first with his version of 'Mary Had A Little Lamb', released by Wings in 1972, but this was a full length album. And although the reviews were positive, it did not parlay into sales. The album was only officially released in the UK (it has been bootlegged the world over) and it failed to chart. It is one of Starr's rarest albums released in the 1970s. Initial copies came with colouring pages for children to enter a contest to win copies of the book.

Ringo does some acting on the record, but it is really the music that is of the utmost interest to fans. 'Living In A Pet Shop' would not have been out of place on *Beaucoups Of Blues*. It is a countryish song, with very interesting backing vocals. Starr's voice is strong and he does sound like he is having fun. 'Scouse's Dream 'is another fun song, with Ringo turning in a convincing vocal, allowing Scouse to dream about being out on his own, and becoming a huge star. This is after he watches the world famous band The Jollys on television, and decides he can do that too. It is also the start of him learning to speak English instead of Animal.

'Running Free 'is about as close to rock and roll as one will get on the album. It is, once again, a fun romp and something that children would clearly enjoy. This is followed by a song from Adam Faith, 'America (A Mouse's Dream)', then Ringo gets to sing about a boat ride ('Boat Ride') and shares a room with the youngest Jolly. He demonstrates his ability to talk (she thinks she is dreaming) and his singing. The band invites him on stage, where he performs the title track, 'Scouse The Mouse'.

Sadly, it is not smooth sailing all the way to America for Souse. After being dropped overboard by a cat, he sends out a distress signal ('SOS', not the ABBA song) and is rescued by a seagull who gets him safely to New York, where he performs the strongest track on the album, 'A Mouse Like Me'. Starr obviously loved the song, as he changed a few words and it became 'A Man Like Me 'on his *Bad Boy* album released in 1978.

Although it did not do well, it did open a door for Ringo, who would be asked in 1984 to narrate the *Thomas The Tank Engine and Friends* television show. This, of course, resulted in him being the star of *Shining*

Time Station from 1989 to 1990. The books and tapes of *Thomas The Tank Engine* have become quite rare and difficult to find.

As 1977 was drawing to a close, Starr was planning for 1978. He had started working on a new album in late 1977 and he was also coming up with an unusual way to promote it, but that would be in 1978. For now, Starr celebrated Christmas with his family and got ready for an interesting 1978.

9

1978 - 1979

Perhaps due to the lack of success of his last two studio albums, Starr focused on his career in 1978. No doubt he was looking for a comeback with his next studio album, and he was more than willing to promote it. Besides interviews, and a tour (which he did not want to launch at this stage of his career), the issue became finding the best way to draw attention to it and getting people going to record stores and buying it. He had said in 1977 that he was considering some personal appearances. Starr told Jim Jerome of *Evening Standard*: "I'm lazy, but I'd like to try it three days a week for a month." That never happened. He also tried to keep Ring O' Records going, which by the end of the year was no longer a viable label.

But this did not mean that he was not willing to help other artists. In fact, he continued to help friends and people whom he admired. Starr was still very much in demand in terms of being a session player and contributing to others' albums.

In January, Lonnie Donegan, the artist who had been such a huge influence on all the Beatles, released a new album, titled *Puttin' on the Style*. The album featured a number of special guests including Rory Gallagher, Elton John, Brian May, Ronnie Wood and Ringo Starr. Starr drummed on two songs, 'Have A Drink On Me (Take A Whiff On Me)' and 'Ham 'n' Eggs'. Donegan was looking for a return to form and his own comeback. Sadly, this was not the album to put Donegan back in the charts. It did receive some positive reviews, but even with the all star cast, it failed to do well, not cracking the charts.

In 2017, Starr said, in an *NME* interview, that Donegan's 'Rock Island Line' was the first song he had learned. "I was lucky because when I started, if you had the instrument, you were in the band. I worked in the same factory as Eddie Clayton, who played guitar, and we'd play in the basement – I had a snare drum, my best friend Roy Chaplin played tea chest bass, and we were a skiffle band. We played weddings for the beer."

'Have A Drink On Me (Take A Whiff On Me)' was released as a single in Europe and failed to chart.

On 3 March 1978, the film *Sextette*, directed by Ken Hughes, premiered at the Cinerama Dome in Hollywood. The film had sat on the shelf for nearly a year before being picked up for distribution by Scorpion

Films (an independent company) and Crown International Pictures, which closed its doors in 1993. The film cost a reported four to eight million dollars, and grossed back only $50,000. The reviews were unkind when it was released. "*Sextette* is a cruel, unnecessary and mostly unfunny musical comedy," was the review in *Variety* (8 March 1978). The film did have far too many low points; Dom DeLuise singing The Beatles' 'Honey Pie' was not an easy watch. The critic also noted that "The remainder of the cast - Tony Curtis as a Soviet delegate to the peace conference, Timothy Dalton as West's new husband, Ringo Starr and George Hamilton as former husbands, among others - will hardly enhance their reputations with this project."

In the film Mae West played a Hollywood starlet who had just married for the sixth time (to Sir Michael Barrington, played by Timothy Dalton) and during their honeymoon, she encounters her ex-husbands, who still carry a torch for her. Starr played Laslo Karolny, an Italian filmmaker. Starr's accent comes and goes, and though he (like most of the cast) overacts, he is quite funny in moments. Keith Moon plays a dress designer, while Alice Cooper is a waiter. Starr does not sing in the film, although much of the cast do get to sing, with West or on their own. To date, no soundtrack has been released.

While Starr was promoting his album *Bad Boy*, he did comment on working with Mae West and the film *Sextette*. During an interview with Robert W. Morgan, Starr said, "The first day of the film, we go on, and no one said anything to me. It was all Mae, Mae, Mae, because it's Mae's movie. So I got crazy. No one told me if I was good, bad or indifferent. It didn't matter. If someone had said, you did terrible, Ring, I would have enjoyed it because it was all just Mae this and Mae that. I hated that day, I hated it! So I called up and said, get me off that film, I don't care, I will pay for the day's shoot. I just can't stand it. I worked four more days with Mae and at the end of those four days, I called up and said 'can I pay to be in the movie?' Because she is dynamite, an amazing woman, just an amazing woman."

Sextette was a failure. It lost a tremendous amount of money for the backers. According to Gabi Shaw of *Business Insider*, "the movie grossed only about $50,000 against an estimated $8 million budget." And it is not an easy film to watch. The critics were ruthless in their assessment and it is not a film that turns up on late night television. It is sad, because it was not only West's last film but also George Raft's. These Hollywood icons from the golden age of cinema were left with this film, which is very light on plot and big on cameos. The film features many actors from Hollywood's golden era, and this is not the film by which they should be remembered. Let's not forget, Mae West on the cover of *Sgt. Pepper's Lonely Hearts Club Band*. For Starr it had to have been a thrill to be with Hollywood royalty, but the film did not turn out as planned.

A month later, another film, in which Starr had a very small role, was released, but this time to extremely positive reviews. The Band's *The Last Waltz* hit the big screens across North America on 26 April 1978. This was a success, and to this day is a highly regarded documentary and concert film. Directed by Martin Scorsese, the film documented The Band's last concert from Thanksgiving, 25 November 1976. Starr came on at the end for the final number and the jam featuring the majority of the artists who participated. Even *Variety* gave this one a good review: "The film is a series of highlights. Except for Dylan, none of the guests perform more than one number with The Band. There are no dull moments and at 115 minutes the picture is tight and exciting." Starr does get a mention in this review. "The group backs up guest artists on another dozen. They include Ronnie Hawkins, Dr. John, Neil Young, the Staples, Neil Diamond, Joni Mitchell, Paul Butterfield, Muddy Waters, Eric Clapton, Emmylou Harris, Van Morrison, Bob Dylan, Ringo Starr and Ron Wood."

The soundtrack album, on which Starr appears, peaked at number 16 on the *Billboard* top 200 album chart. Radio jumped all over the album, especially side six, which featured the last studio recording of The Band. *Cash Box* (22 April 1978) wrote: "The extensive lineup of the world's greatest music figures here attests to the high esteem in which The Band is held by its peers. An indispensable work." *Billboard* were equally complimentary, stating the live album exceeds all expectations of a live album and "...a memorable package were friends of the group whose participation made this an all-star get together. Contributing to the soundtrack are Bob Dylan, Eric Clapton, Neil Diamond, Paul Butterfield, Emmylou Harris, Joni Mitchell, Ringo Starr, Neil Young, Ron Wood, Muddy Waters, Van Morrison, Dr. John, Ronnie Hawkins and the Staples."

Rolling Stone magazine was not so kind. Jim Miller's review for the album was harsh. "There is little here that demands a second hearing. Most of it we have heard before, done better. On this score, some of the guests are at fault...we need Bob Dylan to close with 'I Shall Be Released', on which Ronnie Wood and Ringo Starr join the Band and friends for a choral sing-along."

In the UK the album peaked at number 39, most likely due to the price of the triple album set.

In 1978, Starr also kept busy with Ring O' Records. Suzanne was first out of the gate in January, with her cover version of The Miracles'

'You Really Got A Hold On Me'. Of course, the song was also recorded by The Beatles on their second album, *With The Beatles* (1963). The single was added to Radio Forth and Radio One in the UK for radio play for February and March. *Record Mirror* reviewed the single: "Vocals very reminiscent of Olivia Newton-John. Nothing special" (28 January 1978). Although it was a minor hit in Australia, the song did not chart in the UK or in Europe.

Once again, the single deserved a better fate. Her version is fine, although she did not break new ground with an overly creative arrangement. Unlike her first Ring O' Records release, Russ Ballard did not produce the single; instead it was well-known American producer Dan Schroeder (known for producing James and Bobby Purify). Bergen White (Tony Joe White among others) arranged the song. The B-side, 'You Could Be Right This Time', was written by Todd Cerney, a Nashville writer. The song is fine, and serves her well as a B-side.

After 'You Really Got A Hold On Me', plans for an album on Ring O' Records were scrapped. A catalogue number was assigned, but the company was the issue, not the sales of her singles. Money had started to become a problem and a number of proposed albums were never recorded. Suzanne left Ring O' Records in 1980 and signed with RCA Records.

The next release from Ring O' Records came from Johnny Warman, an artist who had made a name for himself with the band Bearded Lady. Warman remembered: "Phil Lynott used to love our band and watch us, especially at The Marquee club, which we used to ram with about 500 punters." He further added that "Bearded Lady were a band and when they decided that they did not want to perform any more they took all the gear and sold the van after we performed for the last time at The Marquee club and the opening band was The Jam."

He signed to Ring O' Records the old fashioned way, by sending in a tape. "I sent some demos to Barry Anthony, who worked for Ringo," Warman said. He added: "I first met Ringo Starr when I signed to Ringo Records in 1977."

Warman released one single on Ring O' Records, 'Head On Collision', backed with two tracks; one was called 'Mind Games', though it had nothing to do with John Lennon - although Warman pointed out that he had "slept in his and Yoko's Bed for about 6 weeks with a circular mirror suspended 6 feet above me!" while recording at Ringo's Startling Studios. Former Jam producer Vic Coppersmith-Heaven produced the songs. Warman wrote all the tracks.

Warman remembered that Ringo was not involved with the recording or the record, as "he was far too busy with his own career". As such, the record did not receive a great deal of promotion and even less radio play. Sheila 'Scratch' Prophet did review it for *Record Mirror* (18 March 1978). In her review she stated: "An inordinate number of this week's singles sound like exact copies of other people. This one, for instance, is Dan McCafferty (of Nazareth), to the line."

Two of the songs from the single were well known Bearded Lady songs that were popular with their audience: 'Head On Collision' was a finishing number for Bearded Lady, and 'Mind Games', along with 'London's Burning', were part of the Bearded Lady set.

Warman also recorded his debut solo album, *Hour Glass,* at Ringo's home studio. Vic Coppersmith-Heaven produced the album. Although the intention was to release the album on Ring O' Records, and it was assigned a catalogue number (2339 202, Rab Noakes's album had the catalogue number 2339 201, released just before the scheduled release date of *Hour Glass*), it was never released on the label. It was finally released in 1979, after a year of sitting on a shelf, by RCA Records. The label does state that it is an 'Able Label Production', which one will see is an important footnote.

Although things did not work out for Warman during his time with Ring O' Records, he would find success in the 1980s and continued to have a relationship with Starr. He co-wrote four songs for Ringo's 1991 release, *Time Takes Time*. Warman recalled, "We met at his apartment at The Roccabella and worked together with me on acoustic guitar and vocals and we would sit in the sun and it was a magical experience I will never forget." The four songs were 'Don't Go Where The Road Don't Go', 'After All These Years', 'Everyone Wins' and 'Runaways'. Starr revisited 'Everyone Wins' in 2010 for the album *Y Not*.

On 18 February 1978, Ring O' Records released a single by a band named Stormer. The word Stormer is slang for something particularly impressive or good of its kind. The single was 'My Home Town' b/w 'Shake It Baby'. The record attracted little attention; however, Mike Burke, a writer for *The Advertiser (Durham Ed)* noted that the single is "a commercial rocker, and could be a hit given enough airplay" (28 February 1978). Robin Smith, writing for *Record Mirror*, provided the short review: " 'Yellow River' re-visited about four years too late." In advertisements for their shows, it was often noted that they were "Ringo Starr's Latest Signing." The song received a little airplay on Radio One.

"Before Stormer was signed to Ring O' Records, they were actually called Method," Stormer drummer Ron Kelly recalled. "They were signed to Jonathon King's record label, UK Records. Method's manager Kindsay Brown played Tony Chapman, who worked at NEMS, the album. He liked it and went to Terry Condon, managing director of Ring

O' Records." Condon went to see them perform at a club in Yorkshire. The next day the band was sent a contract to sign with Ring O' Records.

The band was to record an album for the label, and in fact there are photos of Starr with the band and the album cover. Sadly, the album was not released. According to Ron Kelly, "Ring O' Records was put into administration by Hilary Gerrard. Hilary went to Ringo and said 'The company has lost a lot of money. We cannot carry on. So the best way we can do this is write it off as a tax loss.' Ringo really didn't want to because he had bands like ourselves. They were all friends of his and he didn't want to do it. However, Hilary was strict... I think the company has lost two and a half million pounds in eighteen months."

It should be noted that Ring O' Records was just one of Starr's companies, which also included Wibble Records, Startling Studios and Startling Productions. Wibble was a record label/production company, of which Ring O' Records was a part. Wibble was part of a long line of production companies Starr was involved with in the 1970s. In the early 1970s, he was involved with a company named Beachport Company Ltd. On initial Ring O' Records releases one sees Beachport on the label. However, Starr had formed Wibble Records to not only be the head of Ring O' Records but also for his own recordings everywhere except North America. Again, the name Wibble pops up on all his Polydor releases. According to Brad Howard and Mitch McGeary of Rarebeatles.com, the original name for Ring O' Records was Reckongrade Ltd., which Starr wisely changed before the initial launch in 1975.

On 18 March 1978, Graham Bonnet returned to Ring O' Records to release his final single for the label. As with his debut album and first three singles, 'Warm Ride' was released on Mercury in most territories, and on Ring O' Records in the UK, Germany and Ireland. 'Warm Ride' made it to number two in Australia, and was popular in New Zealand as well. It was produced, once again, by Pip Williams, and recorded in Ringo's studio. For collectors, there was a twelve inch single sent out to radio and clubs, featuring a long and short version of the song. This coupling was also issued to radio stations on a seven inch single.

The song 'Warm Ride' was written by the Bee Gees and was a song that had been considered for their mammoth album *Saturday Night Fever*. "What happened was they were doing *Saturday Night Fever* at the time, and they had written these songs," recalled Bonnet. "Robin had a song, a rough idea, which he had put down on a cassette machine. The song came to the management office. Barry Gibb worked it all out, put the chords together and made an arrangement. It worked out well, it went to number one in Australia and it was on my second album there. It should have been released in the States."

Sadly the single was not released in the US, where it could have established Bonnet as a solo artist.

Bonnet did not have a hit with the record in the UK. The song became a hit in the UK for Rare Earth, with an almost note for note cover version. Ring O' Records did release a 12 inch, long 'disco' version in the UK, which did get some air time on the radio and, according to *Record Mirror*, was played at discos. It was a "DJ favourite". The B-side of the single was the brilliant '10/12 Observation', which Bonnet wrote.

"It was about something, I made it up, I recorded on the 12th of October, Kip Williams, my producer said, why don't we just call it '10/12 Observation' because I didn't have a title. It is about mysteries we don't understand."

Bonnet's second album, *No Bad Habits*, was scheduled to be released on Ring O' Records, but it suffered the same fate as Suzanne and Stormer. However, he did have a deal with Mercury, who released the album in the Netherlands, Australia (where it peaked at number six) and New Zealand. Bonnet was somewhat disappointed that he only had the one album and four singles with Ring O' Records, and has his view of what happened.

"Ringo's label just went kaput. It just was no longer there. Ringo had all this stuff going on at one point. He was making watches, in fact I had a watch he designed, and a designer furniture shop in London. It bombed too. His manager got me another deal with Mercury. Nothing exciting, it is just how it happened."

Both of Bonnet's albums associated with Ring O' Records were released worldwide on CD in 2016. The CD compilation, titled *Graham Bonnet/No Bad Habits,* features both albums with singles and 12 inch remixes as bonus cuts. It is a great way to get all of Bonnet's recorded output associated with Starr and Ring O' Records. Bonnet would achieve a great deal of success with Rainbow, Michael Schenker Group, Alcatrazz, Impellitteri and The Graham Bonnet Band.

Rab Noakes was a well known Scottish folk musician and during the 1970s he was often seen with the likes of Gerry Rafferty and Lindisfarne. He had been making records since 1970 and had developed a reputation as a songwriter with Lindsifarne and others covering his songs. In fact, he had been signed to A&M records in 1970-1973 and was picked up by Warner Brothers. His last release for Warner Brothers was in 1975. He did not have any hits, but he was well respected, especially in the UK. He was a very influential artist in the British Folk revival in England of the 1970s. In 1978 he signed to Ring O' Records.

"I had made a demo tape over at Gerry Rafferty's house in Kilmacolm over five days in 1976. The tape did the rounds and ended up with Polydor. It was picked up by Terry Condon who said he wanted to take it to his next job. This turned out to be a new label created by Ringo under the Polydor umbrella. The recording was done at Tittenhurst Park which Ringo had access to and where John Lennon recorded 'Imagine', in that big front room. I only met Ringo once, but he did send me a thank you telegram, which I've kept. It was an interesting experience."

The first single by Rab Noakes for Ring O' Records was 'Waiting Here For You', released on 6 May 1978. It was only released in the UK. Rosalind Russell of *Record Mirror* gave it a positive review. "A lovely, haunting song, but it does tend to ramble on. It's not a track I'd have chosen to be a single because it doesn't have the immediacy that's necessary to hold the interest on the radio" (13 May 1978). The single was picked up by Radio Forth, in Edinburgh in Scotland.

The single was a sampler of the new album from Ring O' Records, titled *Restless*. *Restless* was Noakes' second album, and his first since his debut in 1975. *Music Week* noted on 20 May 1978 that Polydor, who distributed Ring O' Records, was pushing this album. It was reported that they were "putting together a major media and in-store campaign to launch the album." It was also noted that Noakes was helping out and planned a tour of the UK with Gerry Rafferty. Further: "Advertising starts May 26 in the Music Press, including Folk News. In Noakes' native Scotland, the LP will be subject to a joint campaign by Polydor and Bruce's Record Shops on Radio Clyde."

Noakes wrote both the A-side and the B-side ('Restless'), and the single, as well as the album, was produced by Terry Melcher (The Beach Boys). The forthcoming album was titled *Restless*, so the title track sits comfortably on the B-side. Fans of British folk will enjoy this single and it has aged quite well. Both songs are well written and produced. Noakes has a fine voice and the songs share similarities with Gerry Rafferty's iconic sound.

Record Week in the 3 June 1978 issue gave the album a lukewarm review. "Without being exceptional, nevertheless consistent, attractive collection of songs." The critic compares the album to Alan Parsons ("Reminds strongly of Alan Parsons"). The album is referred to as "Extremely mellowish, opening with tuneful songs given very imaginative scoring." Further, it is noted that "Noakes writes above average songs without exactly producing basic charisma which makes major hits. Warmly recommended for people liking quality without feeling there must be a necessity for both." Not glowing, but not a bad review overall.

The album even got a small write-up in the US's *Record World* on 5 May 1978. "Rab Noakes returns after a two-year absence to record a new album *Restless* for Ring O' Records. Meanwhile label Guv'nor Ringo Starr issues his Vini Poncia produced album, *Bad Boy*." Sadly, the album was never released in the US, where it might have found an audience.

One more single from the album was released in July of 1978. Two tracks, 'I Won't Let You Down' b/w 'Long After Dark' were issued. It was to gain interest in the album, but failed to do so. The shame is that the album is really quite good and a brilliant example of Scottish folk music at the time, mixed with some pop production. Carolyn Gilbert wrote for the *Dorset Evening Echo* that it is Noakes' "best album" and called his music "original and commercial at the same time". Other critics in other newspapers across the UK offered praise. Noakes would go on to have a respected, strong career, and this album should have established him in the folk world. For whatever reason, it did not.

Rab Noakes passed away on 11 November 2022. He leaves behind an incredible catalogue of music. He was very much at the forefront of traditional Scottish music for over 50 years. Sadly, his album for Ring O' Records did not reflect his passion for folk music. But Noakes was never one to shy away from a challenge or try different music. His album for Ring O' Records is quite wonderful but it is different from his other releases. As a member of Lindisfarne, he continued to expand and explore folk music while incorporating rock and at times prog rock.

'I Won't Let You Down' failed to build any interest in the album and the single failed to chart. It was the last single on Ring O' Records and Noakes would have the only album released on that label in 1978, even though Stormer and Suzanne both recorded albums and were assigned catalogue numbers. Their albums were cancelled. And in August, the label, for all intents and purposes, closed.

In the 23 September 1978 issue of *Music Week*, there was a small article about Ring O' Records. "Ringo is looking for a deal for Ring O' Records," it said. The article further added that the "distribution deal with Polydor ran out at the end of August." The label was dissolved, and was "adapted to a production company called Able Label Productions. Managing director Terry Condon explains: 'We are retaining our artists and placing them with suitable record companies. We are in various stages with different companies for our artists who include Suzanne, Stormer, Johnny Warman, Rab Noakes and Carl Groszmann. Dirk and Stig are already signed to EMI. We are happy to talk to all record companies."

Ring O' Records was Starr's attempt at creating an artist-friendly label, much like Harrison's Dark Horse Records or The Beatles' own

Apple Records. The main, and oddest, difference was that Starr elected to not release any of his own music on Ring O' Records. He could have had an arrangement, like Harrison's, where he was on his label and was distributed by a major label. Perhaps the label and production company would have lasted longer. As it is, the label had a short life and commercially little impact on the rock world. However, it was a springboard for artists who later achieved a level of success, such as Johnny Warman and Graham Bonnet.

Starr should be applauded for his attempt at helping new artists. Unlike Harrison, Starr did not have any direct relationship with the artists he signed to the label, other than Bobby Keys. He found artists the old fashioned way, with unknown and unsigned bands/artists sending in demos. It would have been very easy to have well known friends release music on his label, or even himself, but he was trying to assist new artists, and for that he cannot be faulted.

Starr would try again in 2003 with Pumpkinhead Records, a label he created with his then record producer Mark Hudson. The label released only one album, the critically acclaimed *Fake Songs* by Liam Lynch. Starr drummed on the album and helped promote it. That label folded after one release.

On 19 August 1978 Dirk and Stig (of The Rutles) released the single 'Ging Gang Goolie' b/w 'Mr. Sheen'. Of course, it was really Eric Idle and Rikki Fataar. The song 'Ging Gang Goolie' has its origins in 1905 in Sweden. It was (and is) a nonsense song, usually sung in a round. It was first recorded in 1926 by a group named Lyran, and in 1969 The Scaffold (featuring Mike McCartney) had a minor hit with the song in the UK. The fact that a Rutles offshoot band was on a label financed by Ringo Starr has a certain amount of irony to it. It also speaks to Starr's love of the Rutles project. Remember, Starr did make a brief appearance on *Monty Python's Flying Circus* in 1972.

While Ring O' Records was winding down, Starr was taking his career into his own hands and trying to attract the attention and sales he had had in the first half of the decade. In the 18 March 1978 issue of *Cash Box*, an interesting article appeared announcing Starr was signing with Portrait Records in the US and Canada. He remained on Polydor for the rest of the world. It is interesting, as it would seem that he had not fulfilled the Atlantic Records contract, which had called for five albums. Starr had only released two albums on the label. However, in 1978 he signed with Portrait Records.

Portrait Records was a relatively new label, distributed by Epic in the US and Canada. The label was formed in 1976 by Larry Harris. Harris was the co-founder of the Casablanca record label, which did extremely well with Kiss and Donna Summer. He decided to try his luck again and formed a new label, with a distribution deal through CBS Records (now Sony). In 1976, the initial artists signed to Portrait were Burton Cummings, Joan Baez and the McCrarys. Ringo was the seventh artist signed to the label.

The article in *Cash Box* reported: "Last week came the announcement of Ringo Starr's pact with Portrait, a development that will surely underscore that label's identity as a home for a select number of quality artists. What's more, Portrait's Larry Harris told us, it was Ringo himself who set the wheels in motion with a February 17 call from his organization alerting Portrait to Starr's availability. Needless to say, the label was flattered; as Harris said, 'I can think of no honor that could be greater than for someone of his stature, a man who changed not only music but society as well, to say, Portrait. We're proud, to put it mildly.' Ringo's first Portrait album, *Bad Boy* (produced by Vini Poncia), is due April 17. His NBC-TV special, wrapped last week in L.A. and revolving around an up-dated version of *The Prince and The Pauper*, will air April 26."

The statement that Starr was now available indicates that Atlantic, disappointed with the record sales of *Ringo The 4th*, was willing to negotiate with Starr and make him available. As noted, while Starr had moved on from Atlantic Records, he was still signed to Polydor for the rest of the world (with the exception of a few territories). Elsewhere in the *Cash Box* article, it was noted that Starr had been signed to a long-term contract with Polydor.

The same week, *Billboard* had a similar notice; however, their announcement went into putting Starr's career in some form of perspective. "Ringo Starr to Portrait Records. His first album for the label, *Bad Boy*, is due next month to coincide with an NBC TV Special *Ringo* on April 26. Starr had two top 10 gold albums on Apple (Capitol) in 1973, both of which were produced by Richard Perry, and two less commercially successful albums on Atlantic in 1976, which were supervised by Arif Mardin." The article points out the new album will be produced by Vina Ponca. On 1 April 1978, *Billboard* reported that "Ringo Starr working on his upcoming Portrait album at the Burbank Studios, Vini Poncia producing with Bob Schaper mixing."

The announcement about Vini Poncia was not surprising. Although he was primarily known as a songwriter, he had had some success as a producer. He did extremely well producing Melissa Manchester's self-titled album in 1975. That album proved to be a success, making it to number 12 that year on the *Billboard* Top 200. He also produced Lynda Carter's (TV's *Wonder Woman*) debut album for Portrait Records in

1978. Although he had a history, he was probably best known as Starr's co-writer since 1973, when the two were brought together by Richard Perry. And the pair had a top five hit single with 'Oh My My'.

Bad Boy has an interesting recording history. According to Chip Madinger and Mark Easter, the album was recorded in the Bahamas and Canada for tax purposes. This was Starr's first and only album to be recorded entirely outside of the US or UK, although there were later overdubs recorded in Los Angeles. In the Bahamas, he recorded at Elite Recording Studio, and in Canada he recorded at Can-Base Studio (Vancouver) and Nimbus 9 (Toronto), in the exclusive Yorkville area. Starr later said he moved from Toronto to Vancouver as he was attracting too many fans in Toronto. According to Madinger and Easter, the overdub sessions were completed in Burbank on 8 March 1978. The overdubs included an orchestra led by composer James Newton Howard, who arranged the scores as well at Burbank Studios.

Unlike on his other albums, Starr had a small band back him on the songs. The group was given the name 'Ringo's Roadside Attraction' and included: Ringo on drums and providing lead vocals, old friends Lon Van Eaton and Jimmy Webb on guitar, another old friend, Dr. John, on keyboards, Hamisch Bissonnette (a pseudonym for Dr. John) on synthesiser, Dee Murray (on loan from Elton John's band) on bass guitar and the producer Vini Poncia providing vocals and the arrangements. Reportedly a musician named Morris Lane played organ, although very little is known about Lane. Canadian musician Doug Riley (Dr. Music) arranged the strings. What is significant is that this is the first Ringo Starr album on which he does all the drumming.

In a very odd move, the only musician (besides Starr) who gets credit on the inner sleeve and record notes is Hamisch Bissonnette, which was an established alter ego of Dr. John. The other credits are rather silly pseudonyms: lead and rhythm guitars were attributed to "Push-a-lone" and "Git-tar" respectively, while bass guitar was by "Diesel", and keyboards were credited to "Morris Lane". The album also featured "Vini Poncia's Peaking Duck Orchestra and Chorus, with Horns arranged by Tom of the North."

In speaking with Lon Van Eaton, who appeared on the album, he was not clear as to the reason for the pseudonym. He wondered if there were any tax implications, or was Starr merely being playful? Starr has never commented and there is no documentation as to the reasons.

Once again, Nancy Lee Andrews (Nancy Andrews at the time) took the photo for the front sleeve. Starr took some photographs too, which were used in the inner sleeve. And once again John Kosh designed the sleeve using the photo. "The cover shot was a snap (by Nancy) that I enlarged and added subtle glints to the rings. Then I needed to come up with a logo that seemed suitable." The logo was also used on the UK pressing of the album. Kosh also pointed out that he had nothing to do with the sleeve designs used for singles released in Europe, Japan and Australia.

Andrews recalled how the sleeve photo was taken, and the resulting album titled. "We were on our balcony in Monte Carlo and every evening before we went out for a wonderful meal we would have a little champagne and sit on the balcony. I was sitting there, I used to love to watch the boats come in, ships more like it. We had high power binoculars we bought so we could see what was going on in the bay. So he is sitting there, and we used to get dressed up, and he is wearing this nice suit and shirt and he is holding a beautiful Waterford glass of champagne and I just took a picture of it, just the way it is, framed just the way it is. And a few more pictures of him like that. We got home, I would put all the film in for development. We would put the film in slide trays, and we would sit there and have pasta or something, sit on the floor and give a slide show while we ate dinner. We had friends over, and when that picture came up, he [Starr] went 'Ooooo, wow' and said, 'That's my bad boy,' and he said, 'Yeah, that's it! That's the cover'."

The bulk of the album was recorded over a ten day period in two studios in Canada in November 1977. The musicians then moved to the Bahamas, about which Starr said, "nice days on the beaches, then you get to work at night." This means Starr had a finished album to play to any potential record companies, an unusual practice at the time. Unlike *Ringo The 4th*, which featured songs written by Starr and Poncia, *Bad Boy* had Starr returning to the formula of using several writers.

Although there were tax implications regarding the album and where it was recorded, Nancy Lee Andrews recalled there were other very pragmatic reasons for recording in Canada and Jamaica. "I think it might have to do with time. He could only spend six months out of the year in America, those few weeks he was in Toronto and over in Vancouver as well, gave him weeks he would not use up in America."

She also recalled that Starr took the proceedings very seriously and worked very hard with Poncia on the album (Starr is credited as associate producer). He also quite liked Canada, especially Toronto.

"He worked very hard. I came up for two weeks while he was there. Part of it was done in Toronto. We stayed at the Royal York, what a great hotel. That was just old world, which was right up our alley. And the suite we had there was just 40s, 30s, 50s, just magnificent. We had a good time there. While he was in the studio I would go out with my camera and take a picture of the architecture around the town. I was walking down the street, and I literally bumped into Elliot Gould. We loved Toronto. We used to walk around the streets a lot."

On 18 April 1978, the first single to be released from the album was a cover of the Benny Spellman song 'Lipstick Traces (On A Cigarette)', although The O'Jays had the bigger hit with the song. Starr does not stray too far from the original, although Poncia adds a few surprises. The song was written by Naomi Neville, a pseudonym commonly used by Allen Toussaint. 'Lipstick Traces (On A Cigarette)' was scheduled to be released in the UK, but plans were shelved, and the only single from *Bad Boy* would be released in July. The single was released in North America. It was also released in Europe and Japan, on the Polydor label. In Australia the B-side was the title track, 'Bad Boy'. In Bolivia, it was released on CBS records.

The B-side, a song written by Ponica and Starr, was far more interesting,' Old Time Relovin'. The song featured inspired organ playing from Morris Lane and great vocals from Starr. Perhaps this should have been the A-side. Both tracks were taken from the album *Bad Boy* (which Ringo always referred to as Ringo 'Bad Boy' Starr).

Although *Billboard* did not review it, they did list it in the Recommended Singles section (29 April 1978), and on that date, *Cash Box* did give it a positive review:" The honky tonk piano licks, sit-up beat and familiar progression of this first single from Ringo's new LP, *Bad Boy*, make it a pop sweetheart. The backing horns and vocals are tasty. Ringo's vocals are characteristically well-done." *Record Week* waited until May to review it (5 May 1978) and wrote:" Ringo's TV special last week brought him back into the limelight, and his first single for Portrait could bring him back to the charts. It's a sad but slightly ironic cover of an early sixties Benny Spellman." The critic is referring to the television special that was made to help promote *Bad Boy*, which aired in the US and Canada on 26 April 1978.

'Lipstick Traces (On A Cigarette) 'received scant airplay and did not make the top 100. It peaked on the *Cash Box* and *Record World* charts at 103 on 27 May 1978. That week the *Cash Box* top five included Wings at number one ('With A Little Luck'), as well as Johnny Mathis at number two ('Too Much, Too Little, Too Late'), Olivia Newton-John and John Travolta at number three ('You're The One I Want'), Andy Gibb at number four ('Shadow Dancing'), and Roberta Flack and Donny Hathaway at number five ('The Closer I Get To You'). Given that top five, there should have been a place on radio for Starr as well. It was all but ignored in Canada, and did not make the top 100 in that country.

'Lipstick Traces (On A Cigarette) 'was the second single by Starr that failed to reach the top 100. Although it is an interesting choice and a great song, it was not the best choice as the first single from the album. A stronger song could have been chosen that would have represented the album better and attracted record buyers to the album. Starr did not even perform it in the television special designed to promote the album. Having said that, why it missed with radio programmers and record buyers is anyone's guess. And it deserved a much better fate.

The second single lifted from *Bad Boy* was released on 3 July 1978. It was released only in the US. It was not even released in Canada. Once again *Cash Box* were very kind with their review of 15 July 1978. "Ringo continues his tradition of smooth and likeable pop on this single from his *Bad Boy* album. Produced by Vini Poncia, this song has a lyric about not hiding feelings and a bright arrangement of electric guitars, hiding perky beats and backing strings. Excellent vocals by Ringo." *Billboard* did not review it, but recommended the single.

The song was written by Benny Gallagher and Graham Lyle, who, at one time, were signed to Apple publishing and wrote for the likes of Mary Hopkin. Their version of the song, released in 1976, made it to number six in the UK national chart (number two in Ireland) and made it on to the Adult Contemporary Chart for *Billboard*, hitting number 17. Bryan Ferry's version was well known in the UK.

'Heart On My Sleeve' was Starr's last single on the Portrait label. It was also his last single released in the 1970s in America. He would not release another single until 1981's 'Wrack My Brain'. It was a sad end to the decade for an artist who seemed to have no problems producing hit singles for five years. But more importantly, Starr was loved and embraced by rock fans and radio. He had lost his audience. As for 'Heart On My Sleeve', it is very hard to understand why the extremely well produced and arranged song could not find a home on Adult Contemporary (or easy listening) stations.

Perhaps this should have been the first single. It was featured in the television show and it is one of Starr's best vocals. It is a brilliant song. Reportedly Melissa Manchester sings the backing vocals. The single featured the Starr and Poncia original 'Who Needs A Heart' as a B-side. This song expertly opens the *Bad Boy* album, and is a fine mid tempo rocker. Starr's vocals are strong, as is the production and arrangement. It could have served well as an A-side. It was the second and only other song the pair wrote for *Bad Boy*. As with 'Lipstick Traces (On A Cigarette)', promo copies with mono and stereo mixes of 'Heart On My Sleeve' were sent out to radio stations. It is interesting to note that Portrait did service the single to radio later in the year with the sleeve stating "We believe in this, please listen again". It did not help the single's chances.

In the UK, the only single released from *Bad Boy* was 'Tonight' b/w 'Heart On My Sleeve'. A special promo film was produced for the song, featuring Nancy Lee Andrews guest starring with Starr. According to Andrews, the film was "shot in a castle in France, we were in Monte Carlo at the time, and we drove up the mountains for a couple of hours to this beautiful castle. He was a young French director, and he got it, our love of the old movies."

The song 'Tonight' was written by Ian McLagan and John Pidgeon for the Small Faces reunion album, *Playmates* (1977). Starr would appear on a McLagan solo album, *Troublemaker* (released in 1979, but recorded in 1978 in Malibu). Starr appears on the song 'Hold On'.

Phillip Hall reviewed the single in the 29 July 1978 issue of *Record Mirror*. It was rather harsh and a little cruel. "If Ringo lived in England he'd probably host a Saturday night TV 'spectacular'. He certainly has the right qualifications. He's bland, boring and has a knack of picking reject love songs." The single failed to chart. It was Starr's last record for Polydor, who quietly ended the contract early. Starr recorded only three albums for the label, plus *Scouse The Mouse*, which was not a Ringo Starr album, but for them, that was enough. It should be noted that there was very little promotion for the album or the single in the UK and in Europe. The television film, *Ringo*, intended to promote *Bad Bay*, was not even screened at the time of the album's release in the UK. *Ringo* finally premiered in the UK on 3 January 1983.

Mike Burke wrote a review about 'Tonight' which was published in *The Durham Chronicle, Chester-Le-Street Chronicle* (28 July 1978) and other local newspapers throughout the UK. He was very positive about the song, stating it was "nicely produced...a nice hook" but the only problem, he said, is that Starr cannot sing. He further states that it would have a chance of being a hit, if Starr "could just sing."

One other single, or rather EP, of interest that was released from the *Bad Boy* album appeared only in Germany in 1978. Polydor released a five track EP called *The Bad Boy E.P.* which featured 'Lipstick Traces (On A Cigarette)', 'Bad Boy', 'Tonight', 'Who Needs A Heart' and 'Old Time Relovin'. It collected almost all of the singles released from the album. Once again, sales were underwhelming, and this EP has become quite a collector's item.

Bad Boy was released on 21 April 1978 in the US and 16 June 1978 in the UK. Unlike *Ringo The 4th*, Starr and Poncia only wrote two songs for the album. Starr went back to covering older songs; some songs were very well known, and some were quite deep dives. There is a disco version of The Supremes' 'Where Did Our Love Go', which hit number one in 1964 for The Supremes in the US and number three in the UK.

Starr's version did not really come close to replacing the original version. Starr's version leaned heavily on disco and Starr seemed a bit uncomfortable singing it. The 1980s duo Soft Cell would have much more success with their cover version four years later.

The other cover of interest was a song from *Scouse The Mouse*. Here the song is 'A Man Like Me', replacing the word 'mouse' with 'man'; thus 'A Mouse Like Me' became 'A Man Like Me'. It actually works and is a nice way to end the album. It is a beautiful melody and Starr sings it with conviction and emotion. It is quite lovely. Because *Scouse The Mouse* was only released in the UK, Starr felt confident that no one would know of the original. It was a pretty safe bet that most in the UK would not know of 'A Mouse Like Me', since *Scouse The Mouse* had very limited sales.

Ruan O'Lochlainn wrote the song, and it was the only song on the album not written by Donald Pleasence and Roger Brown. Although he wrote his own music, he was best known as a session player for Bryan Ferry and Jethro Tull (among many others). He died in London in 1988. This was the only song not recorded in Canada or the Bahamas. 'A Man Like Me' was reportedly recorded at Burbank Studios, in Los Angeles, with an orchestration by future soundtrack composer/arranger James Newton Howard. It was also the song chosen to close the television special, *Ringo*.

In between are covers of oldies such as 'Bad Boy', a hit for The Jive Bombers in 1957 (written by Louis Armstrong's second wife, Lil Armstrong, and Avon Young). Starr's knowledge of music history was and is astounding. He knows the music, and no doubt the songs he picked had some emotional contact with him. Again, Starr does not stray far from the original, but still puts his own stamp on it. Starr was so taken by the song that it also became the name of the album. However, as previously noted, Nancy Lee Andrews has another explanation for the album's name.

Two other covers are a little more obscure. 'Hard Times' is by Peter Skellern from his 1975 album of the same name. The *Hard Times* album featured George Harrison on one track ('Make Love, not War'). 'Hard Times' is a standard rocker that harkens back to *Ringo* and *Goodnight Vienna* and would not have been out of place on either album.

The other relatively unknown cover was the song 'Monkey See, Monkey Do'. It was written and released by Michael Franks, but Starr probably knew Melissa Manchester's version from her 1976 album *Help Is On The Way*, which Poncia had produced. Of course, Manchester had sung on two albums by Starr, *Ringo's Rotogravure* and *Ringo The 4th*. She provides backing vocals throughout *Bad Boy* too. The song is a funky rock and roll song. It really does not stand out, and like 'Where Did Our Love Go', it almost feels like filler to complete the album. It really is not up to Starr's usual standards and choice of material. Still, he tackles it in his own style and the end result is a passable rock song.

Bad Boy was not well received by critics, such as *Rolling Stone*'s Tom Carson, who wrote: "To say that *Bad Boy* is a very bad record almost misses the point...Starr's only asset, his bemused, skeptical charm, begins to wear thin. He isn't very likeable anymore, and that is very depressing." He even manages to criticise the television special, calling it "disastrous".

In the UK, John Wishart reviewed the album for *Record Mirror*. "It's almost impossible to hate Ringo and his tired and true product of old songs, other people's hits and a couple of his own efforts," he wrote. "It seems inevitable that Uncle Ringo would become singalong fodder but his drowsy vocals makes the seemingly impossible quite bearable. I'm talking about his revamps of the Supremes' 'Where Did Our Love Go' and Gallagher and Lyle's 'Heart On My Sleeve'. Both of Starkey's own efforts with Poncia are pretty boring. A voice like Ringo's needs something cosy and well known to slip into so that memory takes over and fills in the gaps." He does mention that "the inclusion of 'A Man Like Me' adapted from Donald Pleasence's *Scouse The Mouse* is a bonus."

There were some positive reviews, such as Carol Clark writing in the *Hammersmith and Shepherds Bush Gazette* (29 June 1978): "there is something charming, endearing that makes me want to play it again."

The US trades were a little more positive about the album and the possibility of putting Ringo back on the top again. The review in *Cash Box* in the 29 April 1978 issue stated: "To coincide with his upcoming television special, Ringo has released his first album for his new label. The music is similar to his earlier solo works, featuring bouncy pop tunes, in addition to a fine remake of 'Where Did Our Love Go'. Ringo's voice still has the happy, knowing flavor that seems to link him to his Beatle past. Now, after a couple of disappointments, Ringo looks like a Starr again."

Billboard, in the same week, wrote: "Starr pursues his penchant for sentimental rock with ten cuts which highlight his vocal versatility, ranging from ballads ('A Man Like Me') through rousing rockers ('Hard Times'). Backed by two guitars, bass, keyboards and occasional strings, Starr has emerged with an album smacking more of a 'group' than solo effort - and benefits from the shift. Tasty licks and catchy lyrics pervade, comprising possibly Starr's most commercial LP to date."

On 3 May 1978, *Variety* reviewed the album, referring to it as "interesting". They further noted that "producer Vini Poncia has tailored to the singer's limited vocal abilities. Starr has a lot of positive attributes, some of which manage to come across on vinyl and Poncia has selected a lot of material, writing a couple with Starr, to fit."

Bad Boy peaked at number 97 on *Cash Box* on 10 June 1978, giving him his first top 100 album since 1976's *Ringo's Rotogravure*. On the *Billboard* top 200, it peaked at a disappointing number 129, and failed to chart in the UK and Canada. It did get to number 98 in Australia. The lack of success does not reflect the quality of music or Starr's busy schedule promoting both the album and the accompanying television show. Besides being a guest on Robert W. Morgan's *The Robert W. Morgan Special of the Week* series, distributed to radio stations across America via DIR Broadcasting, Ringo could be heard on WNEWFM, KWST, KMET, KLOS and KVIL AM/FM radio stations. He even appeared on the NBC News segment, '5 minutes with Connie Collins'.

As Starr told Morgan, "If you do anything, you have to promote it. Because there is so much out there now. The days are changing. You can't just sit there and say it will go down, you have to promote it." The television special *Ringo* was a starring vehicle for him, and also a chance to promote his new album, *Bad Boy*. He also on talk shows with Phil Donahue and Mike Douglas (both televised on 17 April 1978). On 1 April 1978, *Manchester Evening News* published an interview with Starr. He reiterated the importance of promotion during the interview. "It's the game you have to promote these days. Everybody has to promote, nobody is big enough not to."

Starr also sat for other interviews in the UK. An interview appeared in the *Manchester Evening News* on 14 June 1978 in which Starr talked about his career and his private life, to a certain extent. "I have a serious side. I'm not a very public person outside the game I'm in. They don't see much of me in public, and that I purposely play."

Cash Box reported on 18 March 1978 that Ken Ehrlich, the veteran producer of such music related shows as PBS' *Soundstage, The Midnight Special, Tony Orlando & Dawn*, had produced the *Ringo* special TV show. The show aired on April 26. It was described as "a contemporary, musical version of Mark Twain's *The Prince and the Pauper*, in which Ringo plays two characters: Ringo Starr the superstar, and Ognir Rrats, a working class youth who sells maps to the stars' homes in Hollywood." Further, Erlich stated that "When we came up with the concept, we then began to build it around Ringo's music, both with songs he did with the Beatles and those he has done since then. So each song in the show has a real identification with Ringo. Secondly, it furthers the story. No song is really 'inserted' in the show."

Andrews not only accompanied Starr during the television show's filming but was also given the job of shooting all of the publicity photos for the special. It was a role that she took very seriously, as it acknowledged her as a photographer. "During the filming, I just shot with my Nikon," she wrote in her book, *A Dose Of Rock 'n' Roll*. "It was more than a feather in my cap because not only did Ringo think I could handle the job, but his producers did as well.'

Andrews remembered that the shoot for the television special took place over twelve days in February 1978, in and around Los Angeles. "Ringo was very serious and focused in this shoot because it was the first television acting role that evolved around his music," she noted. Even though he was very serious about the show, Starr and the cast (and crew) reportedly had a great deal of fun on the set.

According to Nancy Lee Andrews, the show was not entirely Ringo's idea. "While we were in Canada, Ken Erlich and Craig Stereo (one of his sponsors) and the guys from NBC came up, because we could not go down to LA, so they came up. We had dinner at a great restaurant called Winston's. We went there and discussed the special. This was in October. They were wooing him to do the special." Given that Ringo was recording *Bad Boy*, one can assume Starr saw this as an opportunity to promote the album, and vice versa.

The show had a number of very special guests including Angie Dickenson, Carrie Fisher, John Ritter, Vincent Price, Art Carney, Mike Douglas (on whose television show Ringo appeared to promote the album and show) and George Harrison, who is seen briefly at the beginning of the special (making a reference to *The Rutles*, another television programme in which Harrison participated) and narrates part of the programme. The humour in the show often worked, especially Vincent Price hypnotising Ringo. Price's name in the show was Dr. Nancy, a tip of the hat to Starr's fiancé. Also, during the montage for 'Act Naturally', Starr can be seen holding a copy of *Ringo The 4th* in Tower Records.

Andrews recalled: "We need someone to play the doctor, and I said, get Vincent Price. Vincent Price jumped on it, and his name in it was Dr. Nancy. It was an homage to me. He always looked at me like I was the den mother and the doctor."

There was a great deal riding on the special, and not just for Starr. According to Morrie Gelman, writing for *Variety*, NBC's "Neil Israel Hoping to Catch A Star in NBC *Ringo* Special." It was noted that Neil Israel, who created and wrote the programme, saw it as "really an experiment in seeing if there's a way of presenting a contemporary musical in a mass-audience context." Claimed by Israel to be "the first original rock musical for television", it was deliberately pinpointed for audiences who doted on *Laveme & Shirley* and *Three's Company*. The show aired in North America on the NBC Network on 26 April 1978 and made its debut in the UK on 2 January 1983. By then, the album was long out of print in the UK.

Ringo performed live in the special, with musicians who worked on *Bad Boy*. The songs televised were 'Hard Times' and 'Heart On My Sleeve'. Starr and his band reportedly performed 'Act Naturally' and 'You're Sixteen'. Jimmy Webb served as musical director, Dr. John was on keyboards/piano, Dee Murray on bass, and Lon Van Eaton on guitar. Of course, Ringo was on drums and vocals. It was filmed in A&M studios with a very small audience. Nancy Lee Andrews confirmed that the band was recorded live. "That was live, a beautiful set. He always puts together a great band, he knows his music."

Lon Van Eaton confirmed this during our conversation. "We thought we would be playing a track, lip syncing, until we got to the studio, and Ringo said, 'Oh no, we are going live.' The one track that is performed that is not live is the closing number, 'A Man Like Me', with Starr alone in the spotlight. It proved to be a very dramatic ending."

In the television show, there were new versions of 'You're Sixteen' (a duet with Carrie Fisher), 'Act Naturally' (which features the intro from 'A Dose of Rock 'n' Roll'), 'I'm The Greatest' (which features a short drum solo), 'Yellow Submarine', a short version of 'Octopus's Garden' and 'With A Little Help From My Friends'. As noted, 'A Man Like Me' is also featured at the end of the programme, but it was the album version. 'It Don't Come Easy' is featured as background music.

The television show did not do well (it finished in the bottom of the ratings for the week) and received lukewarm reviews. In *Variety*, the critic wrote: "*Ringo*, former Beatle Ringo Starr's first TV special, tried to use a storyline concept as the framework for a musical variety show —in this instance, a rather loose adaptation of the *Prince & The Pauper* premise. The idea is a praiseworthy one, getting away as it does from the usually self-indulgent narrowness of most rock-star forays on the tube, but final execution did not quite measure up to the promise." Further the critic noted that ex-Beatle George Harrison did the voiceover of the Starr-Rrats role-changing story, but did not perform. "That left it all to Starr, who is a rather impassive actor and hardly an exciting singer. His song material, including three tunes from a new album, were in the melodious mainstream of rock material, palatable to wider audiences, but pretty much interchangeable. What Starr lacks in vocal equipment is compensated for by an amiable personality and lack of pretence — so Ringo was pleasant enough watching, without rising to any particular distinction."

The failure of the show and the album, and being let go by Polydor, weighed heavily on Starr. According to Nancy Lee Andrews: "It crushed him, I think it crushed him. It started to crush him, and psychologically depress him." It seemed that Starr had done everything right: there was promotion, the music was of the top quality, and there was a promotional film for the single in the UK. Nothing seemed to work. While McCartney and Wings were topping the charts with *London Town* and 'With A Little Luck' and the Beatles were still selling a lot of records, Starr seemed to have lost his audience.

Undeterred, Starr started to work on a new album, this time with help from Russ Ballard, who was scheduled to not only produce the album but write it for Starr. Ballard was a former member of the group Argent. He had made a name for himself in the 1970s as the lead singer and one of the main writers for that band, but also writing and producing hits for artists such as Roger Daltrey, Hello, Hot Chocolate and Rainbow.

The two worked out of Sweet Silence Studios, Copenhagen, Denmark in July 1978 and four songs were completed: 'On The Rebound', 'She's So In Love', 'One Way Love Affair' and 'As Far As We Can Go'. The project was abandoned and Starr would leave three of the four tracks unreleased. 'As Far As We Can Go' was released in 1994 on the CD re-release of *Old Wave*, as a bonus track.

In 1979, there was some movement with Ring O' Records, or at least the overarching production company of Ringo's. It was also announced in the UK publication *Music Week* (14 April 1979) that Terry Condon had left Able Label Productions (formerly Ring O' Records). His duties at Able would be taken over by Veronica Hall.

Starr did not record any music in 1979, and in fact the only recording that was released that involved Starr was by Ian McLagan. Starr drummed on the song 'Hold On' from McLagan's *Troublemaker* album.

He did appear performing live on a couple of television shows in the US. On 3 September 1979, Starr appeared on the *Jerry Lewis Muscular Dystrophy Telethon*. He was part of a 'Supergroup' featuring Todd Rundgren, Roger Powell, Willie Wilcox, Kasim Sulton (Utopia), Bill Wyman, Dave Mason and Doug Kershaw. They performed 'Money (That's What I Want)', 'Twist And Shout', and 'Jumping Jack Flash'. Ringo even took a turn at answering the phones for about 30 minutes. Interestingly, Paul McCartney and Wings appeared on the same telethon with a promo film for the new single, 'Getting Closer'. This means that

Lewis had three Beatles on his telethon over the years (Lennon appeared in 1972 with Yoko Ono and The Elephant's Memory Band).

Starr also helped out his old friend Ronnie Wood, and played drums for his band (The New Barbarians) for the television show *Midnight Special*. They performed the song 'Buried Alive'. Charlie Watts drums on the studio version (*Gimmie Some Neck,* credited as Ronnie Wood), but Starr filled in for him for the television performance.

Starr made one other concert appearance, this one at Eric Clapton's wedding to Patti Harrison. With all of the musical guests, a jam session during the reception was likely, and in fact Starr joined Denny Laine, George Harrison and Paul McCartney for some songs. Although some photos surfaced, to date, there has not been a tape of the show.

Although Ringo was heard and seen for the commercials for The Who's *The Kids Are Alright,* and seen in the film itself, Starr spent 1979 sorting out his career and making plans. A new album would be started in 1980, with help from his three brothers from The Beatles, and he would also begin filming a movie with his first starring role (*Caveman*). Sadly, he didn't really have many lines, but he was the Starr and the film would be a huge success. But for 1979, Ringo laid low and took account of his career and his life. In April 1979, he experienced a serious health issue; he suffered intestinal problems relating to his childhood bout of peritonitis. He was immediately admitted to the Princess Grace Hospital in Monte Carlo. It was very serious, and according to a number of sources, he nearly died. But, again, demonstrating a great deal of strength, three weeks later he joined Paul McCartney and George Harrison at Eric Clapton's wedding and was part of a jam. The illness did delay the filming of *Caveman*. According to *Variety* magazine, preproduction started in 1979 and filming was scheduled to start in the summer of 1979, but moved to February 1980 due to Starr's health concerns.

There was also a fire which destroyed his priceless collection of Beatle memorabilia, as well as his health issues to deal with, but Starr survived, and faced the 1980s with a plan.

Conclusion

The Ringo Starr story does not end in 1980. Throughout the 1980s, Starr continued to struggle with the changing times and the ever shifting music industry. But he soldiered on, and experienced many highs and new career highlights.

A new Ringo Starr for Christmas became a tradition from my mother. In 1993, the last Christmas we were able to celebrate with her, there was a Ringo Starr CD under the tree (*Ringo Starr and His All Starr Band Volume 2: Live from Montreux*). CDs had replaced vinyl (this album has never been released on vinyl), so my mother kept up with the times, as did Starr, and she bought the CD. Starr, like his music, changed with the times. The tree and the music were much smaller in size, but it was nice to continue the tradition.

The 1970s, like the 1960s, were an ever-shifting minefield. From the time The Beatles called it a day, until 1980, music tastes changed, fads came and went, and for many artists, it was hard to keep up with the ever changing world. And there were no Beatles to lead the way, as there had been in the 1960s. There were huge, mega selling artists, but no Beatles. And yet, there were. Each of the four Beatles paved their own ways in the 1970s and at times changed the musical landscape.

Did Ringo Starr change the musical landscape? In some ways, he did. Many musicians, bands, and record industry types watched what Starr was doing and in that sense, he did influence many artists. His Ring O' Records label gave many artists their break and was their stepping stone to much bigger successes.

For the most part, Starr stayed true to himself. He recorded music that he liked and that interested him. He did not jump on to trends, but rather he had to be proud of the songs that had his name on them. The records may not have sold very well in the latter part of the 1970s, but Starr was proud of them. He did not live in the past; he was open to new music, styles and sounds, but at the end of the day, the music he created was clearly Ringo Starr music. While he worked with many different producers, writers, and musicians, it was his name on the album sleeve or the label of the single. He was the one who made sure the music made it to the airwaves, into the shops and into people's homes.

Starr, like many artists who made the transition from the 1960s to the 1970s, was not alone in trying to re-establish himself. But unlike other artists, he was a former Beatle. The expectations on him (and the other three) were over the top. He was a member of the largest selling and the most influential band in rock history. While the other three had written for The Beatles, for Starr the question was 'what can he possibly do that will be of The Beatles' calibre?' The truth is, none of the four Beatles would ever do anything that critics and the majority of the public would consider as good as, if not better, than The Beatles. Some fans did, but for the most part, it was expected of all four to match their success, creativity, and influence of the 1960s. No one could ever live up to that standard.

Each Beatle went about this in their own way. Sometimes it worked, sometimes it didn't, which is what it means to be an artist. But Starr, who was very much loved, only sang one song per Beatles album, and on three Beatles albums he was not even awarded that. Starr openly admitted that he was not a quick writer, which meant the stakes seemed a bit higher. As with the other three former Beatles, he could easily have worked with well established artists and musicians who were famous and would propel songs into the upper regions of the charts. For Starr it was more interesting and crucial to establish himself first, and then play with the famous friends. Starr was able to rely on other musicians who had a deep respect for his past work with the Beatles, and through collaboration, was able to develop his own artistic voice and practice alongside trusted collaborators.

Starr's trajectory in the seventies was nothing short of unconventional. He kicked off the decade with two albums that, at the time and maybe today, seemed out of character: an album of classic pop music standards and then a country album written by Nashville artists, some of whom were very new to the scene. Then he took a couple of years to figure out his next direction. He released a couple of hit singles, but he waited on recording an album.

Starr experimented with Maurice Gibb of the Bee Gees, and worked with several artists, but he was smart enough to be patient and release his first rock album three years after The Beatles called it a day. In today's music world, three years is nothing, but in the ever changing 1970s three years was like an eternity. And it paid off.

Ringo became a rock star on his own. It is hard to imagine, or conceptualise, the musical landscape of the 1970s. Oldies stations have remodelled the past and neglected some influential artists who still deserve airtime. But in the early 1970s, Starr was a rock star. Music papers and newspapers followed his every move and not *just* because he was a former Beatle. There may have been an element of that, but he was also selling records and working with artists who were selling records. He firmly established himself as an artist.

Over the decade he developed and evolved into a brilliant songwriter, and in the decades to follow he would work on his producing and arranging skills. Truth be told, he was already producing in the 1970s, while not always getting credit for it. In speaking with this author, guitarist David Spinozza noted that Starr was often in the control room following a take and having his input into the production. Let's face it, he learned from the best, George Martin, and was working with equally impressive producers in the 1970s, such as Richard Perry, Arif Mardin, John Lennon, George Harrison, Jimmy Webb, Lou Reizner and Pete Drake. It is an impressive list.

Collaborating was central to his work in the 1970s. One has to be impressed with the number and diversity of artists with whom he worked. He worked with established artists, while also supporting and working with up and coming or independent artists. It did not make a difference to Starr. He loved, and loves, to play, as he continues to work with a great many artists. Starr likes being part of a band. He never felt the need to continually be centre stage. He is just as happy in the background, doing what he loves, drumming. As he told E Street Band's Max Weinberg: "First and foremost I am a drummer. After that, I'm other things... But I didn't play drums to make money. I played drums because I loved them... My soul is that of a drummer..."

Starr said he loved working with his three brothers. He recorded three albums with their individual and collective help and he repaid them by appearing on their records and, in George Harrison's case, concert. It was not even repayment: he enjoyed working and playing with them. When he popped up on stage to give McCartney flowers in Los Angeles, during McCartney's Wings Over America tour, he was showing his support to his friend.

The 1970s was only one decade in Starr's professional life. He continues to make music in the 2020s (his most recent album, *Look Up*, was released in March 2025), and collaboration remains central to his art by working with cutting edge, exciting and new artists. His career has spanned seven decades and he continues to grow as an artist and experiment with his music and image. The 1970s laid the foundation for his solo career and his interdisciplinary artistic practice. It was in the 1970s that he put down the solid framework which has allowed him to create a rich, diverse catalogue spanning various mediums and styles. I would argue that he has not reached his musical peak yet, but all of the work to date would not have been possible without him paying attention to everything around him from 1970 to 1980.

In 1970, Starr was a new solo artist. Like The Beatles, he released two rock singles before he recorded his first rock album. And at a time when it was acceptable to release singles not on any albums, Starr's first two rock singles were stand alone records. This was common practice from the 1960s through to the 1980s (which The Beatles helped pioneer). In many ways, Starr was starting from scratch, and during the 1970s he built his own distinct solo career. He did not rely on the success of The Beatles to carry him through this new decade. He grew as an artist and he built his own confidence.

Ringo Starr was a post-war child, growing up in Liverpool. Although he left the city at a very young age, images from that era have been present throughout Starr's career. His first solo album, *Sentimental Journey*, features songs he sang with his mother and family as a child. He followed this up with a country album (*Beaucoups Of Blues*), a genre of music very popular in Liverpool in the 1950s (and in the present day). *Goodnight Vienna* featured a still from a sci-fi film that Starr would have seen in the cinemas and *Ringo's Rotogravure* paid tribute to a song sung by Judy Garland and a printing process that was long gone.

While Starr successfully launched a solo career with current and progressive music, he never forgot his past. It is found throughout his music, films and art. He certainly didn't dwell in it but it did inform some of his choices. The Ring O' Records model of focusing on singles rather than albums comes directly from the early days of popular music. While The Beatles were in the forefront of creating the album format, Starr looks to a time before to help new artists.

His work is steeped in the past, both his own individual memory and a wider cultural one. In the 1970s, and today, Starr manages to create work containing a tapestry of influences, with a deep understanding that there is a profound importance in finding the balance between staying close to your roots, while also breaking artistic boundaries and barriers.

This was Ringo Starr in the 1970s.

Ringo Starr – Discography

ALBUMS

Sentimental Journey
U.K. - 27 March 1970 (Apple PCS 7101)
North America – 24 April 1970 (Apple SW-3365)

Beaucoups Of Blues
U.K. - 25 September 1970 (Apple PAS 10002)
North America - 28 September 1970 (Apple SMAS-3368)

Ringo
U.K. - 9 November 1973 (Apple PCTC 252)
North America - 2 November 1973 (SWAL–3413)

Son Of Dracula
U.K. - 24 May 1974 (Rapple APL!-0220)
North America - 1 April 1974 (Rapple ABL1-0220)

Goodnight Vienna
U.K. - 15 November 1974 (Apple PCS 7168)
North America - 18 November 1974 (Apple SW-3417)

Blast From Your Past
U.K. - 12 December 1975 (Apple PCS 7170
North America - 25 November 1975 (Apple SW-3422)

Rotogravure
U.K. - 17 September 1976 (Polydor 2302-040)
North America - 25 September 1976 (Atlantic SD 18193)

Ringo The 4th
U.K. - 20 September 1977 (Polydor 2310 556)
North America – 30 September 1977 (Atlantic SD 19108)
Scouse The Mouse   U.K. - 9 December 1977 (Polydor 2480 429)

Bad Boy
U.K. - 21 April 1978 (Polydor 2310 599)
North America - 16 June 1978 (Portrait JR 35378)

SINGLES

'Beaucoups Of Blues' b/w 'Coochy Coochy'
North America - 5 October 1970 (Apple 2969)

'It Don't Come Easy'
b/w 'Early 1970' U.K - 9 April 1971 (Apple R 5898)
North America - 9 April 1971 (Apple 1831)

'Back Off Boogaloo' b/w 'Blindman'
U.K. - 17 March 1972 (Apple R 5944)
North America - 17 March 1972 (Apple 1849)\

'Photograph' b/w 'Down And Out'
U.K. - 24 September 1973 (Apple R 5992)
North America - 24 September 1973 (Apple 1865)

'You're Sixteen' b/w 'Devil Woman'
U.K. - 8 February 1974 (Apple R 5995)
North America - 3 December 1973 (Apple 1870)

'Oh My My' b/w 'Step Lightly'
North America - 18 February 1974 (Apple 1872)

'Only You' b/w 'Call Me'
U.K. - 15 November 1974 (Apple R 6000)
North America - 11 November 1974 (Apple 1876)

'No No Song' b/w 'Snookeroo'
North America - 27 January 1975 (Apple 1880)

'Snookeroo' b/w 'Oo-Wee'

U.K. - 21 February 1975 (Apple R 6004)

'(It's All Down To) Goodnight Vienna'
North America - 2 June 1975 (Apple 1882)
b/w 'Oo-Wee'

'Oh My My' b/w 'No No Song'
U.K. - 9 January 1976 (R 6011)

'A Dose Of Rock 'n' Roll' b/w 'Cryin'' U.K. - 15 October 1976
(Polydor 2001 694)
North America - 20 September 1976 (Atlantic 45-6631)

'You Don't Know Me At All' b/w 'Cryin''
Europe - 15 October 1976 (Polydor 2001 695)

'Las Brisas' b/w 'Cryin''
Mexico - 1976 (Polydor 761)

'Hey Baby' b/w 'Lady Gaye'
U.K. - 26 November 1976 (Polydor 2001 699)
North America - 22 November 1976 (Atlantic 45-3371)

'Wings' b/w 'Just A Dream'   North America - 25
August 1977 (Atlantic 3429)

'Drowning In The Sea Of Love' b/w 'Just   U.K. - 16 September
1977 (Polydor 2001 734)
A Dream'   North America – 18
October 1977 (Atlantic 3412)

'Sneaking Sally Through The Alley' b/w
Australia - (Polydor 2001 753)
'Tango All Night'

'Tango All Night' b/w 'It's No Secret'
Argentina - (Polydor 2001 768)

'Lipstick Traces (On A Cigarette)'
North America - 18 April 1978 (Portrait 6-70015)
b/w 'Old Time Relovin''

'Tonight' b/w 'Heart On My Sleeve'
U.K. - 21 July 1978 (Polydor 2001 795)

'Heart On My Sleeve' b/w 'Who Needs A
U.S. - 13 November 1978 (Portrait 6-70018)
Heart'

   RING O' RECORDS

   ALBUMS

David Hentschel – *Sta*rtling Music*
U.K. - 18 April 1975 (2320-101
U.S. - 17 February 1975 (ST - 11372)

Graham Bonnet – *Graham Bonnet*
U.K. - 09/77 (2320-102)

John Tavener – *The Whale*
U.K. - 09/77 (2320 - 104)

Rab Noakes – *Restless*
U.K. - 05/78 (2339-101)

   SINGLES

David Hentschel – 'Oh My My' b/w
U.K. - 21 March 1975 (2017 101)

'Devil Woman'
U.S. - 17 February 1975 (4030)

Bobby Keys – 'Gimmie The Key' b/w 'Honky
U.K. - 5 September 1975 (2017 102)
Tonk (Parts 1 and 2)'
U.S. - 25 August 1975 (4129)

Carl Groszmann – 'I've Had It' b/w 'C'mon And
U.K. - 3 June 1977 (2017 103) Roll'

Colonel (Doug Bogie) - 'Cokey Cokey' b/w
U.K. - 21 November 1975 (2017 104)
'Away In A Manager'

Graham Bonnet – 'It's All Over Now, Baby
U.K. - 3 June 1977 (2017 105)
Blue' b/w 'Heroes On My Picture Wall'

Graham Bonnet – 'Danny' b/w 'Rock Island
U.K. - 12 August 1977 (2017 106) Line'

Carl Groszmann – 'Face Of A Permanent
U.K. - October 1977 (2017 107)
Stranger' b/w 'Your Own Affair'

Suzanne – 'Born On Halloween' b/w 'Like No
U.K. - November 1977 (2017 108)
One Else'

Graham Bonnet – 'Goodnight And
U.K. - November 1977 (2017 110)
Good Morning' b/w 'Wino Song'

Suzanne – 'You Really Got A Hold On Me'
U.K. - January 1978 (2017 111)
b/w 'You Could Be Right'

Johnny Warman – 'Head On Collision' b/w
U.K. – January 1978 (2017 112)
'London's Burning' , 'Mind Games'

Stormer – 'My Home Town' b/w 'Shake It
U.K – February 1978 (2017 113)
Baby'

Graham Bonnet – 'Warm Ride' b/w '10/12
U.K. – March 1978 (2017 114)
Observation'

Rab Noakes – 'Waiting Here For You' b/w
U.K. – May 1978 (2017 115)
'Restless'

Rab Noakes – 'I Won't Let You Down' b/w
U.K. – July 1978 (2017 117)
'Long After Dark'

Dirk And Stig – 'Ging Gang Goolie' b/w
U.K. – July 1978 (EMI 2852)
Mr. Sheene

Acknowledgements

Writing a book is a solitary job, and at the same time a great many people help and they deserve to be acknowledged.

Special thanks to Andrea Badgley and Linda Badgley with editing, constant support and encouragement and helping me with the book. It could not have been completed without them.

Thank you to Teddie Dahlin and everyone at New Haven Publishing. Thank you for your faith in me and the support in getting this book completed.

The following people gave their time to speak to me about Ringo Starr and I cannot thank them enough. Thank you to: Nancy Lee Andrews, Matt Axton, Dr. Lawrence Blair, Doug Bogie, Graham Bonnet, Ray Connolly, Mike Hales, Ron Kelly, John Kosh, Laurel Massé, Bill Schnee, David Spinozza, Lon Van Eaton, Derrek Van Eaton, Johnny Warman,

Jacques Volcouve, Doug Bogie, Ron Kelly, Linda Badgley, Emily Badgley for the wonderful photos and stories, Mike Hales for his wonderful photos. Thank you Linda Badgley for the author's photo.

Thank you Sarah Healey for the final edits of the book.

Thank you to Alexander Julien, Gary Astridge, John Bezzini, Alan Goldstein, Matt Hurwitz, Piers Hemmingsen and Genevieve Schorr for their help in research and pointing me in the right direction.

A very special thank you to Ruth McCartney for the wonderful Foreword and all of her help and support, and to Angie McCartney, who has been a great source of inspiration and assistance. Thank you both.

On a personal note, thanks to Linda Badgley, Emily Badgley, Servando Moquette (Max), Ian Badgley, Harry Carter, Margarita Carter, Stephen Lussier, Stan Harrison, Margot Steinberg, Donna Stern, Lawrence Stern, Cynthia Stuart, Tony Stuart, Kurt and Ruth Badgley, Kerry and Sue Badgley.

Thank you Andrea for not only putting up with me while I wrote this book (and the many tales of Ringo Starr) but your love, undying encouragement and belief in me. I wish I had the words to thank you. I love you, thank you for your amazing support and love.

And, of course, Sir Richard Starkey.

Bibliography

Alterman, Loraine (25 November 1973). "Ringo Dishes Up a 'Hot Fudge Sundae'." *The New York Times* p. 188.

Axton, Matt. Interview with author, 2i, February 2025

Andrews, Nancy Lee. *A Dose Of Rock 'n' Roll*. (2008) Dalton Watson Fine Books Ltd. Deerfield, Il. 978-185443-230-8

Badgley, Aaron. *Spill Magazine* "Ringo Starr Press Conference" 15 January 2025

Badman, Keith (1990). *The Beatles: After the Break-Up 1970-2000 : A Day-By-Day Diary*. Omnibus Press. 9780711975200

Bangs, Lester. *Rolling Stone* magazine "Yoko Ono/Plastic Ono Band Review" 4 March 1971

https://www.billboard.com/artist/ringo-starr/chart-history/hsi/

Beatlesbible.com https://www.beatlesbible.com/features/tim-bruckner-interview-2015/

Bedford, David (2020). *The Country Of Liverpool. Nashville Of The North*. David Bedford Publications. 10: 183830620X

Blair, Dr. Lawrence. Email with author 9 February 2025

Bogie, Doug. Interview with Author 2025

Bonnet, Graham. Interview with author

Burke, Mike. *The Durham Chronicle, Chester-Le-Street Chronicle* (28 July 1978)

Burton, Charles. *Rolling Stone* magazine, issue # 69, October 29, 1970

Bizzi, Ruth. 10 July 2024. Facebook post

Cairns, D. Shadowplay https://dcairns.wordpress.com/tag/jennifer-jayne/
25 January 2012

Canby, Vincent. *New York Times* "Film: Frank Zappa's Surrealist '200 Motels'". 11 November 1971

Carson, Tom. *Rolling Stone* 'Bad Boy Review'

Cashbox. Cashbox/Singles Review. October 24, 1970.

Castleman, Harry and Podrazik, Walter J. (1975). *All Together Now. The First Complete Beatles Discography 1961 - 1975*. Ballantine Books. 0-345-25680-8-595

Castleman, Harry and Podrazik, Walter J. (1977). *The Beatles Again*. Pierian Press. 0-87650-089-0

Champlin, Charles. *Los Angeles Times* 30 Oct 1974: f1. https://chartmasters.org/ringo-starr-albums-and-songs-sales/#updated_studio_album_sales_comments

Clayson, Alan (1992). *Straight Man or Joker* Paragon House Publishers ISBN - 1-55778-575-9.

Christgau, Robert, *The Village Voice* "Consumer Guide". 7 January 1971

Clark, Carol. *Hammersmith and Shepherds Bush Gazette* (29 June 1978)

Connolly, Ray. Interview with the author. 30 January 2024

Curtis-Horsfall, Thomas (2023). Goldradiouk.com "When Ringo Nearly Reunited The Beatles For His 1973 Debut Album". 27 Noember 2023. https://www.goldradiouk.com/artists/the-beatles/ringo-starr-nearly-reunited/

Dahl, Bill. The London Howlin' Wolf Sessions, MCA Records.

D'Arcy, Matt. *Manchester Evening News* 16 December 1977 "What is Donald Doing In This Company…"

Das, Shyamasundar (2016). *Chasing Rhinos With The Swami - Volume 1* Shyamasundar Das. p. 393. ISBN 978-1495177088.

Daytrippin' magazine

DeRiso, Nick. UCR - Classic Rock & Culture (https://ultimateclassicrock.com/). September 25, 2015

DeRise, Nick, UCR UCR. How Harry Nilsson Steered Toward the Ditch on 'Son of Schmilsson' | https://ultimateclassicrock.com/harry-nilsson-son-of-schmilsson/?utm_source=tsmclip&utm_medium=referral. July 10, 2015

Doggett, Peter (2011). *You Never Give Me Your Money: The Beatles After the Breakup* New York, NY: It Books. ISBN 978-0-06-177418-8.

Drake, Pete. https://www.petedrake.net/

Du Noyer, Paul. https://www.pauldunoyer.com/ringo-starr-interview-1998/

Du Noyer, Paul (July 2001). "Ringo Starr: Champagne Supernova". *Mojo*. pp. 48–54.

Ebert, Roger. https://www.rogerebert.com/reviews/blindman-1972

Engelhardt, Kristofer (2010). *Deeper Undercover* Collector's Guide Publishing. Burlington, Ontario. ISBN 9781-926592-09-1

Fish, Scott K. "Jimmy Webb: Retiring Ringo's 'Sgt. Pepper' Drumset"
https://scottkfish.com/
10 June 2016

Francis, Freddie. Interview
https://historyproject.org.uk/interview/freddie-francis

Gay, Colin. *The Bolton News* 15 September 1977. 'Spin A Disc'.

Gerson, Ben (20 December 1973). "Records: Ringo" Rolling Stone. p. 73.

Giles, Jeff. Ultimate Classic Rock. "When Ringo Starr and Harry Nilsson Made A Movie, Son Of Dracula"
https://ultimateclassicrock.com/ 1 April 2014

Granados, Stefan. *Those Were The Days – An Unofficial History Of The Beatles Apple Organization* 1967 -2002

Roger Greenspun, 'The Screen: Concert for Bangladesh Now a Documentary' *The New York Times*, 24 March 1972, p. 29

Halsall, John. *Daily Post (Merseyside Ed.)* "The Apple Starr With Real Appeal" 15 November 1973. Retrieved Newspaper.com 2 June 2025

Hamil, Peter. *Rolling Stone* "A Long Night's Journey into Day: A Conversation with John Lennon." 6 May 1975

Hard Rock. Ringo discusses his relationship with Marc Bolan
https://www.youtube.com/watch?v=mW0r_ILEYfc

Harry, Bill (2004) *The Ringo Starr Encyclopaedia* London: Virgin Books. ISBN 978-0-7535-0843-5.

Harry, Bill. Sixties City Website. 'Born To Boogie'
https://sixtiescity.net/Mbeat/mbfilms179.htm

Hughes, Howard (2018). Texas, Adios (Cut to the Action: The Films of Ferdinando Baldi) (booklet). Arrow Films. p. 24. FAV177

James, Andrew (2023). *Drumming Is His Madness* Self published. 978–8-8582-6314-2

Jones, Peter (17 April 1971). 'Mirrorpick' *Record Mirror* p. 18

Jones, Peter. *Billboard* magazine "Ringo Starts Label; No Reunion Possible"

Kates, Kristi. *Northern Express* 25 March 2017. "A 70s Start and a New Revival
Local Music: Roger Brown"

Key, Phillip. *Daily Post (Merseyside Ed.)* "Scouse The Mouse Makes it Big" 21 December 1977.

Keys, Bobby & Ditenhafer, Bill (2012). *Every Night's A Saturday Night: The Rock And Roll Life Of Legendary Sax Man, Bobby Keys*. New York, New York. Counterpoint. ISBN: 978-1-58243-783-5

Korinth, Axel. *Stormer The Unreleased Album – Deluxe Edition* Liner notes. Doorwet, Netherlands. 2019 APCOR Books and Records APCOR CD04

Kosh, John. Interview via email March 21, 2025

Leitch, Donovan (2005). *The Autobiography Of Donovan: The Hurdy Gurdy Man.* New York, New York, St. Martin's Press. ISBN: 978-0-31235-252-3.
Lennon, John & Ono, Yoko (2020). *John & Yoko/Plastic Ono Band: In Their Own Words & with Contributions from the People Who Were There.* Weldow Owen Books. ISBN - 978-16818-858-9-6

Madinger, Chip; Easter Mark (2000). *Eight Arms to Hold You: The Solo Beatles Compendium*. Chesterfield, MO: 44.1 Productions. ISBN 0-615-11724-4.

Malton, Leonard. Leonardmalton.com

Marsh, Dave. *Rolling Stone* (RS 187). Keith Moon Review. 22 May 1975, Retrieved 16 February 2025

Marcus, Griel. *Rolling Stone* magazine, issue # 58, May 14, 1970.

Massé, Laurel. Interview with the author. 24 March 2025.

McKee, Emma. Cheatsheet.com. George Harrison Threatened Legal Action Over Ringo Starr's Cover of His Song. 25 November 2022 https://www.cheatsheet.com/entertainment/george-harrison-threatened-legal-action-ringo-starrs-cover-song.html/

Mexican Beatle Blog. https://mexicanbeatle.blogspot.com/

Miles, Barry (2001). *The Beatles Diary Volume 1: The Beatles Years*. London: Omnibus Press. ISBN 0-7119-8308-9.

Mintz, Elliot. Inner-View Interview. August 29, 1977. http://www.beatlesinterviews.org/db1976.00rs.beatles.html

Mojo July 2001.

Morgan Britton, Luke. *New Musical Express* "Ringo Starr Says Working with John Lennon on Plastic Ono Band was 'Best Experience' of His Career" 29th May 2015.
Music Aficionado, The. Website. 1970, The Beatles Part two, 19 August 2023

New Musical Express 12 04 1975

New York Times October, 1973

Nilsson House Website. https://nilssonschmilsson.com/son-of-dracula-210711181613.html

Nolan, Tom. *Rolling Stone* magazine, Issue RS 185 24 April 1975

Pay, May & Edwards, Henry. *Loving John - The Untold Story.* Warner Books, New York, New York. ISBN

Perry, Richard (2021). *Cloud Nine: Memoirs Of A Record Producer.* Orange County, California Redwood Publishing. ISBN 9-781-95210-633-0

Petty, Tom. Interview "New Again, Ringo"

Playboy. October, 1971, Volume 18, Number 10, Page 192.

Q Magazine, September 1998

Rare Beatles. http://www.rarebeatles.com/ringorec/ringo.htm

https://rorint.com/

Record World Single Picks Of The Week. 31 October 1970

Rodriguez, Robert (2010) *Fab Four FAQ 2.0: The Beatles' Solo Years, 1970–1980.* Milwaukee, WI: Backbeat Books. ISBN 978-1-4165-9093-4.

Rodriguez, Robert. Interview with Bill Shnee. https://somethingaboutthebeatles.com/

Ruttenberg, Jay. *Time Out New York* "R-I-N-G-O", 24 July 2003.

Sauter, Donald. Sorrells Pickard on Beaucoups Of Blues. Beatles Pages

Schnee, Bill. Interview with the author.

Sharp, Ken (2024). *Goldmine Magazine.* "Ringo Starr On Anniversaries, Cherished Memories and His Love For Drumming" 7 July 2023

Shaw, Gabi. *Business Insider* "The Biggest Box Office Flops Every Year Since The 70's" 24 June 2025 https://www.businessinsider.com/movie-flops-over-the-years-2018-2#2013-47-ronin-36

Sinkevics, John. Holland Sentinel.Com. 16 May 2014 "Roger Brown talks about the legends he's worked with and the dedication to his craft."

Sirus XM, Ringo Starr Interview, 4 July 2019.

Smith, Alan (24 April 1971). Singles Reviews *NME* p. 20.

Spedding, Chris. http://www.chrisspedding.com/ Retrieved 3 February 2025

Spinozza, David. Interview with the author. 8 December 2024.

Spizer, Bruce (2005). *The Beatles Solo On Apple Records* New York, NY: McGraw-Hill. ISBN 0-07-055087-5.

Starr, Michael Seth. *Ringo With A Little Help.* 2015 Backbeat Books ISBN - 978-1-61713-102-2.

Starr, Ringo. *Photograph – The Very Best Of Ringo.* CD/DVD

Stubbs, Dan. *New Musical Express (NME).* 15 September 1977 "Soundtrack Of My Life: Ringo Starr"

Terrill, Marshall. *Daytrippin'* 2008. "Ringo Starr's former girlfriend, Nancy Andrews, talks about life with Ringo and her book "A Dose of Rock 'n' Roll"". https://daytrippin.com/2022/05/26/ringos-former-girlfriend-nancy-andrews-talks-about-life-with-ringo-and-her-book-a-dose-of-rock-n-roll/

Thegze, Chuck. *The Los Angeles Times* 24 March 1974. 'Richard Pery's Way With An Album'.

Tripplet, Gene. "Hoyt Axton Goes His Own Way" *The Oklahoman* 18 April 1982 (Retrieved 13 February 2025).

Trzcinski, Matthew. Showbiz Cheatsheet. "Why John Lennon Slammed Ringo Starr's Solo Producer". 8 November 2023. https://www.cheatsheet.com/news/john-lennon-slammed-ringo-starrs-solo-producer.html/

TV Guide
https://www.tvguide.com/movies/blindman/review/2000320099/

Variety https://variety.com/1970/film/reviews/200-motels-1200422560/

Vaughan, Adam. "This Day in Music Spotlight: How Doris Troy Became a Beatle Favorite'
Harrison stories, 16 February 2004

Visconti, Tony. *Tony Visconti: The Autobiography: Bowie, Bolan and the Brooklyn Boy*. (2007) Harper 978-0007229451

Watts, Michael. *Melody Maker*. July 31, August 7 and 14th.

Weinberg, Max and Santelli, Robert. (1984) *The Big Beat: Conversations with Rock's Great Drummers* Contemporary Books Inc. Chicago. ISBN 978-0809254859

Warman, Johnny. Interview with the author

Wenner, Jan. Lennon Remembers

Whately, Jack. The classic Ringo Starr song inspired by Marc Bolan. *Far Out* https://faroutmagazine.co.uk/the-classic-ringo-starr-song-inspired-by-marc-bolan/

Wick, Julia. Longreads 'People Let Me Tell You About My Best Friend' 17 April 2015. https://longreads.com/2015/04/17/people-let-me-tell-you-bout-my-best-friend/

Wishart, John. *Record Mirror* 'Bad Boy Review'

Womack, Kenneth (2023). *Living the Beatles Legend: The Untold Story of Mal Evans*. New York, New York. Dey Street Books. ISBN: 978-0-0632-4852-6

www.ingramcontent.com/pod-product-compliance
Lightning Source LLC
Chambersburg PA
CBHW051049160426
43193CB00010B/1118